WE BOYS TOGETHER

TEENAGERS IN LOVE
BEFORE GIRL-CRAZI

We Boys Together

Teenagers in Love Before Girl-Craziness

Jeffery P. Dennis

Vanderbilt University Press
Nashville

11 10 09 08 07   1 2 3 4 5

This book is printed on acid-free paper made
from 50% post consumer recycled paper.
Manufactured in the United States of America
Designed by Dariel Mayer

Frontispiece: Publicity photo from the 1935 motion picture *The
Devil is a Sissy*. Actors from left to right: Freddie Bartholomew,
Jackie Cooper, and Mickey Rooney. © Bettmann/Corbis.

Library of Congress Cataloging-in-Publication Data

Dennis, Jeffery P.
We boys together : teenagers in love before girl-craziness /
Jeffery P. Dennis.—1st ed.
p. cm.
Includes bibliographical references and index.
ISBN-13: 978-0-8265-1556-8 (cloth : alk. paper)
ISBN-13: 978-0-8265-1557-5 (pbk. : alk. paper)
1. Teenage boys in motion pictures. 2. Male friendship in motion
pictures. 3. Teenage boys in literature. 4. Male friendship in
literature. 5. American fiction—20th century—History and
criticism. 6. Male friendship—United States—History—20th
century. I. Title.
PN1995.9.B7D46 2006
791.43'653—dc22
2006032504

Contents

ILLUSTRATIONS

We two boys together clinging,
One the other never leaving,
Up and down the roads going—
North and South excursions making,
Power enjoying—elbows stretching—fingers
clutching,
Arm'd and fearless—eating, drinking, sleeping,
loving.
    —Walt Whitman, *Leaves of Grass*

PREFACE

Select ten people at random, or a hundred, and ask them: "What are the major concerns of teenage boys?" They will, almost without exception, put "teenage girls" at the top of the list. The cultural myth of the teenage boy as hopelessly obsessed with girls is so pervasive that even experts usually treat it as fact, as universal human experience, in spite of the evidence to the contrary.

This book examines the origin of the myth of teenage girl-craziness and explores a time period, before World War II, when boys were not expected to express any romantic interest in girls at all, at least not during middle school or high school. Those who did were considered infantile or effeminate, headaches to their parents and a source of derision to their peers. Instead, they were encouraged to form intimate passionate bonds with other boys or with men, romantic friendships, or homoromances.

Homoromances differed from ordinary same-sex friendships, even of the "best friend" variety, in their intensity, intimacy, and exclusivity. In addition, mass media usually depicted homoromances as permanent, life-long relationships, and emphasized the physicality of the partners, overtly positioning them as objects of desire.

My methodology is content analysis, my objects of interest nearly everything recorded by and about teenagers between 1900 and World War II: psychiatric and sociological data, popular magazine articles, literary novels, memoirs, high school yearbooks. I pay particular attention to mass culture, the serial novels, comic strips, comic books, radio programs, and movies consumed by the teenagers themselves, since they most obviously and graphically encapsulate cultural ideas about what teenagers should think and be.

The careers of a number of young actors who became famous for playing teenagers in the movies will be analyzed in detail, including Jackie Cooper, Freddie Bartholomew, Jimmy Lydon, Mickey Rooney, Frankie Darro, Billy Halop, Leo Gorcey, Bobby Jordan, Sabu, and Johnny Sheffield. They all played characters who pursued intense, passionate same-sex relationships. Some played nothing else. However, their ease or awkwardness at portraying homoromance does not answer the question of their off-screen desire or behavior. Except when otherwise specified, no conclusion about an actor, writer, or director's sexual identity is intended.

Teenagers in the movies were usually played by young adults, and the teenage characters in literary texts, comic strips, and comic books were usually seventeen or eighteen years old, at the end of adolescence rather than at the beginning. However, some texts from the era do describe young teenagers, fourteen and fifteen years old, with an enthusiasm that seems inappropriately lascivious today. These descriptions should be understood within their historical and cultural context, and are not meant to encourage or condone adult erotic interest in minors.

We Boys Together

Teenagers in Love
Before Girl-Craziness

1

TEENAGERS IN LOVE

In the movie *A Dangerous Place* (1995), a preteen martial artist is dismayed to find that his older brother has joined a karate club just to impress girls. "Is that all you think about?" he asks, disgusted. Mom, overhearing, sets him straight: "He's seventeen! Of course it is!" Of course the teenage boy spends 100 percent of his time, every hour of every day, thinking about girls. Of course he joins clubs, plays sports, buys clothes and cars, chooses classes and careers, solely in order to meet or impress girls. He may pal around with other boys, but they are mere placeholders, to be abandoned without hesitation the instant a girl smiles at him. When his parents hear that he has signed up to fight tigers or jump from an airplane, they need only ask, "What's her name?" certain that the answer to every question will always be a "her."

Today this teenage hetero-mania appears almost everywhere, in TV sitcoms and Top 40 songs, in Sunday sermons and college lectures, in advice columns, in *Parents* magazine, in off-hand comments and twinkling asides: "My son is seventeen—you know what *that* means!" And it is presented as undeniable fact, as universal teenage experience, rooted in chromosomes or brain chemistry. It is presented as a fundamental law of the universe, timeless and invariant, as inescapable as gravity.

We know that it is not an undeniable fact. It is not a fundamental law of the universe. Some teenage boys like boys, and even those who like girls do not spend every moment obsessing over them. Teenage hetero-mania is an ideological construct, the hetero dream of a queer-free future revised as a queer-free past, the assertion that whatever might have happened later, in the first garden of pubescence we were all straight. It is the axiom, "No one here is gay," distilled, exaggerated, and repeated so often that one wonders what is being silenced.

Like all ideological constructs, even the most pervasive, teenage hetero-mania must have had a moment of origin—and even, possibly, a time before. Perhaps once, decades or centuries ago, moms did not smugly intone: "He's seventeen—of course it is." Perhaps once teenage boys were *not* expected to spend every moment of every day dreaming of, gazing at, smiling at, showing off for, and trying to kiss girls.

How does one go about finding such a time? Asking real people may be futile, since their memories are thoroughly clouded by how they think today, and besides, there may be few or none left alive who recall that long-ago era. However, we can examine magazine and news-paper articles that discuss teenagers, radio and television programs about them, comic books and serial novels sold to them, and the yearbooks, journals, and diaries that they produced for themselves or each other.

When we examine the mass media of twenty years ago, we find Brat Packer boys single-mindedly obsessed with girls. Thirty years ago, Fonzie of *Happy Days* is joyfully seducing every girl in sight. Forty years ago, Frankie Avalon is endlessly finding salvation in the arms of his beach movie costar Annette Funicello. Fifty years ago, crooners Pat Boone and Ricky Nelson are proclaiming that to be a teenage boy means nothing more than grinning at teenage girls. Hetero-mania is promoted with calm assurance in 1986, 1976, and 1966, and with a sort of anxious fervor in 1956 and 1946. But if we look earlier still, some-thing remarkable happens: utter silence.

In the mass media of 1936, 1926, and 1916, little boys often have girlfriends, and young men just starting out in life spend a substantial amount of stage or screen time wooing young ladies, but teenage boys rarely if ever gaze at, flirt with, dance with, or kiss girls. They rarely if ever groan with longing at a passing beauty or throw off casual com-ments about the profundity of their desire. They rarely if ever have girl-friends. If a girl appears in the story at all, she is a sister, nuisance, or pal.

In *The Time of Your Life,* William Saroyan's 1940 Pulitzer Prizewinning play, all of the lost and wounded denizens of a seedy San Francisco bar express some sort of heterosexual interest, with one exception: Willie, a teenage pinball player. Today he would be characterized as a churning cauldron of heterosexual horniness, but in 1940 he never once looks at or refers to a girl.

In *Boys Town,* a 1938 Oscar winner about a home for juvenile delinquents west of Omaha, five hundred teenage boys work together, eat together, pray together, and bed down together. In a remake today, they would no doubt ogle girls on trips to town, talk about their girlfriends back home, and leer at contraband *Playboys*; the star, Mickey Rooney, just short of his eighteenth birthday, would no doubt fall in love with some delivery girl or caretaker's daughter. But in 1938, there is nothing, not a leer, not a moan, not a murmur of desire, no reference to heterosexual practice at all, except when Mickey refuses to go to movie night because "the guy gets the girl, and they live happily ever after." Who'd want to watch such a disgusting spectacle?

In the Buck Rogers comic strips, radio series, and movie serial of the 1930s, teenage Buddy Deering never expresses any romantic interest in girls. He often pals around with a teenage Martian princess named Alura, but fails to find her in the least alluring.

Between 1926 and 1937, Bomba the Jungle Boy wandered Amazonia in a popular series of boys' books. A teenage Tarzan, later portrayed on screen by Johnny Sheffield of Tarzan fame, he never encounters a single teenage Jane, nor does he express any desire for one.

But it is not only the texts of mass culture. High school yearbooks, popular magazine articles, and scholarly journals in psychiatry and sociology all presume that teenage boys rarely express any interest in girls, and if they do, it is a sign of dysfunction. In a study published in *Child Development* in 1934, about 70 percent of boys admit to having "crushes," mostly on girls, by the age of eighteen.[1] Today most people would find such a revelation absurdly low—surely it's 100 percent—and impossibly late—surely it's at the first moment of pubescence? But in 1934, it seemed horrifyingly high, a wake-up call to the parents and teachers of America.

Looking at these texts is like going through the looking glass. Today the lack of heterosexual interest in teenage boys is intolerable, to be explained away as shyness, dismissed as immaturity, or punished as devi-ance. But in *the time before*, it was the heterosexual interest that signified shyness, immaturity, or deviance. Real, masculine, red-blooded teenage boys were supposed to care only for each other.

DEFINING THE TEENAGER

It is dangerous to view the texts of long-ago cultures through the lens of postmodern academia. There is always a possibility of misreading, of finding themes that the original audiences could never have known, even of misinterpreting social categories. We know that menarche in girls has been coming earlier and earlier, from age fifteen or sixteen in 1800 to age twelve or thirteen today. Perhaps boys in 1916, 1926, and 1936 were similarly late in reaching adolescence.[2] Or perhaps there was no stable category of adolescence at all, and Willie, Mickey Rooney, Buddy Deering, and Bomba were to be taken as prepubescent, as little boys.

But no, the history of adolescence as a social category is well-known. A few scholars argue that it occurred early, in ancient China or medieval Florence,[3] but most agree that it is a product of modernity.[4] Before the industrial revolution, children became adults at puberty or before; a boy of fourteen could take on a man's job, a girl of fourteen could marry. Only in the last years of the nineteenth century did in-dustrialization and an increasingly complex division of labor send most young people out into the world, to seek employment from strangers rather than parents or friends, in factories and offices rather than on the family farm. To compete in the new public sphere, they had to learn subjects that their parents never needed or wanted, like algebra, Latin, bookkeeping, and typing. So instead of facing the world at age fourteen, they had to spend an extra four, five, or ten years in school: Between 1900 and 1940, the high school graduation rate in the United States shot up from 7 percent to 53 percent, and the college graduation rate from 2 percent to 9 percent.

The extra years of education meant that jobs, houses, marriages, all of the benefits and responsibilities of adulthood, had to be postponed.[5] In 1840, a sixteen-year-old boy would likely be an apprentice or a farmer, working from sunup to sundown. He might live apart from his parents; he could marry if he pleased. But in 1940, his sixteen-year-old great-grandson would likely be occupied by school during the day and by games, sports, and homework at night. He could not marry without parental approval, or sign the lease on a house, or drink alcohol.[6] He required nearly as much parental supervision as a child. Indeed, the first generations of adolescent boys, from about 1880 to 1920, lived in a protracted childhood, playing the same games that they had played as twelve year olds, and being supervised as strictly by their parents or *in loco parentis* teachers.

But soon it became obvious that fifteen-, sixteen-, and seventeen-year-old boys were not children. They were adult in features and form; indeed, they were often hyperadult—taller, stronger, harder, more rugged than their elders. They could make decisions, express interests and tastes, plan for the future as well as any adult, or better. They were neither children nor adults, postpubescent yet under adult supervision, negotiating a wide, treacherous, and contradictory gap between innocence and experience, freedom and responsibility. They enjoyed the best of two worlds, or the worst. They were a new social group, adolescents, in-betweeners, later teenagers.[7]

On the heels of G. Stanley Hall's influential two-volume *Adolescence* (1904), psychologists, sociologists, social workers, and educators began to tease out the psychodynamic import of being an in-between. During this period, ethnographers were creating vast taxonomies of human bodies, classifying them according to evolutionary "advancement" from Australian aboriginals up through various Nilotic and Bantu tribes, Polynesians, Native Americans, Malaysians, Semites, and then in rapid succession the Slavs, Greeks, Italians, Celts, until they reached the "pinnacle of human evolution," the Teutons.[8] When they shifted their attention to teenage bodies, we find for the first time discussion of the so-called primary and secondary sexual characteristics that would be drummed into generations of high schoolers in health class: "proper" evolution of face and form from "primitive" childhood androgyny through hypermasculine and hyperfeminine adolescence to a stable, though somewhat sagging adulthood. Parents, teachers, physicians, and young people themselves scurried to categorize the formerly unvariegated masses and to provide them with distinctive social institutions. They built junior and senior high schools, and passed mandatory education laws to keep them filled.[9] They founded or revived 4-H clubs, Sunday schools, Cub Scouts and Boy Scouts, Boys Clubs and Youth Clubs, the YMCA, Hi-Yi, Junior Achievement. They published *Boys' Life* and *The American Boy*. By World War I, people not yet mature were divided quite consistently into three categories: children, adolescents, and young adults.[10]

If adolescence is defined by absence, a liminal space between the two pillars of childhood and adulthood, then precisely which characters or actors in cultural texts should be classified as adolescent may be unclear. For this study, we will use the two characteristics that define adolescence: physical maturity and adult supervision. In written media, a stated age of fourteen will be considered the lowest limit for achieving sufficient physical maturity to be deemed adolescent,[11] except when the author makes an exception: Edgar Rice Burroughs writes that his jungle heroes—Tarzan, Korak, and Azîz—were "fully developed" by the age of ten. In movies, in addition to the age of the actor, we will check for the more overt changes in height, body mass, and voice that signify pubescence. For instance, Johnny Sheffield is not quite fourteen years old in *Tarzan and the Amazons* (1945), yet his muscles have already hardened and his voice has deepened, so he must be taken as an adolescent. In contrast, Dean Stockwell in *Kim* (1950) is nearly fifteen years old, yet his body is so tiny, his voice so delicate, that he must be taken as a child.

The second requirement of adolescence, adult supervision, is even more problematic. Most teenage characters are shown attending high school or junior college, living with their parents or adult caregivers, or traveling with older companions. Other characters will still be classified as adolescent if they appear in a sequence—for instance, five in a series of twelve teenage movies—or if adults specify that they intend to take a parental role in the boys' lives. Frankie Darro does not attend school, and sometimes his parents are absent, but his need for adult supervision is always met early in the film, when a detective or reporter tells him, "I promised your mother I'd look after you." In the absence of statements of custodial intent, we will also look at how the adults treat the character: as a peer or as a "boy," requiring supervision, advice, and support. Many science fiction stories feature young men who are making their own way in the world, but they are clearly distinguished from the adults and so will be classified as at least metaphorical adolescents.

TEEN CULTURE

At first the new breed of adolescents had to make do with childhood toys or co-opt the songs and stories of their collegiate brothers and sisters. But gradually culture industries moved into place, products went on sale, norms and hierarchies developed, and by the 1930s, distinct teen subcultures had emerged. Middle-class girls had a more highly developed cultural apparatus, with more products to buy, more crooners to swoon to, even their own advice columns ("Sub-Deb" in *Ladies Home Journal*, "Tricks for Teens" in *Parents Magazine*), but middle-class boys also had their share of styles, fads, and fashions.[12] They called each other "Dad" and "Jackson" and used phrases like "what's cookin'?" and "get hep!"[13] They wore zoot suits, sweaters autographed by their chums, fedoras cut into spikes (like the one that Jughead in the *Archie* comics has worn ever since). They listened to the big bands led by Benny Goodman, Harry James, and Paul Whiteman.[14] They sang in code to mystify their parents: "Hut-sut rawlson on the rillera," "Mairzy doats and dozy doats." They jitterbugged; they danced the Big Apple and "the La Conga." They had their own preferences in radio stars: Kay Kyser, Spike Jones, George Burns and Gracie Allen, the "Mad Russian" on the Eddie Cantor program. They had their own movies, with teenage protagonists, usually airing on the B-side of double features.

Three main types of teenage boys appeared in American mass culture. The sons of small-town burghers, Anglo-white, native born, middle class, and vaguely Protestant, were Boys Next Door, enjoying domestic comedies and melodramas "close to home." Somewhat farther from "home," the sons of urban immigrants, "nonwhite" Irish or Italian, poor, and Roman Catholic, became Lost Boys in highly stylized tales of juvenile delinquency. Adventure Boys traveled the farthest, beyond the boundaries of Anglo-white Western civilization altogether, to Borneo, savage Pellucidar, or the Moon, for two-fisted action tales or lush colonial fantasies.

Once they had a culture distinct from both children and young adults and a repertoire of mass-culture types and images, teenage boys had become a bona fide social category: physically mature but not socially mature, adult in form yet under adult supervision, with activities, goals, norms, beliefs, and problems mystifying to children, young adults, parents, and teachers. Willie, Mickey Rooney, Bucky Deering, and Bomba were teenagers, virtually identical to Pat Boone and Ricky Nelson in 1956, Frankie Avalon in 1966, Fonzie in 1976, and the Brat Pack in 1986.

But with one significant difference. They were not interested in girls.

ABSENCE OF HETEROSEXUAL INTEREST

This absence of heterosexual interest might be explained by what a 1916 article in *Current Opinion* calls "a fear of the sexual instinct and all its dangers." Medical and popular paradigms of the era gave girls and women no "sexual instinct," or desire for physical intimacy, and little boys no potency, or ability to perform sexually, so their heterosexual romances were safe, all about flowers, moonlight, and sentimental songs rather than bodies pressing against each other in darkened rooms. Young men could channel their desire for physical intimacy into the socially approved goal of marriage, their potency into building a family. But teenage boys presented a problem. They enjoyed quite as much sexual potency as men, perhaps more, yet they were five or ten years away from the possibility of entering a marriage bed. If their desire for physical intimacy arrived shortly after puberty, they would not spend those five or ten years dreaming of flowers, moonlight, and sentimental songs. They would be unchanneled, undisciplined, ravaging beasts, a species with the savage, the immigrant, and the invert. Indeed, early commentators on adolescence made it into a dementia.[15] Didn't Willa Cather warn us, early in the century? She wrote of a Pittsburgh high school boy, lured to New York by the glamour of opera, who meets jaded, decadent men and women, finds desire too great a strain on his sensibility, and kills himself.[16]

It is easier to pretend that the boy has no heterosexual interest whatsoever from the moment his voice first starts to crack to the moment he drives away to college in his tiger-striped jalopy. We find between 1900 and 1940 many examples of preteens with vivid heterosexual obsessions—Booth Tarkington's *Penrod* (1914), Chester Gump and Skeezix in the comics, Jackie Cooper and Alfalfa in the *Our Gang* shorts, Tommy Kelly as *Peck's Bad Boy at the Circus* (1938)—but teenage boys found girls either irrelevant or abhorrent.[17] Frankie Darro grimaces in disgust when a girl he has rescued kisses him on the cheek. Mickey Rooney is asked if he can dance, and he replies indignantly, "Not with girls!" Leo Gorcey brings a female partner to a jitterbug contest, and his friends bug-eye in surprise.

Amid the flurry of professional and pop psychology books that appeared in the first decades of the new century, we find barely a suggestion that teenage boys are ever thunderstruck or even mildly impressed by the sight of the girl next door.[18] In 1907, a few years after the publication of *Adolescence*, G. Stanley Hall informs the readers of *Ladies Home Journal* about "a sad percentage of early private vice," or masturbation, in teenage boys. He does not explain this practice, then considered an extreme physical and psychological danger, as a corollary of desire for physical intimacy with girls, or with other boys, for that matter; it is the result of a perverse introspection, the boy's "unnatural" desire for his own body.[19] Ernest Jones argues that "if the sexual instinct ever plays a significant part in the life of man, it is surely during adolescence," but still he shies away from suggesting that the instinct might lead the boy toward girls; a good Freudian, he theorizes a "pal and gang" stage of sublimated homoerotic interest between childhood latency and adult heterosexual destiny. Sex researcher Havelock Ellis argues that the boy's sex drive does not manifest itself in erotic fantasies or behaviors of any sort, but in "muscular impulses of adventure" or "emotional aspirations in the sphere of art or religion." Heterosexual practice is occasionally documented among nonwhite, urban immigrants, as in *The Revolt of Modern Youth* (1925), but only as a sign of their moral depravity.[20]

Social commentators were happy to document heterosexual interest or practice among young men of college age, but they consistently ignored or dismissed evidence that teenage boys sometimes liked girls. In his influential *Middletown* (1929), a sociological study of Muncie, Indiana, Robert Lynd notes "the apparently increasing relaxation of some of the traditional prohibitions upon the approaches of boys and girls to each others' persons." As evidence, he cites a questionnaire indicating that 44 percent of high school boys have attended "petting parties" (e.g., parties where boys and girls kiss).[21] He registers his disbelief with a long footnote criticizing the methodology of the questionnaire, and finally blames confessional magazines, salacious popular songs, and "the constant witnessing of sex films" for corrupting high school boys who would otherwise have no interest in girls.[22] In *Only Yesterday* (1931), Frederick Allen Lewis documents the decline of the old moral code of premarital chastity: World War I "had not long been over when cries of alarm from parents, teachers, and moral preceptors rent the air. For the boys and girls just growing out of adolescence were making mincemeat of this code."[23] He specifies that they were "just growing out of adolescence," that is, young adults and collegians, to distinguish them from teenagers, fifteen, sixteen, and seventeen years of age, who "certainly" were not making mincemeat of any codes.

Popular literature concurred. The protagonist of Gene Stratton-Porter's *Freckles* (1904), who wanders the Limberlost swamp of northern Indiana and falls in love with a swamp angel, is called a "homeless boy" and a "waif," though he is actually just under twenty, his adolescence over. Though the title character in Stratton-Porter's *Girl of the Limberlost* (1911) is in high school, she does not fall in love with a high school boy, but with a college student, "a young man with a wonderfully attractive face," who is collecting moths to pay for his tuition.[24] In February 1907, an anonymous Mother writes in *Ladies Home Journal* about the time that her son realized that "a girl was really a girl, and not merely the female young of the tribe."[25] It happened when he was away from home for the first time, a freshman in college, eighteen years old. In act 1 of Thornton Wilder's *Our Town* (1938), small-town doctor's son George Gibbs, age fifteen, is merely friendly with Emily from next door; but three years later, a high school graduate, he is in love with her.

In the otherwise heterosexually obsessed F. Scott Fitzgerald, we see little evocation of heterosexual interest before college. In "Bernice Bobs Her Hair" (1920), the youngest of the boys eagerly dancing with girls at a party is sixteen years old—but he is mentioned because he is an oddity among the college students and law-school graduates. "The Four Fists" (1920) begins at the posh Philips Exeter Academy, where teenage Samuel Meredith has no girlfriends, just a "close friend and constant companion" in his roommate. Then it quickly fast-forwards through college to Wall Street, where, in young adulthood, "his diversion was—women."[26]

In real life, even eighteen-year-old boys "just growing out of adolescence" were often loathe to let on that they enjoyed the company of the other sex. At Everett High School in Washington, the class of 1925 was immortalized in the yearbook by little mottos next to their names. Five of the seventy-three graduating boys were tagged with an interest in girls: "Girls are nice!" "Girls are his hobby!" "Put me among girls and I am happy!" But the other sixty-eight omitted heterosexual interest in favor of more manly mottos: "A bold, bad man!" "He's fast—head and feet both!" And some even make public disavowals of heterosexual interest: "Tall, dashing, quick, and fair, spurns all girls with vigilant care!" The 1928 Terre Haute *Otterian* notes a fondness for boys among most of the senior girls at Otter Creek High ("If flirting is a sin, pray for her!"), but never a fondness for girls among the boys. The absence of heterosexual interest is so thoroughly assumed that it is joked about only once: "I don't go with girls because I don't want to disappoint so many." Nor does the school itself appear to have a vested interest in pushing boys and girls into social activities together. There are many parties, a junior-senior banquet, and a "moving picture show," but no dances, no proms. In 1928, gazing awestricken at girls was not required of teenage boys. Nor was it expected.[27]

GIRL-CRAZINESS AND GIRLISHNESS

When a teenage boy who did like girls appeared in mass culture, he was framed as deviant, an effeminate contrast to the real, red-blooded, masculine boy who "spurned all girls with vigilant care." He was jeered, blackmailed, and ostracized. He was asked, "What kind of flower are you?" and "Can I borrow your lipstick, dearie?" His peers called him "honey-boy," "panty-waist," "mollycoddle," and "Percy," and the adults, "sensitive," "gentle," "artistic," and "sweet." Andy Hardy was psychoanalyzed as suffering from an "unconscious fixation on youth." Henry Aldrich was subject to pummeling by bullies and tense heart-to-hearts with his parents. His buddy Dizzy usually tolerated his eccentricity, with the expansive, self-conscious tolerance that one sees today in straight high schoolers reaching out to their gay classmates, but sometimes even he couldn't take it anymore and yelled, "What the heck's the matter with you, anyway?"

Babbit, the hero of the famous Sinclair Lewis novel (1922), worries when his son Ted, "a decorative boy of seventeen," offers to give two girls from his high school a ride to a chorus rehearsal. "I hope they're decent girls," he muses. "I wouldn't want him to, uh, get mixed up and everything." His wife suggests that he take Ted aside and give him a little talk about "Things," but he rejects the proposal: "no sense suggesting a lot of Things to a boy's mind." He assumes that no seventeen-year-old boy could possibly experience heterosexual desire unless he is manipulated from outside. The next summer, Babbit discovers Ted at one of those infamous "petting parties," but still he blames the girl next door for "enticing" him, refusing to believe that any eighteen-year-old boy could want to kiss girls of his own accord.[28]

A boy just short of his seventeenth birthday does fall for a girl in Eugene O'Neill's *Ah, Wilderness!* (1933), but he is an unrepentant sissy. O'Neill tells us that there is "something of extreme sensitiveness . . . a restless, apprehensive, defiant, shy, dreamy, self-conscious intelligence about him." He reads too much poetry, especially sexual anarchist Algernon Swinburne and gay icon Oscar Wilde, whose trial and incarceration for "the love that dare not speak its name" was still freshly scandalous in 1904 (the date of the plot). "He's a queer boy," his mother muses. "Sometimes I can't make head or tail of him."[29]

THE HOMOROMANTIC ARCADIA

But the teenage boy was not defined by an absence waiting to be filled. He fell in love. Sometimes in scholarly texts, and sometimes in the hints and glimpses of high school yearbooks, but most often in mass culture: Between 1900 and 1940, many, perhaps most Boys Next Door, Lost Boys, and Adventure Boys fell in love with each other. They were not merely best friends: They shared more emotional intensity than that of the truest of true-blue chums; more physical intimacy than any stage convention or cultural norm allowed for the expression of mere camaraderie; and more exclusivity than any homosocial bond, with other suitors either dismissed or sparking jealous arguments. Fade-out scenes often showed them walking side by side into the future, suggesting a permanence unusual for teenage couples of any sort, in any era. In fact, the intensity, intimacy, exclusivity, and permanence of these partnerships resemble nothing in mass culture so much as adult heterosexual romances. Conventions were copied, line by line and beat by beat, with dramatic first encounters, coy flirtations, and falling-in-love montages, with tearful breakups and reconciliations in drama, humorous misunderstandings in comedy, and daring rescues in adventure, all ending with the promise of marriage, or at least permanent association. They were teenage homoromances.

In the days before homophobic contempt for male affection became commonplace, real teenage boys (and girls and adults) often experienced same-sex "crushes" with the intensity, exclusivity, and no doubt the intimacy that distinguished homoromance from homosocial friendship.[30] At Columbus High School in southern Indiana, the class of 1929 was immortalized in the *Log* by rhyming couplets. Of seventy-five senior boys, four are assigned an interest in girls, but a dozen or more are lauded for same-sex loves astonishing in their passion: "a friend who knows and dares to say, the brave, sweet words that cheer the day," and "With such a comrade, such a friend, one could walk 'til journey's end." The "Low-Down" in the Clarksville, Tennessee *Purple & Gold* of 1933 records "talking about girls" as one senior boy's favorite pastime, but the vast majority prefer football, driving trucks, reading about airplanes, and "following around boys." In the category "seen with," a few boys are paired with girls, but the vast majority are "seen with" various boys, suggesting onlooker interest in exclusive pairings similar to today's gossip about which boys and girls might "like" each other (J. R. Meek is especially scandalous, "seen with a negro boy").[31] But doubtless most of these bonds lacked permanence: When the boys became men, they would scatter to colleges and careers, abandon their crushes to yearbook memories, and spend the rest of their lives being "seen with" women.

Bildungsroman of the prewar era often portray boys at boarding school enjoying intense, intimate, and exclusive bonds, but again they lack permanence. In Somerset Maugham's *Of Human Bondage* (1915), for instance, the teenage Philip falls in love with a male classmate named Rose:

> Soon they grew accustomed to the two walking into chapel arm in arm or strolling round the precincts in conversation. . . . Philip at first was reserved. He would not let himself yield entirely to the proud joy that filled him; but presently his distrust of the fates gave way before a wild happiness. He thought Rose the most wonderful fellow he had ever seen. His books now were insignificant; he could not bother about them when there was something infinitely more important to occupy him. . . . Philip was happy.[32]

When Rose breaks up with him, Philip is devastated. He hates school, hates his classmates; he toys with the idea of entering the clergy, where celibacy would save him from the pain of falling in love again. Then he passes the Sixth Form (the equivalent of twelfth grade), enrolls at Heidelberg University, and falls in love again—but not with a boy.

But the teenagers of mass culture somehow managed to find a place of permanent residence, an Arcadia. The distant pastoral valleys of Arcadia first appeared in Virgil's *Eclogue II*, about a shepherd named Corydon who longs for the beautiful Alexis, and ever since people have sought a place where their same-sex loves could last forever, without being hidden, denied, or drowned out by the roar of heteronormative expectation. In *Joseph and His Friend* (1869), the lovers seek a valley where "there is no force to drag you back, when you are there." In *Maurice* (1913–1914), the lovers abandon Edwardian Oxford for "a deserted valley for those who wish . . . to be left alone." André Gide found Arcadia in *Saül* (1906), the biblical tale of David and Jonathan, and Kenneth Grahame in *The Wind in the Willows* (1908), the fable of the Mole and the Water Rat.[33] And between 1900 and 1940, anyone who read a story or saw a film about teenage boys could find it, in homoromances that were not only intense, intimate, and exclusive, but offered the promise of permanence.

The primary teenager in the story or film is described in none-too-subtle erotic terms: He is handsome, devastatingly so, and superlative after superlative praises his massive chest, broad shoulders, muscular legs, and so on. In visual media, there are endless scenes of the teenager swimming, changing for athletic contests, or stripping down for bed, while the camera or the artist lingers lovingly over his massive chest, broad shoulders, muscular legs, and so on. Adults and teens not involved in a homoromance rarely received such attention. Since most teenagers in mass culture were framed as seventeen or eighteen years old, and actors who portrayed them several years older, we need not presume ephebophilia in the gaze; the gaze is directed at a man. Yet it is possible only because the character is *not a man*. Several scholars have argued that children in mass culture are fetishized through the rubric of *innocence*: They are presumed neither potent nor desiring, so they can be erotic without the possibility of sex.[34] Perhaps teenage boys could be fetishized through the rubric of *power*: They were presumed potent but not heterosexually desiring, so their eroticism provided a safe place for the expression of same-sex love, an Arcadia.

Explaining the Homoromance

Teenage homoromance is not a matter of deciphering subtexts and codes: It is drawn so explicitly and so joyously, in so many venues, and so much to the exclusion of heteroromance that one is astounded. Of course, it does not reflect real life: Many teenage boys in 1916, 1926, and 1936 liked girls, and those who liked boys had to keep their desire carefully hidden, if they even managed to acknowledge its existence. It is an ideological construct, the axiom "No one here is straight," presented nearly as often and nearly as aggressively as the axiom "No one here is gay" would be after the war. And as with all ideologies, we must ask who desires it or who profits by it. Who wants to dream of Freddie Bartholomew and Jimmy Lydon gazing at each other in *Tom Brown's School Days*, or of the comic book Human Torch rushing to the aid of his teen sidekick? Who stands to increase their wealth, status, and power by promoting or buying into the myth that all teenage boys long for other boys or men? There are three possibilities.

First, some or many of the writers, artists, producers, directors, and actors might have been themselves gay, or at least subject to an un-named, unacknowledged desire for same-sex intimacy that they trans-posed onto the nostalgic freedom of adolescence. Explaining the text through the author's own desire has a venerable history in literary and film studies.[35] However, with marriages of convenience so common and journalists of the era vowed to silence, locating actual same-sex practice requires confessionals or gossip, and it is impossible to locate unnamed and unacknowledged desire. Still, we find that men who preferred the company of men, regardless of their desire or practices, were generally more adept at homoromantic performance than men who preferred the company of women. Frankie Darro was a man's man, a "woman-hater" throughout his life in spite of his two marriages, and in dozens of movies he has no trouble at all conveying homoromantic intensity and intimacy. But Mickey Rooney was uncommonly woman-oriented, with nine marriages and innumerable heteroromances to his credit, and in his few homoromantic movies—*Little Lord Fauntleroy, Thoroughbreds Don't Cry, Life Begins for Andy Hardy*—his emotional intensity seems stilted and forced, and he conveys intimacy through awkward grabs and jokes.

The extent of the physicality in the portrayals of the teenagers also differs from artist to artist, suggesting a biographical element in mass media homoromance. Under Ford Beebe's direction, Billy Halop spends most of the running time of *Junior G-Men* (1940) shirtless or in his underwear, but when Lewis D. Collins directs the sequel, *Junior G-Men of the Air* (1942), the actor remains fully clothed throughout. In the *Andy Hardy* series, Mickey Rooney rarely lets more than ten minutes of air-time pass without taking off his clothes, but in the concurrent *Henry Aldrich* series, Jimmy Lydon never so much as fumbles with a button.

The production of teen culture supports the biographical thesis. Books, movies, radio programs, magazines, and comics about teenagers were largely produced by bargain-basement publishers and studios, and ignored by critics or else reviled as mindless trash: The *New York Times* reviews only two or three of the hundred-plus Dead End Kids, East Side Kids, and Little Tough Guys movies, and those reviews ooze with contempt. As Buhle and Wagner note, "[A]rtists on the bottom rungs of the genres often had a freer hand than their more exalted counterparts."[36] Frankie Darro's work for the Poverty Row Monogram, Mascot, and Republic studios always involves homoromance, but in Paramount's *Three Kids and a Queen* (1935) he asks a girl to marry him, and they kiss. Also, these texts were produced very quickly, a book in two weeks, a movie in five days. The lack of rewrites and multiple takes meant that goofs, slips, faux pas, and ad-libs were retained, resulting in considerable slippage between personal biography and fictional worlds. The Dead End Kids were infamous for breaking character, missing marks and cues, horse-playing, generally acting themselves, and Frankie Darro infuses his movies with asides and ruminations that seem irrelevant to the situation he is portraying.

Offscreen desire may play a role in fictional presentations, particularly in the artists who portray teenage homoromance most adroitly or with the greatest physicality, or who continue to portray it once teenage heteroromance has become common. However, it is difficult to believe that all artists working in teen culture were sublimating offscreen desire, or that they stopped suddenly in 1945 or when their characters grew up.

A second possibility is the newly created homosocial public sphere. In one of the key texts of modern queer theory, Eve Sedgwick points out that in the mid- to late nineteenth century, when boys no longer learned their father's trade or took apprenticeships under family friends, they had to seek jobs from men they didn't know, in the offices and factories of the city.[37] That is, they had to incite the interest of potential employers, all strangers, almost all male. In the days before the credentialing and skill-checks of modern human resources, these potential employers judged them on their pleasant appearance and demeanor, on their attractiveness. The dynamic of homosocial flirtation and seduction obviously parallels a homoerotic relationship, with economic capital a metaphor for sexual congress: The man offers the boy a place in the capitalist workforce and receives an attractive protégé in exchange, just as the *erastes* of ancient Greece offered boys training in social skills, the opportunity to participate in adult society, in exchange for sex.[38]

Many of the homoromances in mass culture take place not between peers, but between teenage boys and men, especially during the war. They occurred primarily in visual media such as *Terry and the Pirates*, superhero comics, and Frankie Darro's teen sleuth melodramas, and they tended to display the teenager's body more openly, and with more sensuality, than homoromances between peers. The domestic sphere could take care of itself: Boys had to learn about their destiny in the male-dominated public sphere, where older and younger men worked together, fought together, cared for each other, loved each other. When Captain America is shown rescuing his teenage sidekick from menacing Nazi monsters, it becomes a little easier for a teenage soldier to entrust his life to a foxhole buddy.

This explanation is provocative, but one suspects that the intensity, intimacy, and exclusivity of the homoromance would be poor preparation for the calm cordiality of the business office or for the stoic efficiency of the battlefield. Also, the young adults in mass culture who actually consorted with the older men in offices or on battlefields rarely fell in love with them; theirs was a world of cheesecake pinups in lockers and wolfish flirtations with the girl behind the counter at the drug store. Evidently only teenagers were an appropriate object of adult male desire.

A third possibility is a reaction to the feminization of culture. In the early days of the twentieth century, white, Euro-American male civilization, though lauded as "the pinnacle of human accomplishment," was thought to threaten a man's soul.[39] Its technology—providing food that one doesn't have to hunt, houses that one doesn't have to build—bred men who were indolent and weak. Its luxury made them foppish and vain. Civilized relations, where one tips one's hat and makes small talk with friend and enemy alike, made them two-faced and undependable. Mothers, sisters, girlfriends, and wives only compounded the problem, dressing their charges in satin instead of buckskin; force-feeding them green-carnation decadents like Oscar Wilde and Ernest Dowson when they would really rather be reading Zane Grey Westerns; dragging them to literary salons, operas, light operas, and Chautauqua lectures on aesthetics when they would really rather be bare-knuckle boxing.[40] Earlier generations of men might retain their masculinity by lighting out for the territory or by working with their hands and muscles, but by 1912 there were no territories, just states—the streets of Laredo were no wilder than the streets of Pittsburgh—and physical labor was increasingly giving way to white collars and soft hands in offices.

The younger generation of boys was the worst off, since it not only lacked a frontier, it was spending an extra four, five, or ten years in school, surrounded by girls, taught by women. Many real-life remedies were offered to help boys become adequately masculine in spite of it all: the YMCA, the Boy Scouts, high school and college athletics, secret clubs and fraternal organizations, fishing and hunting as pastimes rather than livelihoods, Sunday-school lessons about Jesus the muscleman.[41] And in mass culture, the most potent remedy to feminization was found in the arms of a chum.

Certainly, rejection of the feminine can help explain the sensuality of the verbal and visual depictions of the teenagers: hard, "clear-eyed" adolescence contrasts vividly with soft, befuddled adulthood, eroticized wilderness with staid civilization. It may explain the proliferation of teenage "woman-haters" in mass culture. However, one wonders why it necessarily requires homoromance. Real, red-blooded, masculine boys must be tough, stoic, aggressive, and independent. When they swoon over each other, link arms, and gaze into each other's eyes, surely they are displaying just as much unmanly tenderness as the dandies who swoon over girls.

No doubt all three factors, and others, contributed to the homoromantic Arcadia, a curious world where the desire between men, elsewhere thought impossible or deviant, was acknowledged and celebrated, but only if one or both of the partners was *not yet* a man.[42] The next chapters outline the origin and growth of the homoromantic Arcadia among Boys Next Door, Lost Boys, and Adventure Boys in American mass culture during the first decades of the twentieth century, and its startlingly quick demise afterward.

2

Main Street
The Boys Next Door

Sinclair Lewis introduces *Main Street* (1920), his mildly ironic view of small-town life, with a celebratory prologue:

> This is America—a town of a few thousand, in a region of wheat and corn and dairies and little groves. . . . The story would be the same in Ohio or Montana, in Kansas or Kentucky or Illinois, and not very differently would it be told Up New York State or in the Carolina hills. Main Street is the climax of civilization. That this Ford car might stand in front of the Bon Ton Store, Hannibal invaded Rome and Erasmus wrote in Oxford cloisters. What Ole Jenson the grocer says to Ezra Stowbody the banker is the new law for London, Prague, and the unprofitable isles of the sea.[1]

We still dream of this America: small towns with steepled churches and picket-fence cottages, a grid of Elm and Oak Streets encased in a womb of green fields, where everyone knows you and most everyone likes you, where you are born, live, and die within a few blocks' walk of parents, grandparents, your boss, your minister, and your high school science teacher. This sense of gemeinschaft, of elemental belonging, probably never existed. It is a nostalgic fantasy, invented late in the nineteenth century by the arbiters of mass culture production and distribution, white, middle-class, native-born Protestants, as their control over the world loosened.

Between 1880 and 1940, the small-town and rural population of the United States declined from 82 percent to 43 percent, due partially to small-town boys and girls seeking their fortunes in the big city, but mostly to an influx of immigrants. In 1903 alone, over eight hundred thousand hopefuls docked at Ellis Island and other points of entry. Most were not white, a category the taxonomists of the day granted only to those of Teutonic "stock": They were Irish and Italian, Greek and Bohemian, Polish and Semitic, from the quaintly antique kingdoms ruled by the Hapsburgs or Hohenzollers or the last of the Tsars. Only about a fifth belonged to "proper" Protestant churches; the rest were Roman Catholic and Jewish, with a scattering of Muslims and Eastern Orthodox Christians. Less than 3 percent were trained for middle-class jobs, managers, professionals, or technicians; most were working class or poor, craftsmen or laborers, and a quarter had no occupation at all.[2]

The arbiters of culture deemed the new immigrants barbarians, with icons and idols instead of the rational Protestant God, cacophonous babbling instead of good grammatical English, and leering vulgarity instead of small-town decorum. Unchecked, the "inferior races" would dilute and eventually erase the Teutonic qualities of intelligence, ingenuity, and enterprise, even if they were strictly segregated in Little Italys and Lower East Sides. They could not help but add social disorganization and spiritual malaise to the melting pot. Sociologists studied immigrant communities not to explore the process of intercultural contact but to brainstorm ways to slow the degradation of Anglo-American "stock." The National Origins Act of 1924 decreed that 86 percent of the immigrants admitted each year must come from northwestern Europe, but native-born Anglo-white Protestants already comprised less than a fifth of the U.S. population, and immigrants and their children a third, more in urban areas.[3] They were already taking positions of authority, as politicians, industrialists, and journalists; they had all but invented Hollywood and Tin Pan Alley.[4] The Boy Next Door originated in this power struggle, in an attempt to demonstrate the "superiority" of small town over city, native white over immigrant, Protestantism over superstition, connectedness over rootlessness, gemeinschaft over gesellschaft.

STRONG AND STURDY

Between 1880 and 1930, hundreds of serial novels were produced for middle-class youth in the United States. Later they would be marketed to children and younger teenagers, but in the absence of radio adventures, comic strips, comic books, and movie serials, they formed a substantial part of every middle-class high schooler's entertainment budget.[5] There were girl and adult protagonists, but the lion's share of series starred Boys Next Door, white middle-class native-born Protestants with go-getter names like Strong and Sturdy, Hale and Hardy. In at least one novel per year, sometimes five or more, they scored touchdowns and won Boy Scouting trophies. They thwarted jewel thieves and counterfeiters. They invented automobiles and aeroplanes. They fought in the Revolutionary War. They single-handedly won the Great War.

The Boy Next Door heroes are not described in much detail, but the two or three adjectives they receive always suggest physical perfection, in contrast to the hulking, dissolute, unattractive villains. They are *extraordinarily* handsome, *immensely* muscular, strong, sturdy, erect, lithe, well-formed, and "well-knit." In *Jack Winters' Gridiron Chums* (1919), we read that "Big Bob stretched out his massive arms . . . as though to call the attention of his companion to his splendid physique." In *The Radio Boys at the Mexican Border* (1922), the chief Boy Next Door has "long legs, flat hips, trim waist, deep chest and broad shoulders and a flat back . . . altogether, he was a striking figure." And their attractiveness is not lost on the other characters (or, one assumes, the readers). In *The Dare Boys of 1776* (1910), teenage patriot Richard Dare is given an audience with a highly appreciative General Washington: "When [Washington's] eyes took in the handsome face, the fine physique and perfect poise of the youth, he gave a slight start and eyed him keenly and somewhat searchingly, with considerable interest."[6]

The overt physicality of the Boys Next Door is coupled with a near total rejection of anything feminine. A small percentage of the protagonists have girlfriends, particularly if they are approaching the end of their high school careers, and occasionally a sidekick is assigned heterosexual interest as a mildly derogatory character tag, like being fat or wearing glasses. In *The Darewell Chums in the Woods* (1908), a boy named

Fenn smiles at a girl: "The other chums laughed, for Fenn was rather "sweet" on the girls, and Jennie was an especial favorite with him. But Fenn did not like to have his failing commented on."[7]

Usually, however, there is no question: Girls are simply not of interest. In *Roy Blakely* (1920), the titular Boy Scout sets out to write a book about his adventures, and he is asked if there will be girls in it. When he avers that there will be, his friend yells, "Good night! I see your finish!" But Roy means only that he will mention his sisters, and critique them for deficient masculinity at that: "One thing about girls," he writes, "They can't throw a ball. They can't whistle, either."[8]

The boys' book heroes usually move in a pack of chums, but some also have "particular friends," with a bond that others recognize as exclusive, with the emotional intensity and physical intimacy that evoke homoromance rather than camaraderie. In *Chums of Scranton High* (1919) there are five chums, but two are particular friends, called "Damon and Pythias" or "David and Jonathan" to evoke literary or biblical antecedents for the social category. They are inseparable, two boys living only for each other as they attempt to best the rival school at the sport du jour.

When "particular friends" appear in a book series, the last installment usually shows them continuing to share their lives as adults. Harrie Irving Hancock's *High School Boys* (1910) traces the sports and scouting exploits of "Dick and Company," six Boys Next Door who all study, work, and play together; but each has a particular friend, so they are actually divisible into three homoromantic couples. Simultaneously with his description of their adolescent exploits, Hancock traces the adventures of each pair of particular friends through college and adulthood. In the *Dick Prescott* series, the titular character and his particular friend Greg Holmes enroll at West Point together, where they endure hazing, sadistic superior officers, failed tests, bullies, fights, and false accusations, all the while rejecting other potential suitors. After graduation, they become *The Boys of the Army*; evidently they are able to request assignments as a couple, since there is never any question that they will remain together forever.

The *Annapolis* series follows a second pair of particular friends, Dave Darrin and Dan Daltzell (or "Danny Grin"), through the U.S.

Naval Academy. In the book recounting the adventures of their junior year, they rather surprisingly get girlfriends, but then they graduate and continue through the *Dave Darrin* series as young adult naval officers, with not a girl in sight and not a hint that they will ever want to marry and lead separate lives. After a climactic battle in *Dave Darrin at Vera Cruz* (1914), they stand on the bridge of their battleship together:

> "We had an interesting time while it lasted," declared [Dan] Daltzell, with a broad grin.
> [Dave replies:] "There is a world full of interesting times ahead of us. We'll find time in every quarter of the globe."[9]

Meanwhile, the third pair, Tom Reade and Harry Hazeltine, two "bronze-looking, erect young men," skip college to become *The Young Engineers*, supervising civil engineering projects and solving mysteries in Arizona, Colorado, New Mexico, and Nevada. They age several years beyond high school during their five-book series, but they always share a room or a house; they never date girls, flirt with girls, or discuss the possibility of "settling down." Evidently they are settled down already.[10]

CHILD STARS GROW UP

There were very few teenagers on the silent screens of the Jazz Age. Unaware of suitable plots or any potential audience for adolescent actors, studio publicity departments tried to maintain a facade of pre-pubescence as long as possible, dressing their stars in little-kid costumes, closeting their teenage activities, even doctoring their birth certificates and destroying old biographies. Thus, actors usually leapt directly from freckle-faced kids to pampered collegians, with no sojourns in high school in between. Sometimes they even interspliced roles. In 1917, for instance, Mary Pickford's sickly brother Jack played a down-and-out boxer in *Jack and Jill*, Pip as both boy and man in *Great Expectations*, and the prepubescent Tom Sawyer in the film of the same name.

Soon, however, child actors became too numerous and too popular to shuffle them from tot to young adult without arousing attention. In 1935, there were fifteen hundred hopefuls on the rosters of Central

Casting, with fifty more registering every day, dragged in by mothers certain that their talent would instantly cure the family's money woes (one mother in Michigan put her daughters, aged eight and ten, on a bus to Hollywood with $7 in their pockets, instructing them to send for the family as soon as the mansion was ready).[11] Perhaps a hundred managed to find steady work, and less than dozen—Shirley Temple, Freddie Bartholomew, Jane Withers, Bobby Breen—became famous, but those few were superstars, carrying the studios through the Depression almost single-handedly with singing, dancing, and cutesy-pooing movies dedicated to promoting a single theme: It's better to be poor than rich. The poor (but never the *immigrant* poor) are more moral, more intelligent, more attractive, more enterprising, and certainly much happier.

Rich women may enjoy their status, becoming bossy dowagers who deserve pies in the face, but every rich man, his soul deadened from endless wheeling and dealing, longs to be poor again, to enjoy the elemental belonging of the small town or farm. Sometimes he sneaks out of the mansion to visit wrong-side-of-the-tracks pals, like Jiggs in the *Bringing Up Father* comic strip, but more often his joie de vivre is restored by a poor child. He takes up with a tattered, smudge-faced boy or girl that he can hold and cuddle, bathe and dress—and the cuter and sweeter, the better. Perhaps aware that the oldster's interest is a ticket out of the ghetto, the child flirts outrageously, eye batting, dimpling, falling asleep on his lap. The intimacy and exclusivity of these relationships signifies family rather than romance The child is neither desiring nor potent, and the adult desires emotional rather than sexual congress, a family rather than a lover: The movie fades out with adoption rather than marriage (the Victorian era was likewise awash with images of eroticized children and with writers whose biographers have spent a century clearing them of the charge of real-life pedophilia).[12]

As these child superstars entered adolescence, fans were watching their every move so closely that a pretense of either prepubescence or maturity was impossible: They had to be cast as teenagers. Girls were not a problem, since the cherubic-charming shtick was actually a stereotypic femininity that would work for them at any age; the objective of their flirtation merely changed from acquiring a father to acquiring a boyfriend. However, boys had a more difficult transition. Audiences got somewhat queasy over the prospect of cherubic-charming fifteen-year-old boys: Politeness, cheerfulness, clean clothing, and grammatically correct speech signified the mollycoddle and the pansy. Boys Next Door had to be hard, tough, muscular, manly. They did not sing, they did not dance, they were not cute or sweet. But how could they toughen up without losing their fan base?

AMERICA'S BOY

Born September 15, 1922, the blond, pug-faced Jackie Cooper started acting at age three and saw his first success as a precocious kindergartner in Hal Roach's *Our Gang* comedy shorts. In 1931, his famous uncle, director Norman Taurog, cast him in *Skippy*, an adaptation of the comic strip about kids and dogs and the lunacy of adult society. Jackie's ability to shed realistic tears on cue (augmented by authoritarian directing: Taurog threatened to shoot his dog if he failed to deliver) won him a Best Actor Oscar nomination and catapulted him into the ranks of Hollywood royalty. *Sooky, The Champ, When a Fellow Needs a Friend*, and *Treasure Island* followed, all box-office toppers. By 1934 Jackie had his own fan magazine, half a dozen Big-Little book titles, and enough advertising tie-ins to shame Little Orphan Annie. He was invited to dinner at the White House, where he acted the celebrity, and Franklin and Eleanor Roosevelt the awestricken groupies. He had a put-on blind date with notoriously decadent Talulah Bankhead, who thought she was getting adult hunk *Gary* Cooper but didn't mind being seen on the arm of the world-famous twelve-year-old instead. Armies of hysterical fans screamed, fainted, and grabbed at his clothes with the mania later reserved for teen dreams and boy bands. He was "America's Boy."

Jackie's preteen characters—Skippy, Midge, Dinky, and Scooter—were Boys Next Door in training. They were native-born Anglo-white Protestants, though in real life Jackie came from Irish Catholic and Jewish roots. They lived with loving parents or parent-substitutes, though in real life Jackie recalls his father as absent, Norman Taurog as a tyrant, and regular costar Wallace Beery as cool, critical, and abusive. They were "popular with dozens of buddies," though in real life Jackie had no close male friends, just coworkers, fans, toadies, and hangers-on.[13]

Skippy, Midge, Dinky, and Scooter were no adventurous scamps, no pint-sized troublemakers like Penrod or Our Gang. They did get into scrapes, but only to complicate the plot; they drew the crowds by being gentle, kind, trusting, polite, affectionate, and mawkishly sentimental. They were constantly hugging, kissing, and crawling into the laps of older men (fathers, surrogate fathers, or total strangers), and they unleashed torrents of tears at the slightest hardship or misunderstanding. Depression-era audiences loved hardship and misunderstandings: Jackie's character reconciles with his alcoholic father; he consoles an orphaned buddy; he's a handicapped boy who wants to be a regular fella; he is torn between his biological father and his stepdad. When Peck's Bad Boy, a gilded age Bart Simpson who hurricaned through decades of newspaper stories, novels, and silent movies, got the Jackie Cooper treatment in 1934, he became a crocodile-tearing good boy who gets blamed for his cousin's mischief. A contemporary advertising flier illustrates the none-too-subtle change in the archetypal Bad Boy:

From the trembling lips of a heartbroken boy tumbled these words, when he thought the Dad he loved had failed him: "If they don't want me, I don't want them!"[14]

Since the whole world was gazing ardently at Jackie every moment of every day, his pubescence became a public event. In *Tough Guy,* filmed from November 1935 to January 1936, the thirteen-year-old Jackie's voice is beginning to deepen and his chubby cheeks are beginning to thin,[15] and the box office is declining: Audiences are falling out of love with him and in love with Freddie Bartholomew, only one and a half years younger but still able to play a passive, feminine, affectionate, and trusting child, not a teenage mollycoddle. So Jackie struggled to reinvent himself as an "all-American Boy," a hard, masculine boys' book hero. He spent hundreds of hours at the gym, becoming an expert boxer, wrestler, and swimmer. Movie magazines published photos of him in boxing trunks or skimpy swimsuits, displaying a hard-packed muscularity that made adult beefcake star John Garfield look downright scrawny. Boys and men rarely appeared shirtless on camera in the days when nudity was a signifier of barbarity, permissible only in the working classes, so instead Jackie wore tight dark-colored T-shirts that accentuated his V-shaped torso and mountainous biceps. But even with a stunning boys' book physique, he had become so thoroughly promoted as vulnerable, sensitive, and clingy that audiences simply wouldn't accept him as tough—not even tough as a façade to hide a sensitive soul—so he was still asked to make with the waterworks, or at least produce a tearstreak or two, in every picture.

Within the Hollywood community, there was considerable speculation that the teenage Jackie's sensitivity and his many friendships with girls signified that he was gay. Whispered "anecdotes" had Jackie and former costar Wallace Beery caught with their pants down or arguing over who would wear the wedding dress, and once at a nightclub, brash blue comedian Milton Berle spotlighted him as a "fag" to gales of humiliating laughter. These jokes and rumors apparently had a profound effect on Jackie. In his later years, in spite of his otherwise liberal politics, he has made some mildly homophobic statements, and he has never formed a close friendship with a man, perhaps out of a fear of what masculine intimacy might signify.[16] He had his first heterosexual experience at the age of fourteen, when Mickey Rooney, his costar in *The Devil is a Sissy* (1936), took him to visit a prostitute,[17] and he spent the rest of his adolescence obsessively allowing himself to be "seduced" by female classmates, costars, and older women (including diva Joan Crawford), all eager to brag to their friends about how they had deflowered Skippy. But in the movies, heterosexual practice was antithetical to teenage masculinity, so Jackie proved himself a real boy by taking roles as street kids or military school brats who form intense, intimate, exclusive bonds with peers, including Martin Spellman, Freddie Bartholomew, Hally Chester, and Gene Reynolds.

THE MALE SHIRLEY TEMPLE

Born March 28, 1924, son of a British soldier and his estranged wife, raised first by his grandparents and then by Aunt Myllicent (who mollycoddled him into all of the dandyisms of the upper crust), Freddie Bartholomew was spotted by a talent scout while on holiday in New

York in 1934. His audition consisted of walking into David O. Selznick's office dressed in period costume and announcing, "I am David Copperfield." Entranced by his British accent, angelic face, and china-doll fragility, Selznick immediately invited the boy onto his lap, gave him a hug—a tender gesture rather out of character for the man-eating producer—and signed him up, not only for the starring role in *David Copperfield* (1935) but for a seven-year contract. He had arrived at precisely the right moment to fill the vacuum left by Jackie Cooper's pubescence, and soon he was bringing $1,000 per week home to Aunt Myllicent (three hundred times the average construction worker's salary of $33). He had become the "Male Shirley Temple." Studio executives were clamoring to hold him on their laps and offer him roles, mostly in fancy-dress costume dramas appropriate to his upper-class British accent: *Anna Karenina, Professional Soldier, Lloyd's of London, Kidnapped*. Regardless of the literary classic mined for the plotline, there was only one theme: A sweet, gentle, trusting, affectionate boy flirts outrageously with a gruff older man until his heart melts, he invites the boy onto his lap, and they form a sort of alternative family. Perhaps Freddie needed one: His private life was stormy.

In 1936, Freddie's mother suddenly realized that she loved the little superstar and showed up in Los Angeles to wrench guardianship away from Aunt Myllicent. His father and grandparents soon followed with their own claims of undying affection and desire for guardianship. Freddie spent the next three years in court, testifying in twenty-seven separate lawsuits filed by various family members against each other. Finally he was ordered to give his birth parents 20 percent of his earnings, but there was little left: Paying for all the lawsuits left him nearly broke, and the roles were drying up as he grew too old to comfortably fit on men's laps.

The adolescent Jackie Cooper tried to he-man his way from childhood cuteness to boys' book masculinity, but when Freddie entered puberty, he embraced his cuteness, making it a plot device: He played rich-kid dandies, weak, effeminate, and miserable until a buddy taught them how to catch baseballs, get their clothes dirty, and use slang, transforming them from mollycoddled honey-boy to tough, masculine Boy Next

Door. In effect, he *became* the rich man who finds elemental belonging by hugging a poor boy. However, an adolescent, both potent and potentially desiring, cannot easily defer the erotic from an eroticized bond.

The transformation to Boy Next Door begins early, in *Little Lord Fauntleroy* (Selznick International Pictures, dir. John Cromwell, 1936), about an heir to a British estate raised in poverty because his father is dead and his wealthy, miserable grandfather disapproves of his mother (a commoner named "Dearest"). Masculinizing Little Lord Fauntleroy would be a hard job: In Francis Hodgson Burnett's original novel, published in *St. Nicholas Magazine* in 1885, poor Cedric defined the word "mollycoddle" by being endlessly kissed, cuddled, coddled, and cloyed at by the smothering Dearest. In the 1921 silent movie, Mary Pickford played both mother and son, suggesting that they were two species of the same gentle, feminine spirit. Through the 1920s, millions of cooing middle-class mothers forced their sons into outrageous "Little Lord Fauntleroy" outfits: velvet coats with extra-wide lapels, frilly blouses with lace collars, and knee pants, all topped off with huge blond shoulder-length curls.[18] In 1936 a few mothers were still insisting on such outfits, their exclamations of "How precious!" deafening them to the sounds of their sons being pummeled in the schoolyard. Even the name Cedric came to signify the sissy: Soprano-voiced comedian Hugh Herbert swished unmercifully as Uncle Cedric in *Colleen* (1936).

Freddie's Cedric, nicknamed "Ceddie" to avoid the pansy connotations, has abandoned the girlish curls and frilly, lacy outfits of the earlier Fauntleroys, but still he is fragile, petite, and overpolite, and he finds the mean streets of Brooklyn inexpressibly gauche—and dangerous—until he is rescued from some bullies by the tough, English-mangling street kid Dick Tipton (fifteen-year-old Mickey Rooney, then best known as the Irish rapscallion Mickey McGuire in Our Gang–type comedy shorts). Both fatherless, both outsiders—Ceddie because he is too refined for Brooklyn adolescents, Dick because he is too vulgar—the two become instant "particular friends." Dick does teach Ceddie a bit about rough-and-tumbling, but their scenes together more often involve lying side by side, discussing their dreams, or else simply gazing at each other with mute longing.

When Ceddie is forced to move to England to live with his wealthy and therefore miserable grandfather, he and Dick endure a long, painful good-bye. The inarticulate Dick says, "Gee, I wish you didn't have to go. I really wish you weren't going." As a parting gift, he gives Ceddie a drawing of four muscular boxers, that is, a beefcake poster, simultaneously marking Ceddie's newfound toughness and the physicality of their bond. The beefcake poster does not appear in the original novel, nor in the 1921 silent version, nor in the recent versions starring Ricky Schroeder and George Baker.[19]

In England, Ceddie does not pollyanna the estate with his kind, gentle sissihood, like the child stars did; instead, he impresses his grandfather, the dour Earl of Dorincourt, with his masculine traits, his open, honest manner and lack of fear. Meanwhile, back in Brooklyn, Dick reads long letters and mopes about. "I wish he was here," he moans. "Gee, I wish he was here." He gets his wish at the end of the movie, when Ceddie invites him to come live in England on the estate. The homoromantic bond has proven permanent.[20]

As a teenager, Freddie Bartholomew was unable to stave off some media fussing about how much of a "he-man" he was. A 1938 article in the *New York Times* praised his macho interests: "two dogs, a workroom full of tools, a gasoline scooter, and a penchant for swimming and football."[21] But in his movie roles, he continued to play china-doll sissies who form strong bonds with he-man chums. Or try to. In *Listen, Darling* (MGM, 1938), Freddie plays an extremely fey Boy Next Door with an ultramasculine name (Buzz), who spends most of his time with his best friend Pinkie (Judy Garland) and her mom Dottie (Fay Wray). Film historians and video boxes today often misidentify Buzz as Pinkie's boyfriend, and the two actors were in fact in the midst of a holding-hands romance at the time, before Judy Garland moved on to more mature boyfriends and Freddie moved on to more clandestine affairs.[22] However, director Edward L. Marin took great pains to ensure that the two teenagers express no romantic interest in each other. Pinkie sings "Zing! Went the Strings of My Heart," which became a "love at first sight" standard, to her mother.

The Four Musketeers (Buzz, Pinkie, Dottie, and a wise-cracking little brother) embark on a cross-country trailer trip with the goal of finding Mom a husband so she won't be forced into a marriage of desperation with a stuffy banker. But Buzz searches far more assiduously than one would expect from a mere attempt to fix up a friend's mother. He interrogates each new prospect as if *he* expects the intimate involvement. At a campsite, he meets handsome lawyer-photographer Richard Thurlow (Walter Pidgeon), and Buzz can barely control his enthusiasm. He asks so many questions and comes on so strong that Thurlow suspiciously asks: "What is it that fascinates you so [about me]?" Forced to deflect attention away from his own desire, Buzz accuses him of being "a woman hater." "Why, do I look like one?" Thurlow counters.

The term "woman-hater," coined during the Renaissance, originally meant a man who refused to marry because he found the social company of women distasteful, regardless of whether he enjoyed bedding them or not. Through the first years of the twentieth century, masculinity in both boys and men included some degree of "woman-hating." Men who befriended or socialized with women were ridiculed as inappropriately feminine, as frilly, perfumed fops, as traitors to their sex; playwright August Strindberg tells us that they "purchase the woman's favour by delivering up the heads of their friends on silver chargers; and they absorb so much femininity, that they see with feminine eyes and feel with feminine feelings."[23] Often they were suspected of being sexually "deviant," like Valentino in the 1920s or Jackie Cooper in the 1930s. But Thurlow's assumption that one can tell a woman-hater by distinguishing physical characteristics suggests a new association.

Perhaps by 1938 it was the woman-hater, not the woman-lover, who was suspected of deviancy. According to the myth, the woman-hater rejected women as social companions because he was unable or unwilling to bed them. He was so inappropriately feminine that he could not experience the attraction of masculine to feminine that formed the basis of heterosexual desire. Instead, he was attracted to the masculine, to other men. Thurlow asks Buzz if he has any inappropriately feminine traits that might mark him as a "woman-hater," that is, as gay. Buzz immediately backtracks and says "no."

Thurlow grudgingly accepts an invitation to dinner (only after Buzz tells him that a single adult woman will be there as well), but then he changes his mind and drives away. Buzz feels personally betrayed and snippily dislikes him for the remainder of the film, promoting a staid banker as a potential husband instead and grimacing with disgust when Thurlow and Dottie finally kiss. Clearly he was shopping for a male companion of his own, but the heteroromantic main plot stymied his plans.

After *Listen Darling*, Freddie Bartholomew played scrappy sissies who ignore girls and buddy-bond with Mickey Rooney (*Lord Jeff*, *The Devil Is a Sissy*), Jackie Cooper (*The Spirit of Culver*, *Two Bright Boys*), and Tim Holt (playing his older brother in *Swiss Family Robinson*). Then, in the spring of 1940, sixteen years old, tall, thin, brittle looking, and as feminine as a young Quentin Crisp, he landed the most important buddy-bonding role of his life, in *Tom Brown's School Days* (RKO, dir. Robert Stevenson).

The original novel by Thomas Hughes (1857) predates boys' book series, but it has never gone out of print, so it would have been quite familiar to the audiences of 1940. Robert Drake writes that it became "one of the more influential texts for emerging gay writers, or writers with a gay sensibility," the inspiration for dozens of novels set in fondly recalled or envisioned private schools, where the love between boys is agonizing in its intensity: "Arthur was lying on a sofa by the open window, through which the rays of the Western sun stole gently, lighting up his white face and golden hair. Tom remembered a German picture of an angel which he knew . . . never til that moment had he felt how his little chum had twined himself round his heart." Presumedly the authors intend for these loves to presage the "true" heterosexual loves of adults or else to demonstrate the spiritual love of Christ for his people ("through hero-worship, to the worship of Him who is the King and Lord of heroes," Hughes tells us).[24] But nevertheless they embody homoromance in every detail except permanence. The movie version would condense the variety of same-sex loves to concentrate on a single pair.

A tall, slim seventeen-year-old named Jimmy Lydon, veteran of a few Broadway plays and a few minor films (including a feature-length commercial for Westinghouse), beat out fifteen hundred other boys in a nationwide contest for the role of Tom, "the typical American boy" even though he is still scripted as upper-class British. He expresses his typical American boyhood by being stoic, courageous, and adventurous;

by displaying himself as an object of desire (his shirt comes off twice—it never would again, on screen); and by ignoring girls. The daughter of a local shopkeeper appears in several scenes and plays a pivotal role in the plot, lending Tom her parents' carriage when he needs to escape, but Tom never gives her a second glance. Instead, he falls in love with a brittle, aristocratic upperclassman.

Freddie Bartholomew's East takes the initiative in the courtship, approaching Tom the moment he gets off the train, showing him around, taking him by the arm or shoulder, and gazing at him with the same rapt ardor he bestowed upon Mickey Rooney's Dick in *Little Lord Fauntleroy*. He gives Tom a picture of two ancient Greek warriors shaking hands, marks them as "Brown" and "East," and captions it "Friends Forever," a gesture reminiscent of the burly boxers his Ceddie received a few years earlier, marking both the physicality and the permanence of their bond.

East carefully dismisses or outwits Tom's other suitors. When they go out for "murphys" (baked potatoes sold as a snack), he protects Tom from a groping, leering boy named Tadpole.

> Tadpole: Is this the new fellow? Nice looking, isn't he?
> Tom: How do you do?
> Tadpole: (Looks him up and down.) Hungry, thank you.

A more violent threat comes from Sixth Formers (high school seniors), led by the bestial Flashman,[25] who shouts "fag!" to summon Tom to do his chores and homework, or to summon him for bouts of dangerous hazing. In Victorian England, the term referred to a bullied underclassman (because one of his jobs was fetching "faggots" of wood), but in the United States in 1940 it was more commonly used as derogatory slang for a gay man (because another of his jobs was to be buggered by the upperclassmen). One wonders how American audiences reacted to the shouts of "fag." Were homoromantic bonds already becoming suspect, as being a "woman-hater" had become?

When Tom is accused of "telling tales," the worst crime in the boys' honor code, East breaks up with him, tearing up the picture and sending Tom his half. Even after Tom is found innocent, East refuses to take him back, using oddly romantic rhetoric: "I'm not interested in you or anything about you! I never want to see you again!" Adult women in movies of the era rely on the phrase "I never want to see you again" to angrily break up with their boyfriends, but this is nearly the only example of its use among buddies. Obviously, Tom and East are not buddies, but homoromantic partners: Their relationship is emotionally intense, physically intimate, and exclusive, and but for their breakup, it would be permanent. The movie ends years later, when Tom and East encounter each other by accident at the tomb of their beloved head-master. Tom asks, "Can't we be friends?" and East grudgingly shakes his hand, thus giving closure to their romance. In the original story, Tom stands at the tomb alone. Only in the 1940 are Tom and East homoro-mantic partners, so only in 1940 do they require closure.

THE VIOLIN PRODIGY

Ronald Sinclair, or Ra Hould (a take on his real name, R. A. Hould), was born in Dunedin, New Zealand, on January 21, 1924, three months before Freddie Bartholomew. But he spent his childhood performing professionally as a violinist, only arriving in Hollywood in 1936, when he was twelve years old. He would have only a year or two to charm audiences before being afflicted with adolescence, but he looked so much Freddie Bartholomew's younger, softer, cheerier twin—with the British accent, angelic face, and china-doll fragility that made audiences swoon—that Republic rushed him immediately into movies about little boys aching to crawl onto the laps of older men. In 1937, he won the heart of a physician in *Doctor's Diary*, a tough-guy gangster in *Dangerous Holiday*, and a cowboy crooner in *Boots and Saddle*, all before summer vacation.

Later in 1937, in a stunning display of one-upmanship, MGM asked Ronald to take the role scripted for Freddie Bartholomew in *Thorough-breds Don't Cry* (dir. Alfred E. Green). He plays Roger Calverton, a Brit-ish aristocrat who has nothing left of his fortune but a racehorse. He and his grandfather relocate to America to seek their fortunes. He ap-proaches superstar jockey Timmie (seventeen-year-old Mickey Rooney) outside the locker room with a "proposition." He means a job offer, but

Timmie thinks he is a gay groupie making a pass at him and snipes, "Get lost, gunsel."[26] After the initial misunderstanding is cleared up, Timmie accepts the job and quickly warms up to the younger boy. They begin to "date," going to movies, dinners, and horse shows together. Cricket (Judy Garland), daughter of the landlady at the local jockey boardinghouse, is also sweet on Roger, and she and Timmie compete openly for his affection. But Timmie is somewhat more aggressive.

When Roger falls off his horse during a jockeying lesson, Timmie insists on doctoring him: He makes Roger lie on the bed with his pants down and begins enthusiastically rubbing liniment into his legs and thighs, stopping just short of his buttocks. Roger protests that he feels fine and tries to get up, but Timmie exclaims, "I'm just getting started!" and forces him down again. Timmie's obvious joy in the physical contact seems much more than medicinal, and one wonders what else he intends for the afternoon. Cricket evidently wonders the same thing: She stands outside the door and sings to distract them. In an astonishingly vivid scene, Roger keeps jumping off the bed and pulling up his pants, trying to choose the girl over the boy, and a frustrated Timmie keeps jerking Roger's pants down and throwing him on the bed again.

Eventually the two older teenagers stop competing and woo Roger jointly. Though Roger agrees that he might marry Cricket someday, his salvation does not come through the promise of future heterosexual respectability but through learning manliness from Timmie: He becomes an accomplished jockey and canny racing speculator, shifting from effete, Old World inherited money to American capitalism. In the last scene, the three friends and their guardians drive away in a horse van, singing gleefully as they embark not on a marriage but on a horse-racing business.

Ronald was not particularly busy during the war, as scrappy sissies were going out of style and Mickey Rooney was grabbing up all of the good adolescent roles. Ronald played the young Ebenezer Scrooge in *A Christmas Carol*, a sissy conned by the Dead End Kids in *They Made Me a Criminal*, and the boy King Edward in *Tower of London*, before getting what he thought was a big break at Columbia with *The Five Little Peppers and How They Grew*, an adaptation of the first volume of the popular book series (1881). Ronald played Jasper King, a rich boy who befriends the poor family in spite of his father's snobbish disapproval. Contrary to studio expectations, the movie was not a hit, and the presence of an aging child star did little to boost ticket sales. In the three sequels, the role of Jasper King is minimized.

Prey to the same large-scale elimination of scrappy sissies that felled Freddie Bartholomew, Ronald acted for the last time in *Desperate Journey* (1942) playing one of several Allied soldiers shot down behind enemy lines in Poland. Although he is twenty-two years old, he is still playing a "youngster." He expresses no interest in girls and buddy-bonds extensively with Errol Flynn (who was infamous for his behind-the-scenes exploits with sweet young things of both sexes[27]). In the 1950s Ronald started a new career as a film editor, adding his talents to *The Amazing Colossal Man*, *Attack of the Puppet People*, *The Raven*, *Sergeant Dead Head*, and many other movies. He was married for thirty-one years and died in 1992.[28]

WHAT HAPPENED AT MIDNIGHT

In the 1930s, competition from movies, radio, and pulp magazines demolished the market for serial novels—the number of series titles diminished from seventy-six to seven, the audience shifted downward from high schoolers to children and young teens, and the football and scouting exploits all but vanished in favor of globetrotting adventure. But the most famous boys' novel series survived and even thrived: the *Hardy Boys,* introduced in 1927 by the Stratemeyer Syndicate with the usual "breeder set" of six volumes.[29] Frank and Joe Hardy, high school–aged sons of the famous detective Fenton Hardy, begin by butting into their father's cases but soon find trouble enough on their own: They capture smugglers and counterfeiters, thwart spies and evil cultists, and investigate haunted houses that aren't really haunted after all.

Although they are both in the same year of high school, the Hardys are a year apart in age. They share the Herculean musculature and breathtaking good looks standard in boys' books, but their personalities are complementary: The older Frank is reasoned, logical, and serious, while the younger Joe is impetuous, emotional, and something of a jokester.[30] Since the *Hardy Boys* managed to endure and even prosper through the 1930s and 1940s (and on to today), while other boys' book series failed, we may conclude that they provided something unavailable in the movies, radio programs, and comic books of the era.[31] Perhaps what they provided was homoromance, even after girls came to dominate the thoughts and lives of other Boys Next Door.

The *Hardy Boys* series displays several progressive innovations, such as a multiethnic cast (the boys' friends include the Jewish Phil Cohen and the Italian Tony LoPrieto) and the freedom to like girls without ridicule: Frank has a "favorite among all the girls of his class," Callie, and Joe has "an attachment" to Iola.[32] However, Callie and Iola appear in only four of the ten installments published between 1930 and 1939 (and once more by allusion), and never as girlfriends. No individual boy-girl dates are planned or discussed, no romantic attachment fuels any plot, and the only fade-out embraces occur between siblings. Callie and Iola dance with the Hardys at parties, invite themselves along on their picnics, and run into them downtown, not so much objects of heteroromantic desire as emblems of the "ordinary time" that frames the call to adventure.

In the first six installments, the brothers also have particular boy friends, whom they do invite out on dates, to picnics and movies and camping trips. Frank favors chubby, good-natured Chet, who frets over household chores, befriends girls, and eventually goes to art school. Joe favors Biff, with "muscles like steel," who dislikes household chores, dislikes girls, and plays every school sport (he is named after a famous boxer relative). The choices of boy friend clearly complement their own gender polarization, masculine Frank with feminine Chet, feminine Joe with masculine Biff. Later, however, Biff is demoted to a minor character, and Chet becomes a ubiquitous best friend, confidant, tagalong, and comic relief. After the mystery is solved and explained, he returns the Hardys to ordinary time by saying something about sitting down to dinner or else, "We've heard the story. Now let's dance!" He no longer favors either brother. The Hardys no longer have particular friends; instead, as Kismaric and Heiferman state, they "live for each other."[33]

The Hardys sleuth out clues together, piece together mysteries together, befriend the innocent and excoriate the guilty together, and in the frame stories attend all of the parties and picnics as a pair; one has to read through a great many pages to find a scene where they separate by choice. They touch wrists and shoulders; they finish each other's sentences; they express a world with a glance. At least once per story, one of the brothers is captured, tied up, and threatened with torture or murder, and he is rescued by the other brother. The two share the intensity, intimacy, and exclusivity of homoromance, and perhaps the permanence, since they never discuss their immanent entry into adulthood, except to vaguely declare that they want to become detectives. All that separates them from homoromance is the fraternal bond: Their passion is the passion of brothers, not of lovers.

Why are Frank and Joe brothers? By boys' book convention, they should be strangers who meet for the first time as competitors on a high school gridiron or else in darkest Africa, when one saves the other from being sacrificed to the Leopard God. Even the Hardy series must fudge a bit with the backstory, alluding vaguely to an "illness" that kept Frank out of school for a year to explain why Frank and Joe are in the same grade. For that matter, why *must* they be in the same grade? They are rarely shown in school, so it would make little difference except to establish that they cannot bear to be apart for even the fifty minutes of an algebra class. Real brothers sometimes require time alone or with other friends. Not the Hardys.

Men in mass culture are often cast as brothers when the plot requires that they care deeply for each other, when one will be rescued or have a deathbed scene, since the fraternal bond allows for an intensity and an intimacy that would otherwise signify romance. But the Hardys display none of the easy jocularity, the good-natured ribbing, the posturing and the bullying of real brothers, in mass media or in real life. They behave precisely as if their bond is romantic rather than fraternal, as if they are in love.

The oddly placed girlfriends and the unconvincing fraternal bond suggest a desire for homoromance diluted by a discomfort unknown in *The Moving Picture Boys*, *The Radio Boys*, or *Dick and Company*. Teenage boys could love each other because they presumably were incapable of desiring each other; once homoerotic possibility was recognized, they must be given girlfriends, or transformed into brothers, or both. By the time the *Hardy Boys* premiered in 1927, writers were evidently aware that teenage boys could not only love each other, but become lovers. Sex had entered the homoromantic Arcadia.

In the same way, Jackie Cooper's movie roles in the late 1930s step back a bit from the homoromance, giving his same-sex loves some heterosexual competition. In *Gangster's Boy* (Monogram, dir. William Nigh, 1938), Jackie plays Larry Kelly, a type with the ultracompetent Boy Next Door heroes of the book series. He is a whiz-kid valedictorian, a letterman in every sport, yet also a fun-loving regular fella: He drives a jalopy covered with graffiti, plays the drums in a swing band, and litters his speech with goofy expressions like, "Who do you think you are? Anyhow?" He is, of course, stunningly handsome, so thoroughly desired by the guys, gals, teachers, and townsfolk that they always look like they want to rip his clothes off and ravish him on the spot, but he is devoted to his long-term "particular friend," Bill Davis (future Broadway star Tommy Wonder). "We'll always be together," Larry exclaims in a tender moment, and indeed after their high school graduation they plan to enroll at West Point together and embark on a military career as a couple, like Dick Prescott and Greg Holmes in the H. Irving Hancock stories.

When Larry transgresses the homoromantic rule of exclusivity by dating a girl (Bill's sister), Bill seems to resent the competition: Every time Larry swoops in for a kiss, Bill finds some excuse to interrupt them. He also tries to deflect Larry's newfound heteroromantic inclinations by claiming that pictures of girls are not allowed in cadets' lockers at West Point: "You're not supposed to waste time thinking about girls . . . you've got important things to think about!" This may or not be true, but Larry does not challenge him.

The somewhat strained homoromance is further interrupted when Larry's father, Knuckles, returns from an extended "business trip" up the river and confesses that he is actually a reformed gangster, just released from prison (perhaps the name "Knuckles" should have provided a clue). When the townsfolk discover the terrible secret, they turn into slathering bigots. No gangster's son has the right to sully their town: They kick Larry out of the nightclub where he's performing, refuse to applaud after his valedictory speech, and forbid their children from seeing him. On the night of the big dance, Bill and his sister both sneak out of the house to see Larry, both positioning themselves as "dates," as competitors for his affection. But then the sister is forgotten, and the rest of the movie is traditional homoromance.

Driving home from the big dance, they accidentally hit and injure a small child. Bill was at the wheel, but Larry claims responsibility, recognizing that an arrest for reckless driving will ruin either of their chances of being admitted to West Point. But Bill is unwilling to let Larry sacrifice his career. They posture and argue about who will take the blame until the judge uncovers the truth and exonerates them both, intoning that they have "learned a lot about friendship." But really it is the adults who have learned a lot. Larry and Bill already knew that they were ready to fight and die for each other, that their bond far transcended any momentary flirtation with girls. Instead of a heteronormative clinch, the movie ends with the boys gazing at each other with eye-shimmering affection. In less than five years, such a gaze would be impossible among Boys Next Door.

3

DEAD ENDS
THE LOST BOYS

Poor boys in fiction always turned out to be misplaced heirs until 1866, when Unitarian minister Horatio Alger, ejected from his parish on Cape Cod after taking liberties with a sixteen-year-old, moved to New York to live in exile. As he wandered down the mean streets where Walt Whitman had sought male companionship only a few years before,[1] he was startled by the huge number of "street Arabs." There were between ten thousand and forty thousand teenagers, mostly Irish, some Italian, Jewish, and Bohemian, even a few Anglo-white, living in flophouses or on the streets while working as bootblacks, pickpockets, newsboys, and rent boys. They were not children, like the pitiable doe-eyed "street urchins"; they were nearly men, strong, powerful, and savage. Their clothes were mismatched and ragged; they stank of tobacco and sweat. They stared with dark-eyed malice, or flashed the oily, insincere grins of con artists, or sauntered their availability as rough trade.[2] Yet beneath the smudges and rags, the malice and deceit, Alger saw something of value in them, something beautiful.

He had been writing fluff books like *Bertha's Christmas Vision* (1856) and *Nothing to Do: A Tilt at Our Best Society* (1857), but now he had a new goal: to demonstrate that poor boys deserved adult attention just as much as middle class boys. The best social engineers of the era (all white, middle-class, native born) believed that juvenile delinquency was the result of biological disposition: Some people were simply born dull-

witted, slothful, and depraved, while others were born intelligent, indus-
trious, and morally upright.[3] But Alger was an avid physiognomist who
associated virtue with beauty, and these homeless teenagers were just as
handsome, muscular, and "clear of eye" as the sons of Boston Brahmins
back home. Even more so. He returned to his flat and started to write:

> In spite of his dirt and rags there was something about Dick that
> was attractive. It was easy to see that if he had been clean and well
> dressed he would have been decidedly good-looking. Some of his
> companions were sly, and their faces inspired distrust; but Dick had a
> frank, straight-forward manner that made him a favorite.[4]

Alger was not alone in his interest in immigrants. Tin Pan Alley
churned out dozens of sappily sentimental adulations of Irish immigrant
girls: "Sweet Rosie O'Grady" (1896), "My Wild Irish Rose" (1899), "Peg
O' My Heart" (1913), "The Daughter of Mother Machree" (1915), "The
Daughter of Rosie O'Grady" (1918). Irish, Jewish, Dutch, and Scandina-
vian immigrants frolicked on the silent screen. *Abie's Irish Rose* (1922),
about a Jewish boy married to an Irish girl, became one of early Broadway's biggest hits, with 2,327 performances.[5]

The Lost Boy grew out of this undisguised voyeurism. Where the
Boy Next Door was middle-class, Anglo-white, Protestant, with dual
parents and a picket-fence home, the Lost Boy was working-class or
poor, usually Irish Catholic, usually fatherless and often motherless, living in a bare tenement or on the streets. He led a savage, chaotic life,
his manliness threatened not by effeminizing civilization but by vio-
lence and corruption, the "social disorganization" that would lead to
hypermasculinity or effeminacy in adulthood. Yet because he was *not
yet* a man, he presented no threat to the arbiters of mass culture. Indeed,
his Arcadia became more blatantly erotic than that of the Boys Next
Door, a Dionysian idyll where conventions were turned upside down
and the hidden was brought to light. The descriptions of the hero as
"very handsome" became a salacious leer, and the bond between teenage boys or between boys and men moved from the coyly flirtatious to
the palpably sensual.

RAGS TO RICHES

Horatio Alger's first Street Arab novel, *Ragged Dick: or, Streetlife in New York with the Bootblacks* (1868), became a runaway bestseller and a critical success. Never particularly inventive, Alger spent the rest of his life writing the same novel over and over, merely changing locations and incidental details, and adding some violent scenes to compete with the cowboys and masked detectives in the penny dreadfuls. He was prolific, chugging through three or more novels per year (six in 1888 alone) without the benefit of a ghost-writing syndicate, but he never found the success of *Ragged Dick* again. His main income came from tutoring children. He lived in penury in boarding houses, among the Street Arabs that he loved, and died in obscurity in 1898.[6] His books were forgotten until after World War I, when the market for boys' serial novels was heating up and Simon & Street reprinted them, not as edifying do-gooder tales but as gripping mysteries full of danger and intrigue. The marketing ploy worked, and soon many middle-class boys were requesting or purchasing copies of *Paul the Peddler*, *Phil the Fiddler*, *Fame and Fortune*, and *Luck and Pluck* to sit beside *Don Sturdy* and the *Chums of Scranton High*.

Though Alger is associated with the rags-to-riches motif, his hero typically does not rise from poverty to power through all-American industriousness, pluck, and ingenuity. He acquires his "wealth," usually a clerical job or a place in a private school, only because a wealthy benefactor takes an economic-erotic interest in him, in a parallel to the avuncular-erotic interest that the wealthy benefactor takes in the child star.[7] However, most of the stories do not dwell on the adult-teen relationship; the plots are usually constructed around a romantic bond between two immigrant boys or else between an immigrant and an Anglo-white rich boy.

In his seminal critique of postmodernism, Jameson argues that cultural products serve to "manage desire in social terms, negotiating between wish-fulfillment and repression, or to arouse fantasy content within carefully symbolic containment structures, which defuse the awakened (dangerous) desires."[8] Alger does not mask his physical attraction to the Lost Boys he creates; like Boys Next Door, they are described continually and glowingly as handsome, manly, erect, clear-eyed, and so on. But placing them in the arms of peers while benevolent adults look on suggests that what he desires is less the body of the boy than the glimpse of a permanent, exclusive, same-sex romance that, as an adult, he is denied. He gazes at the boys gazing at each other, just as the boys' book writers (and readers) looked to Arcadia for expression of the same-sex bonds that in real life they found impossible or undesirable.

For instance, in *Facing the World* (1917), sixteen-year-old orphan Harry Vane runs away from his abusive guardian and meets an itinerant magician, Professor Hemingway, who notes approvingly that he is "well-built . . . healthy and strong" and hires him as an assistant. However, their bond lacks passion and intimacy, even the familial intimacy of boy and surrogate father. They are business partners. Harry starts singing to entertain the crowds between acts, but soon his physique draws more crowds than his voice: "[H]is fresh, attractive face and manly appearance won him a welcome in all the towns on their route."[9] Two years pass, and Harry's winning combination of beefcake and dancehall numbers has made him the star of the show. He and the professor embark on a voyage to Australia, where they will be touring.

During the voyage, the Professor is absent, explained away as seasick, and Harry goes cruising. He responds coyly to the flirtations of the foppish Montgomery Clinton, but quickly decides that he prefers Jack, a boy his own age or slightly younger. Clinton jealously disapproves of the match, but Harry is insistent: "Don't you think he is a good-looking boy, Mr. Clinton?" The fop has to admit that Jack is good-looking.

Jack has many other suitors: He "was a general favorite on board, as is apt to be the case with a boy, if he possesses any attractive qualities." The captain, a morose Byronic figure, is especially interested in him and keeps assigning extra duties to keep him too busy to see Harry. When they manage to meet anyway for a late-night rendezvous, the captain in a drunken rage tries to shoot Jack, but Harry intervenes and pulls him out of danger.

> "You have saved my life!" [Jack] said. "I will always be your friend. I would lay down my life for you."

"It's all right, Jack," said Harry, rather shyly. "You would have done the same for me."

"Yes, I would," answered Jack, heartily, "But there's no one else who would have done it for me."

When the ship is damaged in a storm, the captain and many passengers take to lifeboats, but Harry, Jack, the professor, and a few others decide to stick it out. Clinton stays because he is afraid of the tiny lifeboats, and he makes himself useful by doing the cooking for the little party. Since the captain is gone, Jack and Harry can be more open about their courtship, and "they grew still more intimate." Now we see that the professor was never a homoromantic partner, as he does not grumble or complain about Harry and Jack. He is not jealous; he has not been replaced.

The ship eventually runs aground on a desert island, where Harry and company meet some other castaways, establish a gleeful Yankee democracy, run afoul of the now-deranged captain, and after many more adventures are rescued. The professor makes his way back to America, to reconcile with a never-before mentioned wife, but Harry and Jack, now permanent partners, decide to go on to Australia after all. Alger concludes: "Here we may leave Harry and Jack to pursue their course to such eminence as they may desire from the characteristics they have portrayed in this narrative." Whatever that means, it is clear that Alger frames adult romantic interest in teenagers as either humorously ineffectual (Clinton) or dangerous and destructive (the captain), but always unrequited. Only the two teenage boys can share a permanent, exclusive, intimate bond. In Alger's world, only peers can experience homoromance.

WILD BOYS AND BOXERS

During the Depression, when thousands of boys set out on the road and the first fears of juvenile delinquency arose, the old model of teenagers as either handsome and innately good or ugly and innately bad had to be revised. Now crowded tenements, abusive or indifferent parents, and the lack of green fields produced the bad, the indolent, and the ugly, and the job of the adult benefactor was not to reward the boy's innate virtue but to draw him away from the unhealthy environment, sometimes through a literal trip to the country, sometimes through starting a basketball team or youth choir. As a consequence, the homoromance occurred less typically between peers than between a youth heading down the wrong path and an adult determined to save him. Junior Durkin played a new-style Lost Boy in *Hell's House* (1932) and *Manhunt* (1933), and Frank Coghlan Junior played one in *The Little Red Schoolhouse* (1936), but the most prolific of all the Lost Boys on film was Frankie Darro.

Born December 22, 1917, in Chicago to a family of circus performers, Frankie was a movie star by the age of five, playing the titular waif abandoned by his mother in *Half-a-Dollar Bill* (1923). He specialized in Westerns—*Judgment of the Hills, Tyrant of Red Gulch, Phantom of the Range,* over fifty before he hit puberty—often playing pure, innocent Indian boys who bond with cowboy heroes. He had a dark, handsome face with hard features perfect for the wind-swept desert, and he was compact, agile, and athletic, perfect for leaping onto a horse or out of a burning building. Though he lacked the china-doll fragility of a child star and rarely wept over misunderstandings with Dad, he could weep over more serious matters, such as frontier death and destruction, and still maintain his toughness. Close-ups of Frankie's tear-streaked face become as familiar to audiences as Jackie Cooper's pout, and he often parodied them later in his career.

Since he was never a cherubic-charming child star, Frankie did not have to reinvent himself in adolescence. There were few movie-magazine articles about his he-man interests, and he evidently felt little pressure to demonstrate that he was heterosexual. One finds no evidence of adolescent heteroromance at all, except for a brief, mysterious engagement to Virginia Gumm (Judy Garland's sister), when they were both students at the Lawlor Professional School in Hollywood. When other Hollywood teens of the era reminisce about groups of pals bargaining with prostitutes, leering at lesbian performance acts, or waking up in bed naked together after nights of unspecified carousing, his name is absent.[10] Frank Coghlan Junior, Frankie's sometime costar, does recall seeing him at a brothel. He is naked except for a towel tented by an erection, and he is dancing around with nylon panties on his head. But even this single fleeting glimpse, recalled sixty years later, seems to be clowning rather than an expression of heterosexual desire.[11] Frankie spent his adolescence riding the range, or occasionally inner-city streets, as a wounded boy who finds solace in the arms of adult father figures: George Brent, George G. Lewis, Jack Mulhall, and Gene Autry.

In 1936, when he was seventeen years old, Frankie began a series of nine "thrill-o-dramas," produced by Maurice Coon for the Poverty Row studios, Ambassador and Monogram.[12] Most were adapted from stories by Peter B. Kyne, who wrote about men's men—cowboys, sailors, and lumberjacks—brawling and bonding in all-male enclaves, with an occasional invalid mother or baby sister thrown in for bathos. He even wrote one called *Man's Man*. Frankie plays smart-aleck street kids, usually the orphaned sons of Irish immigrants, who become involved with glamorous Anglo-white adults, usually Kane Richmond (a square-jawed beefcake actor, veteran of many two-fisted actioners, and later a fashion designer). They are stable owner and jockey's little brother in *Racing Blood* (1936), reporter and snoopy kid in *Tough to Handle* (1937), state trooper and snoopy kid in *Young Dynamite* (1937).[13] But Frankie's on-screen persona treats Kane Richmond much differently than he did his earlier adult costars. Instead of the eye-gleaming hero worship of a boy seeking a father or a big brother, he displays the clumsy overtures, hypersensitive jealousy, and maudlin sentimentality of a first love. And Richmond responds with smoldering looks, gazing at the body rather than the bond; Frankie may not be his first love, but neither is he a potential little brother or surrogate son.

The change was monumental, marking a shift from peers to men as the objects of teenage boys' desire. During the war, adult-teen homo-romance would come to dominate among Lost Boys and eventually Adventure Boys as well. It is important to note that they do not signify ephebophilia, since the teenagers in question were usually played by fully grown adults and scripted as seventeen or eighteen, of legal age. Also, there is usually a structural reversal, in which the teenager becomes dominant, takes charge of the relationship, in effect becoming "the man," while the adult becomes passive, swoons, in effect becoming "the boy." The two thus become equals.

The adult-teen homoromance was emotionally intense and physically intimate, but it was rarely exclusive: Kane Richmond also fell in love with a woman. Frankie generally lives with his older sister, who has one or two early scenes with Richmond and then reappears at the fadeout to melt into his arms. The nod to heteronormativity serves to deflect the new awareness of homoerotic potential, like making Frank and Joe brothers in the *Hardy Boys* series. If Richmond marries Frankie's sister, then he and Frankie can be together tomorrow and the next day, and every day for the rest of their lives, loving each other deeply and passionately, because they will "really" be brothers, and they can pretend that this is the relationship they wanted all along.

Though the adult may suddenly back away from the homoromance by "realizing" that he is in love with a woman, the teenager remains firmly in the homoromantic Arcadia throughout. Most movies in the series have a girl hanging around with a crush on Frankie, for him to reject with varying degrees of callousness. Most of the teenage-boy movies of the Depression era eliminate girls from the script altogether, except as older sisters, so the question of heteroromance never comes up, but it is rare for a Boy Next Door or Adventure Boy to actively reject the advances of a girl. Yet Lost Boy Frankie does it over and over, proclaiming himself a "woman hater," ordering the girl to get lost, complaining bitterly when he is forced into a dance or a date; in fifty-two movie appearances between 1930 and 1939, his character has an explicit heterosexual romance only once, in *Three Kids and a Queen* (1935). An internet biography suggest that "this element was part of his character's hilarious charm,"[14] but, as we have seen, a lack of heterosexual interest in the teenage boy was perfectly ordinary; its opposite, girl-craziness, was portrayed as hilarious, roughly the equivalent of dressing the boy in drag today. Frankie's assertion of woman-hating is an expression of adolescent masculinity, marking him as tough and strong in spite of the heterosexual triangulation necessary for the plot.

Born to Fight (1936) reverses the triangulation, giving Richmond no heterosexual interest while Frankie is "seen with" girls twice: He appears driving a car with a girl next to him and a boy-girl couple in the other seat, evidently on a double date; and at a party, he "steals" an older man's date and dances briefly and awkwardly with her, perhaps as a joke. Elsewhere, the movie emphasizes homoromance. On the lam after he clobbers a gangster, boxer Tom "Bomber" Brown (Kane Richmand) takes an interest in the homeless adolescent Baby Face (Frankie). They set up housekeeping, and Bomber suggests that Baby Face could make a good living as a boxer (after all, he already has the name for it). Several years pass—the heterosexual liaisons occur after Baby Face has grown up—while we see the standard boxing and backstage plot of fame, hubris, dramatic fall, and a realization that "there's no place like home."

However, Bomber and Baby Face share an intimacy and an intensity unknown in other boxer-manager teams. *Palooka* (1934) lacks any scenes where the manager and the boxer (Jimmy Durante, Stu Erwin) walk off with their arms wrapped around each other's waists, or enfold each other in full-body hugs, or sit pressed together on a bench, drawing their faces so close together that they seem preparing to kiss. *Kid Galahad* (1937) never shows the manager (Eddie G. Robinson) sharing a house with the boxer (Wayne Morris), or cooking him breakfast, or asking "How did you sleep?" or working twelve-hour shifts at a gas station to pay for his training. In *Golden Boy* (1939), the manager and the boxer (Adolphe Menjou, William Holden) do not break up, realize how much they mean to each other, and then reconcile with teary-eyed abandon. Bomber and Baby Face do.

Devil Diamond (Ambassador, dir. Leslie Goodwins), released January 15, 1937, oddly gives the boy an unrequited crush on the man. This time gangsters take an interest in adolescent Lee (Frankie Darro) and offer to train him as a boxer. They're really using the boxing academy as a front for a jewel heist. Living at a boarding house during his "training," Lee becomes quite taken with fellow boarder Jerry Carter (Kane Richmond), a government agent working undercover, and though Jerry is not sure at first if Lee is accomplice, pigeon, or gunsel, he soon warms up to the boy and reveals his true identity. Now sharing a secret life, the two spend many scenes heart-to-hearting and going on long walks together. When Jerry also begins courting a girl, Lee roils with jealousy. What does he need a "dame" for? Why can't it be just the two of them? One night Jerry fails to appear at the boarding house at his usual time, and Lee stays up late waiting, along with Yvonne (Rosita Baker), the landlady's daughter. Finally Jerry shows up:

> Lee: [Anxiously.] Where you been? I've been looking for you.
> Jerry: Out for a walk. Want anything special?
> Lee: [Hesitates.] No . . . I just wanted to say hello.
> Jerry: Okay—hello. [Goes upstairs.]
> Yvonne: [Frustrated.] Is that all you wanted to say to Jerry? Hello?

A moment later, Lee musters up his courage and scoots up the stairs after him, but even when they are alone, he is altogether afraid to say whatever needs to be said. He stares and stumbles, and mutters incoherently about wanting to become a junior g-man, until Jerry gets frustrated and asks him to leave. Lee's inability to express his interest in Jerry is counterbalanced by his very vocal disinterest in Yvonne: He rebuffs her with snide remarks, tells her in no uncertain terms to "scram," accepts a date with her only when Jerry offers to double. The movie ends with the bad guys subdued and Jerry in a clinch with his girl, while Lee looks on in rather obvious distress. There has been no physical intimacy, no exclusivity, no promise of permanence; the passion has been all one-sided. Yvonne swoops in to kiss him on the cheek, and he grimaces as we fade out to dreams deferred.

DEAD END

On August 24, 1937, the most popular Lost Boy movie of the Depression era premiered: *Dead End* (Samuel Goldwyn), the film version of Sidney Kingsley's heavy-handed Broadway play about how criminals are made, not born. It was scripted by infamously radical Lilian Hellman (*The Children's Hour, The Little Foxes*) and directed by William Wyler (*Dodsworth, Wuthering Heights*), and it starred box-office big-shots Humphrey Bogart and Joel McCrea. Innocent of this backstory of political and sociological bandstanding were the five "Dead End Kids" from the original play, child stars grown into teenagers and young adults when no one was looking. None really came from Dead Ends: Billy Halop was a radio cowboy named Bobby Benson, Gabriel Dell a radio crooner, Huntz Hall a graduate of New York's Professional Children's School, Bobby Jordan a boy model, and Leo Gorcey the well-seasoned son of vaudevillians. Yet they created a myth of the Lost Boy as a wisecracking, irreverent noble savage, a myth that endured in hundreds of films, radio plays, pulp stories, and novels for nearly twenty years, until Marlon Brando and James Dean summarily ended its reign.[15]

Dead End takes place within a single day and night on a single block in Manhattan near the East River, where the poor Irish immigrants in their tenements and the ultrarich Anglo-whites in a high-rise apartment complex peer out windows at each other. Dave Connell (Joel McCrea) grew up in "this rat's nest" and tried to escape by studying architecture, but he has returned, unable to find work. Meanwhile, his friend Marty Martin (Humphrey Bogart) grew up to become a gangster named Baby Face and has returned to lie low for awhile. A group of neighborhood boys, all teenagers,[16] immigrants' sons and orphans, zooms across the set. They spend the day swimming, playing cards, fighting, assaulting sissies, offending the sensibilities of the rich, and posturing for the approval of "big men." The men, in turn, take an interest in the boys and compete for their attention.

Frankie Thomas stripped down to swim in a lagoon and Frankie Darro was occasionally filmed in his undershirt, but in *Dead End* bodies are displayed blatantly and continuously. Before five minutes have passed, Tommy (Billy Halop), a dark, earnest seventeen-year-old, rushes out of his tenement apartment wearing overalls and no shirt. It's a hot day, so he and his friends decide to go swimming in the East River, an excuse to spend the first third of the movie in their underwear, displaying their adolescent physiques extensively, if not obtrusively. Diving into the East River is not essential to the plot; their interactions could have worked just as well fully clothed. But, as many authors have noted, bodies of water signify the boundary between civilization and savagery, childhood and adulthood, the liminal space of adolescence itself.[17]

At midday, they put on clothes—only the clown Dippy (Huntz Hall) remains shirtless—to play cards and beat up the sissy, but afterward they strip down again. Tommy drops his pants and converses awhile in his underwear and, in case we haven't gotten a good enough look, gets grabbed by a rich man from the high rise so he can squirm and twist, muscles straining. Reuter notes that in the 1930s, hirsute, swarthy, and sweaty physiques denoted working-class "brutes," but the Dead

End Kids are smooth, lean, and very pale, their bodies almost glowing against the dark, sooty backdrops, suggesting that they do not belong there.[18] They belong in an angelic world, in an Eden unsullied by sin (Bobby Jordan's character is even named Angel). One is reminded of the somewhat more bucolic setting of Thomas Eakins's *Swimming*, where Berger locates in the adolescent nudes "a reassurance of an essentialized masculine identity." Yet they represent something more, an elemental connection with each other, sensuous, intense, and physical, erotic but preromantic. They are not yet separated into homoromantic pairs, like the Boys Next Door, not yet constrained into exclusivity and permanence. They are Dick and Company before they graduate and pursue separate lives, Frankie Darro among his chums in *Phantom Empire* (1936) before he settles down with Kane Richmond.[19] They are a pack.

Wlodarz notes a similar exuberant nudity in the opening sequence of *Sleepers* (1996), set similarly in Hell's Kitchen, with four boys swimming, playing in the spray of a fire hydrant, and sunbathing "side by side in a near fusion of flesh." But he argues that the latter film specifically associates youthful purity with masculinity and therefore with heterosexuality ("free from any taint of sexual or psychic depravity").[20] And certainly *Dead End* does not. The boys exhibit no interest in heterosexual coupling, except for a taunt from Spit (Leo Gorcey) at a rich girl who can't find her boyfriend: "Won't I do?" When they see rich couples dancing on a balcony, they pretend disgust: "Look, they're dancing like they like it!"

But they are quite aware of same-sex erotic practice. When they taunt the sissy with "what are ya, a boy or a goil?" evoking the classic intersexed pansy of 1930s comedies,[21] they add a sexual dig. Angel thrusts his pelvis backward and forward, not side to side as he would to signify girlishness—he is emulating coitus, pretending that he wishes to have sex with the boy. He has been to reform school and knows about the same-sex practices there; when Tommy is arrested, he offers explicit advice on whom to hook up with and whom to avoid.

Early in the film, the kids encounter a new boy, who is acting the mollycoddle by rocking a baby carriage. He and Tommy exchange shy smiles, but the others try to strong-arm a quarter out of him. He only has three cents, so they grab him, throw him to the ground, pull up his shirt, and start to pull down his pants. There is a close-up of his waist with many hands on his belt, one cupping his crotch. He struggles wildly. At that moment an adult intervenes and surely prevents a sexual assault. Amazingly, the boys' homoerotic language and behavior was toned down by the censors.[22] In Kingsley's original play, dirt is rubbed directly into the boy's privates, and in other scenes the boys playfully grab at each other's zippers.[23]

Awareness of same-sex practice was common among Lost Boys in fiction as well. Studs Logan, the fifteen-year-old Irish-Catholic boy in James T. Farrell's *Studs Lonigan* trilogy (1938), has a girlfriend: "[H]e got soft, and felt like he was all mud and mush inside; he held his hand over his heart, and told himself 'My Lucy'!" There are older men in his world whose caresses and invitations to lonely places give Studs "an awful feeling," in contrast to the joy he feels in homoerotic horseplay with his chums. They grab at each other's crotches and jerk open the buttons of each other's pants, presumably to expose their sex organs. They play kissing games, and not only with girls: "Dan kissed Bill . . . it was funny. [Bill] kissed Tubby, who blushed with embarrassment, and they nearly all split their sides laughing."[24]

Many critics have noted the homoerotic subtexts in gangster films; according to Borde and Chaumeton's classic study, film noir was characterized by anguish, malaise, a loss of psychological bearings, and "a nebulous and polymorphous" eroticism.[25] Often that eroticism becomes fixed as same-sex desire or, as Jack Shadoain notes in homophobic contempt, "a tinge of abnormality."[26] In real life, same-sex practice cemented the bonds of many gangs of the period, and "respectable" middle-class men through the 1930s sought working-class partners for their homoerotic liaisons.[27] But why is the homoerotic activity here located among teenagers?

The ideological constructs of "the homosexual" and "the adolescent" were created at the same time, around the turn of the century. They were both conceived of as underevolved, atavistic groups that required intervention, diagnosis, and redemption to take their place in the glorious white, male, European, heterosexual future.[28] So it is not surprising that the two models intermingled, "the homosexual" perceived as a perpetual adolescent poised on the brink of adult responsibility, and "the adolescent" perceived as possibly queer, poised on the brink of adult heteronormativity.

DEAD END KIDS

After *Dead End,* Billy Halop and company were stars. As Lee and Van Hecke state, "[T]he six little toughs rode the movie merry-go-round to fame and fortune."[29] Lost Boys, teenage delinquents with hearts of gold and a propensity to hero-worship gangsters, began to proliferate in mass media. Sometimes they still traveled in preromantic packs.[30] Sometimes they enjoyed peer homoromances, very occasionally contrasted with a girlfriend: Gang leader Jackie Cooper cries over the death of his beloved male sidekick and gives a quick cheek buss to "girl friend" turned girlfriend. Frankie Darro bonds with Bobby Jordan in reform school. Frankie Thomas virtually ignores homoerotic potential to flirt with a girl.[31] But most often boys were paired with men. Frankie Darro plays basketball under the supervision of crusading public defender Paul Kelly, who spends many, many scenes watching him on the court and in the locker room but ends up in a clinch with his sister. Frankie is redeemed by the love of a police officer, who, again, falls for his sister. He is wooed into studying medicine by a hunky prison doctor (who, for a change, does not fall for anyone's sister). Copyboy Bobby Jordan chooses a newspaper reporter over his gangster brother. Billy Halop, as Humphrey Bogart's gunsel, finds a new boy friend in Sing Sing, whereupon the jealous Bogie tries to rub him out.[32]

The original Dead End Kids also favored adult-teen homoromance over peers, packs, or the glimmers of heterosexual desire. *Angels with Dirty Faces* (Warner Brothers, dir. Michael Curtiz), which was released on Thanksgiving Day 1938, considerably intensified the adults' emotional and erotic investment in the teenagers. Gangster Rocky Sullivan (James Cagney) takes an interest in the Dead End Kids and talks them into playing basketball at the parish gym. As they wash up afterward, the camera moves to a close-up on their tight athletic torsos bent over the communal wash basin, and then on Rocky, gazing with obvious interest. Later, Rocky wants to give Soapy (eighteen-year-old Billy Halop) an envelope for safekeeping, so he lifts up Soapy's shirt, pauses to look at his chest and belly, and then shoves it far down inside his pants. Since Soapy retrieves the envelope later by merely pulling it from beneath his shirt, the frontal shove was unnecessary, a barely displaced gesture of erotic intimacy.

Meanwhile, Rocky's childhood friend Jerry Connelly (Pat O'Brien), now a priest, competes with him for the boys' affection with equally erotic zeal: He confiscates a deflated basketball from the back of one boy's shorts and in the process pulls back the elastic and leers at his buttocks before snapping it back into place. Most Depression-era child stars rehabilitated adults by displaying innocence and dimples, but here the adult epiphanies are caused by the boys' toughness, suspicion, and sheer physical attractiveness. Leske notes likewise "an administering gaze that is longing, desirous, and erotic" among the armies of crusading child savers, well-wishers, and big brothers who were administering hugs to real-life street kids during the period.[33] Casting one of the adults as a priest and giving the other a romance with someone's older sister ensured that everything was "square," but only after the teenagers themselves were presented as objects of obsessive desire.

They Made Me a Criminal (Warner Brothers, January 1939, dir. Busby Berkeley) contrasts the sensuality of the pack with the focused intimacy of adult-peer homoromance. Johnnie Bradfield (John Garfield), a prize fighter on the lam after he is wrongfully accused of murder, stumbles onto an Arizona date farm occupied for some reason by the Dead End Kids. While Johnnie, the nominal star, occasionally displays a presentable physique, the Kids do not seem to own clothes: They box and swim in short pants, strip down to work the date farm, strip down for bed.

Again, the Dead End Kids never display the slightest interest in girls, but they seem quite aware of same-sex practice. When they need money to buy some boxing gloves, they spy foppish rich kid J. Douglas Williamson (fifteen-year-old Ronald Sinclair) playing with a camera while he waits for his chauffeur to complete an errand. They offer to teach him to play poker and then cheat so he will lose. But why do they play strip poker—surely any game would allow them to acquire the camera—unless they have a special interest in seeing the boy with his clothes off? Spit (Leo Gorcey) keeps his arm wrapped around the boy's shoulders throughout the game, leering at him and after each loss helping him remove his jacket or unbutton his shirt. He brings a fever-ish urgency to the scene; it is hard not to imagine that he wants more from J. Douglas Williamson than his clothes or his camera.

Johnnie keeps his hands firmly attached to one or another of the Dead End Kids at all times, but he seems especially drawn to Tommy (Billy Halop). In a pivotal scene, they all go swimming in an irrigation tank (evidently the Kids had to go swimming at least once in every movie, even if it was set in the desert). When the water level unexpect-edly goes down, they are trapped, unable to climb out. Johnnie physi-cally holds onto Tommy throughout the crisis and rescue. But the mo-ment they get home, he confesses his love for Tommy's sister in a scene that seems absurdly unprecedented, since the man and woman have spent barely a moment of screen time together.

Tommy responds favorably to Johnnie's homoromantic interest. Taking charge of the courtship, he suggests that they go away together, since "lots of guys go in pairs." During the Depression, hobos often traveled as older-younger couples: The older would provide the street-smarts and protection, and the younger sex.[34] But perhaps what he is really suggesting is a permanent domestic partnership. Near the end of the movie, as Johnnie prepares to run away to avoid capture, Tommy again importunes him to come along. When Johnnie refuses, Tommy stows away under the rails, an extremely risky procedure, willing to risk his life to stay with a partner. Finally Johnnie gives in and tells him, "Let's go!" It's not clear if he has decided to stay or to take Tommy with him, but the older sister has been forgotten. The movie fades out to the two walking along the railroad tracks together with their arms around each other, the permanence of their bond expressed at last.

4

Rocket to the Moon
The Adventure Boys

By 1920, books about Adventure Boys wandering through Africa, Tibet, or Borneo were far outselling books about Boys Next Door scoring touchdowns or Lost Boys landing clerical jobs, perhaps because the real Age of Exploration was over. On December 14, 1911, when Norwegian explorer Roald Amundsen and his team stood on the South Pole, Euro-Americans had officially been everywhere and seen everything, except for a few backwaters not worth the trip. The Union Jack was flying over a quarter of the world's total inhabited land area, and the French Tricolor over another 10 percent. Belgium occupied the Congo, Holland the East Indies, Italy Somaliland, Portugal Mozambique. Indeed, it was hard to find a territory in all the world free of anthropologists, missionaries, and capitalists. There was nothing left for explorers to do but book charter tours.[1]

The United States was no imperial slouch. It occupied Alaska, Hawaii, the Philippines, Nicaragua, Panama, and many islands and atolls, and it sent out as many anthropologists, missionaries, and capitalists as the European powers. The much-lauded "Western Civilization" meant Anglo-America just as much as Northwestern Europe. The first volume of the Harvard Classics, Dr. Charles W. Elliott's famous "Five-Foot Shelf of Books," featured writings of the American Founding Fathers (the *second* volume featured the ancient Greeks). Kipling's famous summation of the "White Man's Burden" was not about French West Africa or the British Raj, but about the Philippines, placing the United States on the custodial side of a cosmic division of humanity into white-civilized and brown-savage:

> Go, bind your sons in exile
> To serve your captives' needs
> To wait, in heavy harness
> On fluttered folk and wild—
> Your new-caught, sullen peoples
> Half devil and half child.[2]

The "new-caught, sullen peoples" did not submit quietly. Through the first decades of the twentieth century, there were riots and organized protests in Africa, India, and Southeast Asia. Writers sought to establish national vernaculars. Members of indigenous religions sought recognition, and Christians sought new, native forms of expression. Jomo Kenyatta, later the first president of Kenya, was organizing the Kikuyu Central Association. Jawaharlal Nehru, later the first president of India, was in jail.

Just as the Boy Next Door and the Lost Boy arose in a struggle over white and nonwhite, native born and immigrant, the Adventure Boy arose in a struggle between isolation and empire. He demonstrated the utility—indeed, the necessity—of American intervention into the barbaric, heathen world.[3] Boys Next Door and Lost Boys might occasionally sleuth out a mystery at a mountain lodge or an uncle's ranch "out west," but they stayed within the confines of the United States. Adventure Boys had unlimited horizons: They could dive for sunken treasure in the South Seas, fight ivory poachers in the Belgian Congo, discover a lost city in the Andes, and even blast off to Venus.[4] In ordinary time they might be either middle-class or poor, small-town or urban, Anglo-white or Irish (some were even Arab and South Asian); such sociological nitpicking was irrelevant when their playing field was the whole world. Their adversaries were less likely to be gangsters, spies, or jewel thieves than "Jivaros" seeking additions to their shrunken head collections, "Hindoos" loathe to allow the Sacred Eye of Kali to take its rightful place in a museum in New York, or evil Euro-Americans fomenting discontent among the otherwise docile Waziri.

AMONG THE CANNIBALS

Adventure Boys in serial novels tend to be somewhat bigger and stronger than Boys Next Door or Lost Boys, perhaps because more feats of physical prowess are required of them. J. W. Duffeld carefully establishes that the chief radio boy of *Radio Boys in the Thousand Islands* "was only seventeen years old, but as big as a man . . . he lacked one inch of being six feet tall, and he wore size eight shoes."[5] Adventure Boys tend to be breathtakingly handsome, though their sidekicks sometimes suffer from fat, eyeglasses, freckles, or red hair. And girls are usually absent, even as sisters and classmates in the ordinary time that frames the adventure. Edgar Stratemeyer, owner of the Stratemeyer syndicate that produced many novel series, argued that he was merely reflecting the lack of heterosexual interest in his mostly-male readership: In fan letters, "the boys want to know what the hero is going to do in the next book . . . the girls, with scarcely an exception, want to know how soon the hero of that particular story is going to marry his best girl."[6] But adult male adventurers, though equally popular among teenage boys, were constantly rescuing and then wooing brassy girl reporters, glamorous spies, and jungle queens. It was only the teenage boy character who had to be excused from any hint of the feminine, lest he be branded a namby-pamby and a sissy.

Sometimes girls do appear in the frame stories, but not as dance partners or objects of shy grins. At the beginning of *Don Sturdy in the Land of Volcanoes* (1925), a rich kid named Brock Harrington, "a big, hulking fellow of eighteen with pale blue eyes set in a weak and dissipated looking face," is trying to force a girl into his car.[7] Don Sturdy rushes to the rescue, and Harrington vows vengeance, setting off the chain of events that fuels the plot. But no heterosexual romance, not even a flirtation, results. Instead, the girl vanishes from the narrative, and Don and Teddy, his freckled, redheaded sidekick, sail to Alaska. There they rescue each other from being drowned at sea, mauled by grizzly bears, suffocated by volcanic ash, incinerated by lava, and stabbed by a murderous Harrington henchman, and when they are both safe again, they celebrate with purple-prose exultations: "You can't keep a good man down,' jubilated Teddy, as he laid his hand affectionately on Don's shoulder."[8]

Tahara, the *Boy King of the Desert*, the *Boy Mystic of India*, and so on (1933), is actually an American named Dick, who discovers that he is the reincarnated god of a North African tribe. He travels the world in search of his destiny, accompanied by a large, unwieldy entourage: Dan, his fat, good-natured sidekick; their fathers, a professor and a financier; two native bodyguards; and a tomboyish young lady named Rex. The narrator admits that Dick and Rex make "a stunning-looking couple," and the two frequently rescue each other from danger, yet "neither treated each other as more than a chum." Still, even the hint of hetero-romantic potential seems to limit homoromance: Dick never treats Dan as more than a chum, either.[9]

Adventure Boys endure many more dangers and hardships than Boys Next Door or Lost Boys, with many more last-minute rescues and scrapes with death (even Frank and Joe Hardy were rarely sched-uled for human sacrifice atop Aztec pyramids). As a consequence, their bonds often transcend those of Boys Next Door and Lost Boys in both emotional intensity and physical intimacy, becoming more sensual, more erotic. And more exclusive. Adult adventurers had sidekicks, but their homoromantic potential was diffused by the many young ladies who caught their eye, and as soon as they returned to the "real" world of skyscrapers and business suits, the sidekick quietly made himself scarce. The moment their aerial glider lands at Shopton Airport, young adult adventurer Tom Swift all but shoves his sidekick Ned out of the way in his haste to rejoin Mary Nestor in her garden.[10] But Adventure Boys and their sidekicks find no other loves on their journey, and at the end of the day they remain together.

In Roy Rockwood's *Great Marvel* series (1906), teenagers Mark Sampson (a muscleman like the Bible hero) and Jack Darrow (an intel-lect like Clarence Darrow) share a homoromance so blatant that collec-tor Jessica Amanda Salmonson rather nastily suggests "a psychological thesis on whether boys' series publishers & writers weren't a tad per-verse."[11] In the main stories, they explore the North Pole, the South Pole, the Earth's core, and various planets in the solar system, just as

Tom Swift might, but when they return to the frame of ordinary time, they do not abandon each other in search of girlfriends. The books conclude with either a coyly described intimacy or an assurance that their bond is permanent. In *Five Thousand Miles Underground* (1908), the boys return from the Earth's core laden with diamonds, and they decide to invest their newfound wealth in college educations. What will become of them after college, Mark wonders. "We'll take another trip!" Jack exclaims. The two clasp hands, and the narrator hastily retreats.[12]

Mark needn't worry—they'll be together forever. As the series progresses, they complete high school, then college (UECC, Universal Electrical and Chemical College), and become professional inventors, without anyone ever suggesting that they should find women and commence separate lives. In the last book of the series, *By Spaceship to Saturn* (1935), they are middle-aged professors at UECC and still living together. They have taken an interest in two of their young astronomy students, Lucky and Phil, who embark on the adventure while the adults sit by the fire and reminisce.

In first *Don Sturdy* novel (1925), fifteen-year-old Don is searching for his missing parents in the wilds of the Sahara when he encounters a boy, Teddy, being held captive by some brigands. He mounts a daring rescue. Since they are both missing one or more parents, it is only logical that they join forces. But even after Teddy's father is found, they stay together. Even after Don's parents are found, they stay together. They move to Hillville, New York, where they attend high school together and live with or near Don's "bachelor uncles." Every so often they embark on a new adventure involving pirates in the Sargasso Sea, giants in Patagonia, headhunters in Borneo, gorillas in Africa, or renegade Aztecs in Mexico, and afterward they always return to lives of happy domesticity. They never discuss the possibility of one day parting. Their homoromance is permanent.

Adventure Boys in fiction usually travel under adult supervision, no doubt because they are too young to realistically traverse the globe by themselves. However, they rarely establish adult-teen homoromances; instead, the adults have often established same-sex partnerships of their own.[13] In the *Don Sturdy* series, Don and Teddy globetrot with Don's bachelor uncles, an archaeologist and a big-game hunter. The brothers of Don's mother and father, respectively, they probably met in adulthood, when Don's parents were courting. We are not told why they decided to live together—money certainly wasn't an issue—or why neither ever mentions a lady friend. They are simply permanent partners whose bond precludes other loves. The practice serves to domesticate homoromance, making it not only present in the quotidian world, but commonplace, as ordinary to Adventure Boys as teachers, homework, and the "big game" to the Boy Next Door.[14]

LORDS OF THE APES

Some Adventure Boys need not travel from Hillville to the jungles of darkest Africa: They were born there. They were abandoned to the wilderness as infants, and they grew up alone, with only madmen or apes to look after them. Perhaps they had a literary antecedent in Mowgli, the boy raised by animals in the Kipling story, or in Romulus and Remus, the boys suckled by wolves who grew up to found Rome, but they were really born in *Tarzan of the Apes*, scribbled on the backs of old envelopes by failed writer Edgar Rice Burroughs and published, after many rejections, in the bargain-basement pulp *All-Story* in October 1912.[15] The cover illustration, a long-haired, loincloth-clad man fighting a lion, differs from the usual pulp covers in two ways. The lion fighter is extremely muscular, nearly "cut" in bodybuilder's lingo, in an era when most pulp heroes were pictured as svelte. And he is rescuing a man, not a lady. Readers could learn no more of the situation until they bought a copy for fifteen cents, but they could easily conclude that the jungle was a site of masculine intimacy. They would not be mistaken: Jane Porter does appear as an object of the Ape Man's romantic interest, but in the end she rejects him. Meanwhile he spends a great deal of time rescuing a man who turns out to be his cousin, and his salvation comes not through a "Me Tarzan—You Jane" epiphany, as in the movies, but through several chapters of domestic happiness with a "handsome Frenchman" named D'Arnot.[16]

The Return of Tarzan appeared in 1913, followed by The Son of Tarzan, The Beasts of Tarzan, and twenty more. Burroughs wrote about many muscular heroes on weird worlds—John Carter on Mars, Carson Napier on Venus, Tanar in Pellucidar—but Tarzan overshadowed them all and soon spun out of control, becoming arguably the most famous literary creation of the twentieth century. There were eleven silent movies and innumerable talkies, with the Lord of the Apes portrayed by Elmo Lincoln, Buster Crabbe, Herman Brix, and Johnny Weissmuller. There was a syndicated comic strip by 1929, and a radio program by 1932. There were comic books, Big Little Books, marketing tie-ins, spoofs. And imitators: *Bomba the Jungle Boy* (1925), *Morgo the Mighty* (1930), *Tam Son of the Tiger* (1931), *Kwa of the Jungle* (1932), *Ozar of the Aztec* (1933), *Sorak* (1934), *Ka-Zar* (1936), *Ki-Gor* (1939), and dozens more, avoiding midair collisions as they swung from the trees only because they grew up in different jungles, roaming Brazil, Malaysia, India, the South Seas, and the "tropics" of Alaska and the South Pole.[17]

Adventure Boys are always more muscular than the comparatively scrawny Lost Boys and Boys Next Door, but when they are raised in the jungle, every sense of proportion, balance, and feasibility vanishes. Jan of the Jungle, from Venezuela, is "a handsome, superbly muscled lad, with a straight, athletic figure, broad shoulders, narrow hips, and the features of a Greek god." Sorak, from British Malaysia, is "broad-shouldered, slender-waisted, and muscled like a blacksmith . . . [a] bronzed and blue eyed Hercules . . . the incarnation of physical perfection." Illustrations rarely live up to the textual hyperbole—cover art depicts Bomba as a skinny preteen in a leopard skin, while inside the book we hear that his "muscular development was amazing," with "rippling ridges on [his] arms and legs." However, Og Son of Fire (1921), who roams the savage jungles of 500,000 B.C. in the pages of *Boys Life*, becomes increasingly muscular in each illustration, until by the mid 1930s he has the impossibly buffed physique of a modern bodybuilder.[18]

There is no social category of adolescence in the jungle, since there is no gradual increase in responsibility and independence. For this reason, Burroughs brings his feral heroes, Tarzan, Korak (*Son of Tarzan*, 1916), and Azîz (*The Lad and the Lion*, 1938), from boyhood to adulthood in just a paragraph or two. But sometimes the Jungle Man spends a significant amount of time, even his entire book or movie career, as a teenage Adventure Boy. Then the central paradox of adolescence is exaggerated: He is neither civilized nor savage, neither adult nor child, neither fully naked nor fully clothed. Or perhaps he is both. White but raised in savagery, he can display the "superiority" of white Euro-American civilization yet avoid its mollycoddling weakness.

Bomba the Jungle Boy, raised in Amazonia by a "half-mad naturalist," spends the first ten books of his series searching for his long-lost birth parents. They turn out to be Andrew and Laura Bartow, an artist and an opera singer, respectively, members of two of the more effeminate professions that civilization offers, and they originally named their son Bonny, a fey equivalent of "beautiful" rarely bestowed upon boys in 1910, except those predestined to become mollycoddles. Perhaps it is fortunate that Bomba was lost as a child and spared the feminizing threat. In the jungle there are no artists, no operas, no Aubrey Beardsley or Oscar Wilde, no coed high schools. There are no mothers, sisters, or girlfriends telling the Adventure Boy to bathe or to settle disputes with words rather than fists. In fact, there are usually no women at all (since savage was coded as masculine and civilization as feminine, natives were usually portrayed as exclusively male). Not a native, yet free from feminizing civilization, Bomba grows up superior to both, a superbly muscled jungle Adonis at the improbable age of fourteen.

When girls appear in the jungle, the Adventure Boys befriend them, protect them, but never long for them. In his magazine fiction, Og Son of Fire never encounters a female Neanderthal. A girl named Nada appears in the radio series (1934) and in the Big Little Book (1936), but as a foster child, not as a potential girlfriend.[19] Sorak occasionally meets a girl, and his sidekick Dick, the product of mollycoddling civilization, suggests that he might pause long enough to fall in love, but the bronzed and blue-eyed Hercules always responds with an indignant denial of heterosexual interest. Bomba meets girls as well, somewhat less frequently, and he treats them with calm cordiality, never with hetero-mania.

Sometimes the Adventure Boy does "grow up" into heterosexual practice. Jan of the Jungle is raised in the Florida Everglades by a mad scientist who thinks feral children might turn into superhuman killing machines. At the age of sixteen Jan escapes and somehow ends up in Venezuela, where a Haitian named Borno takes an interest in him. Just as D'Arnot civilized Tarzan, Borno civilizes Jan, teaching him to speak

English, giving him a loincloth to wear, and fretting and fussing over him like a maiden aunt. "His huge hand was gentle as that of a woman," we are told. The bond is intimate and remarkably tender, but even more gender-polarized than the masculine-feminine pairing of Freddie Bartholomew and Jimmy Lydon. Jan is hard-bodied, straight-edged, empirical, logical, "masculine," while Borno, no longer the bringer of civilization, becomes "feminine," soft and voluptuous in body, fuzzy and superstitious in mind.

About halfway through the novel, Jan is captured by savages intent on burning him at the stake, and Borno rushes to the rescue. Now Borno is no longer a trembling, superstitious native, no longer a servant. The colonizer-colonized dynamic has been broken, and they must regretfully part. Jan wanders the jungle alone for many months, until he turns eighteen and, adequately grown up, he spies Ramona, a girl "more lovely than the fairest jungle flower . . . too fragile to be dangerous, too beautiful to be destroyed."[20] She requires rescue from a pouncing jaguar, and in that instant Jan has civilization thrust upon him. The 1935 movie serial adaptation, *Call of the Savage*, skips over Borno: Seven-year old Dickie Jones transmutes instantly into twenty-one-year-old Noah Beery Jr.

Bomba the Jungle Boy never reaches adulthood, so he never must abandon his native partner, Gibo. They are far more intimate than Jan and Borno: They are always throwing their arms around each other's necks, grabbing arms or shoulders, sleeping cradled against each other—and there are coy hints of erotic as well as emotional attraction. Obviously Bomba, as the epitome of physical perfection, is intensely attractive to everyone, but why should he be attracted to Gibo, when natives are uniformly described as hideous? Yet the colonizer must find the colonized attractive, an object of desire, if their bond is to take on a gender-polarized masculine-feminine dynamic.

Bomba saves Gibo's life a dozen or more times per book, and Gibo not infrequently saves Bomba's life. When only one has a chance to escape, he adamantly refuses, insisting that they must remain together to the end. In *Bomba the Jungle Boy on the Underground River*, each believes that the other has died, and when they are reunited after many pages, "Their delight at finding themselves together was beyond all words. The frightful loneliness that had weighed both of them down was a thing of the past."[21] Neither ever forgets the gap between them: Bomba is always masculine/colonizer, Gibo feminine/colonized. Yet beneath this racist dynamic we can see quite clearly a homoromance that is never disrupted by heterosexual desire.

So powerful is the correlation between heterosexual desire and adulthood that only one of the Adventure Boys raised in the jungle, Og Son of Fire, manages to grow up *without* falling in love with a fair flower of maidenhood. Perhaps he is spared because in 500,000 B.C. white Euro-American civilization does not yet exist; he himself creates it, story by story, personally inventing everything from agriculture to the bow and arrow. In a 1924 story, Og helps a boy named Ru journey to the Valley of Fear to rescue his brother, a captive of the Great Snake. When the crisis is resolved, Og and Ru decide to stay together. Soon they are portrayed as permanent partners, hunting, fishing, fighting monsters, toppling tyrants, and rescuing each other from an endless array of savages bent on human sacrifice or cannibalism. And, almost by accident, they grow into men. They settle down with an amenable tribe, sharing a cave without adult supervision. They participate in tribal discussions and disputes as adults, "Little Bowman and Big Bowman." Eventually they adopt a young boy named Tao, an artistic sort who has invented cave drawings, just as Mark and Jack in the Great Marvel series grow up, live together, and nurture boys of their own.

THE DREAM OF ASIA

Depression-era pulps loved to invoke the unimaginably ancient and unimaginably decadent civilizations of the Orient: the cities all warrens of harems, opium dens, dungeons, lairs, and oubliettes; the rulers all fat, bejeweled, and lecherous; the people childlike; the laws brutal; the religions by turns esoteric and superstitious. There the White Man's Burden mandated that Yankees triumph not over savagery, as in Africa and Amazonia, but over decadence. Beginning with the first incursions of Europeans into India and China in the sixteenth century, but certainly intensified as colonial powers began to wane in the 1920s, the Orient was imagined as labyrinthine, duplicitous, effeminate, and drowsy with age, in sharp contrast to Western self-fashioning as straightforward, straight-edged, manly, and vigorous.

To avoid the minutiae of contemporary political struggles, the Orient was usually romanticized into the distant past worlds of Hyperborea and Atlantis, the distant future world of Xiccarph, or the aging jungle cities of Mars. H. P. Lovecraft writes of "Celephais, in the Valley of Ooth-Nargai, beyond the Tanarian Hills," where galleys "sail up the river Oukranos past the gilded spires of Thran," and "elephant caravans tramp through perfumed jungles in Kled," where "forgotten palaces with veined ivory columns sleep lovely and unbroken under the moon."[22] That is, Istanbul, Samarkand, and Shiraz writ large.

Placing Adventure Boys in realms of Oriental myth allowed for a lushly sensual homoromance that still establishes the superiority of white Euro-American civilization over Asian and Middle Eastern "decadence." In Lovecraft's "The Quest of Iranon" (1921), a young man wanders a stern, unfriendly world in search of the city of Aira, where there are "men to whom songs and dreams . . . bring pleasure." He meets "a young boy with sad eyes" who also dreams of escape, to a city where "men understand our longings and welcome us as brothers, nor even laugh or frown at what we say." They travel together, happy in a way yet always longing. They grow old together and finally die, never finding their true home.[23]

Often the outskirts of these unimaginably ancient cities were teaming with mighty thewed, sword-wielding barbarians—Henry Kuttner's Elak, Clark Ashton Smith's Tiglari, Robert E. Howard's Conan, Brak, and Kull. They were as feral as Tarzan, combining the strength and vigor of savagery with Anglo-white moral "superiority." The plots usually articulated a masculine/feminine colonizer/colonized myth, with the muscleman rescuing a naked woman (prominently displayed on the magazine cover) from some effeminate, ruby-ringed satrap. Fellow musclemen appeared only as bullies, cads, or, at best, untrustworthy companions who ended up betraying the hero. Some authors suggest that this distrust of masculine intimacy was a psychological residue of the bullying and abuse the authors suffered as bookish, shy children in redneck towns; Robert E. Howard fumed over his grade school "enemies" throughout his life. However, it also marks heterosexual de-

sire as the defining quality of civilization—except when the barbarians are Adventure Boys rather than men. Then they rescue no naked
women and their same-sex bonds are true.[24]

Robert E. Howard's Conan the Barbarian spends his seventeen
stories in *Weird Tales* rescuing the requisite naked woman and being betrayed by men, except in the only story set in his adolescence,
"The Tower of the Elephant" (1933).[25] About sixteen years old, a "tall,
strongly made youth" with "broad, heavy shoulders, massive chest" and
so on, Conan has traveled from the Teutonic fatherland of Cimmeria
(modern-day Scandinavia) to ancient, decadent Zamora (southern Russia). He sneaks into the Tower of the Elephant with the hope of stealing
a fabulous jewel hidden there. At this point, plot conventions decree
that he find a naked woman. Instead, he finds a naked man.

An alien named Yag-kosha, elephant-headed but otherwise human,
has been blinded, crippled, and imprisoned in the tower by an evil sorcerer. They become friendly, and Yag-kosha asks Conan to rescue him
through the strange-sounding expedient of cutting out his heart. Conan
never hesitates about killing monsters and enemies, but he will not kill
a friend, and complies only when Yag-kosha assures him that he will
not die. In fact, he uses the magic of the heart to take revenge on the
evil sorcerer, and then, restored to his original strength and beauty, he
jubilantly flies away to join his companions on his home planet.

This story is fascinating because it precisely mirrors the adventures
of the adult Conan, only transformed from hetero-erotic to graphically homoerotic. In the shimmering tower, the adult Conan would
find a female object of desire (naked, beautiful, benevolent) contrasted
with a male threat (clothed, hideous, evil). However, the teenage Conan
finds a male, both object of desire (naked, benevolent) and threat (blind,
crippled, aged, with a hideous face "of nightmare and madness"). Then
ritualized death and resurrection removes the threat, leaving only desire:
Conan perceives the new Yag-kosha as beautiful.

Even the hints of heterosexual intimacy that the adult Conan often
enjoys with the naked ladies he rescues[26] are mirrored when the naked
Yag-kosha gets to "know" Conan—sexual knowledge, perhaps—by caressing his chest and shoulders with his soft phallic trunk: "[I]ts touch
was as light as a girl's hand," Howard tells us, suggesting a tender, gentle

sexual congress. Conan's desire here is for the male, a yearning for masculine intimacy that must be sublimated beyond all recognition among the adults in Cimmeria—and in Depression-era America—but can be expressed freely, with only a veneer of euphemism, during the paradox of youth.[27]

GATES OF DREAM

In 1928, boys and teenagers could find adventure only in serial novels, pulp fiction, and an occasional silent movie, but just ten years later, in 1938, they could choose from a huge assortment of new, cheap entertainment sources: radio, science fiction magazines, comic strips, comic books, and movie serials.[28] In *Beyond the Gates of Dream* (1969), anthologist Lin Carter describes a Depression-era childhood of endless joy. Every day after school he runs home to turn on the radio and find out if "the Skipper and Simba . . . had yet penetrated the lava wall around the mystery isle to confront the villainous Madame Shark and recover the stolen idol of Kali." On Saturday he stops at the newsstand to see if the new *Startling Stories* has arrived, with Leigh Brackett's novel *Sea Kings of Mars*, and then it's on to the Rialto Theatre for the latest installment in *The Adventures of Captain Marvel*, followed by the swashbuckling main feature, *The Mark of Zorro*. On Sundays he spends "a delicious hour" over the comics page "to see how Flash Gordon made it over the snowfields . . . and to linger over another picture of the lovely Queen Fria of Frigia."[29] Though Carter's interest in Queen Fria and the bikini-clad lady who illustrates *Sea Kings of Mars* may have been based on heterosexual desire, most of his adolescent media consumption—radio series, comic books, comic strips, movie serials—had Adventure Boys endlessly forming passionate, intimate bonds with each other or with men.

By 1934, 60 percent of American homes had at least one radio, and producers were starting to move beyond sports and fireside chats to present a wide variety of genres: soap opera, sitcom, variety, game show, Western, horror, thriller, and mystery. The adventure programs were usually broadcast in the late afternoon for the after-school amusement of preteens. There were Western heroes (*Red Ryder*, *The Lone Ranger*), masked crime fighters (*The Green Hornet*, *The Shadow*), white men in jungles (*Jungle Jim*, *Tarzan*), and space explorers (*Captain Midnight*, *Flash Gordon*), but hardly a teenager in the bunch, either as star or as sidekick. When shows with teenagers, like *Terry and the Pirates* or *Og Son of Fire*, did air, they failed to draw an audience and were swiftly cancelled: Evidently preteens wanted to see men, not boys. The only two successful teenage adventure programs, *The Air Adventures of Jimmie Allen* and *Jack Armstrong, All-American Boy*, paired the teenager with an adult hero.

Though newspaper comics had been a high priority for readers ever since *Hogan's Alley* first appeared in Hearst's *New York World* in 1895, not until the 1930s did syndicates allow for national distribution of comic titles and did cheap printing costs allow for the meticulously drawn naturalism customary in adventure strips. *Tailspin Tommy* and *Tim Tyler's Luck* began in 1928, *Buck Rogers* and *Tarzan* in 1929, and soon family and working-girl strips like *Gasoline Alley* were practically overwhelmed by stalwarts squashing native rebellions in the jungles of Africa, freedom-fighting in the far future or the distant past, or exploring the center of the earth. Since the intended audience was more varied, so were the heroes: There were men working alone (*Buck Rogers*), men with men (*Tailspin Tommy*), men with teenagers (*Red Barry*), teenagers with teenagers (*Tim Tyler's Luck*), and even the occasional child (*Dickie Dare*). However, with few exceptions they were all heavily muscled and half-naked, unwieldy masses of bulging biceps and tight-packed chests; Sunday morning must have been the pictorial equivalent of an afternoon on Muscle Beach. When the men worked solo or were paired with other men, they—like the barbarian heroes in the pulps—spent most of their strips rescuing curvaceous, scantily-clad women. But when one of the partners was a teenager, they rarely rescued women or had women fall in love with them; they lived only for each other.

Movie serials were adventure, science fiction, or mystery stories with twelve to fifteen episodes of about twenty minutes each, shown amid the cartoons and newsreels prior to the main picture to incite audience interest and ensure that they would return for the new installment "at this theatre next week." A few cliffhangers were produced in silent movie days, and a few as late as 1953, but the golden age of the movie serial began around 1937 and lasted to the end of the war, when Columbia, Republic, and Universal invested substantial sums of money and talent on some ninety-six different serials. Like the comic strips and radio series (and often based on them), movie serials had stalwart heroes visiting weird worlds, fighting monsters, and inevitably rescuing and falling for a savage princess, scientist's daughter, or tagalong girl reporter. A heteroromance followed, with a fade-out marriage proposal in Chapter Thirteen. When the stalwart was a teenager, however, he rescued no reporters or princesses. Instead he inevitably fell in love with a man.

JIMMIE AND SPEED

The Air Adventures of Jimmie Allen began on the radio in 1932, when a "wide-awake, clear-eyed youth of seventeen" wandered onto the field at the Kansas City Airport and drew the interest of race-pilot Speed Robinson. In the earliest episodes, they stay close to home, where Speed tests experimental planes and takes stunt-flying jobs, and Jimmie takes flying lessons—every lesson repeated word for word in the dialogue, the technical details presumably mesmerizing to audiences in the early days of flight. But there was not much room for adventure in Kansas City, so soon the pair was flying across the world to tangle with spies, gangsters, cannibals, and "sinister Orientals." There were Jimmie Allen–brand model airplanes, Jimmie Allen Flying Clubs with some three million members, and Jimmie Allen Air Races, model airplane expositions, held annually in cities across the Midwest. Jimmie and Speed appeared in a Big Little Book, *Jimmie Allen and the Air Mail Robbery*, and in a movie, *The Sky Parade* (1936), with Jimmie Allen "playing himself."

Neither Jimmie nor Speed have a girlfriend or express any interest in acquiring one.[30] They live together, sharing meals and a bedroom in the airport pilots' quarters, and perhaps a bed. When Jimmie hears a mysterious sound in the middle of the night, he whispers for Speed to wake up without any moving-across-the-room sound effects, as if they are lying in close proximity, and then Speed tells him to put on his "trousers and shirt" so they can investigate, as if they have been nearly naked.

Although their bond is intimate, exclusive, and permanent, the partners shy away from displays of emotional intensity. When Jimmie loses a wheel during his first solo flight (in an act of sabotage, naturally), Speed flies up in another airplane, leaps into his cockpit, lands them safely, and then praises *him*: "You certainly came through at the right time, Jimmie!" But the teenager didn't do anything but yell for help. When he tries to reverse the praise ("You know, Speed, that was a wonderful thing for you to do . . ."), Speed summarily cuts him off. Obviously the rescue itself signifies a degree of emotional intensity, but in a serial novel, the pair would be getting all doe-eyed and mushy. The intended audience may be a factor in the reticence; *Jimmie Allen* was broadcast after school for the preteen secret-decoder-ring crowd. Presumably passion was beyond their ken: Only teenagers and adults would understand, or desire, a stumbling, husky "if anything were to happen to you. . . ."

JACK AND UNCLE JIM

Jack Armstrong (1933), the All-American Boy responsible for selling millions of bowls of Wheaties during his seventeen years on the radio, started his life as a Boy Next Door, a football hero at Hudson High, but the call to adventure came early. In a 1934 continuity, Jim Fairfield, a government agent, pilot, explorer, and all-round tough guy, swooped down for a visit on his private plane, the Silver Albatross. He invited his niece and nephew, Betty and Billy, on his new assignment, a search for a kidnapped scientist, and, as their best friend, Jack tagged along. Uncle Jim and Jack found something inspiring in each other, or else globetrotting adventures drew more listeners than a rival team stealing Hudson High's playbook, and soon the high school plotlines were abandoned as man and boy (sometimes with Betty and/or Billy, often not) embarked on month-long continuities in Africa, China, Tibet, Morocco, Easter Island, and Zamboanga.

Many commentators, even those who listened to the series during its original run, mistakenly think that Uncle Jim was *Jack's* uncle and believe the relationship to be as familial as that of Don Sturdy and his avuncular "parents," but Uncle Jim is definitely not kin. Civic responsibility was still associated with homosocial desire rather than the heterosexual practice that drew Tarzan and the barbarians to their Janes,[31] and Jim has "taken an interest" in Jack. But his interest is decidedly more than homosocial: He never mentions a wife or girlfriend back home, and he is always complimenting his teenage charge on his good judgment, his bravery, and his "young muscles."[32] Their relationship is intimate, exclusive, and no doubt permanent, but again it lacks emotional intensity: There are few of the post-crisis gasps of "I thought you were . . ." that Don Sturdy shared with Teddy, or Bomba with Gibo. Again we might blame the preteen audience. On the comics page enjoyed by children, teenager, and adult alike, homoromantic intensity was never a problem.

TIM AND SPUD

Tim Tyler's Luck (1928) began as a comic strip about a young teenager living in an orphanage, where he was burdened by presumably humorous spells of bad luck. Then he met an older boy, Spud, and they decided to set out on the road together. Their gag-a-day adventures took a serious turn when they wandered onto the field of Sky Lane Airways. Experienced pilot Roy Fleet offered to teach them to fly and incidentally introduced them to the same world of globetrotting intrigue that Jack Armstrong was concurrently enjoying with Uncle Jim, and Jimmie Allen with Speed. However, he did not display a significant homoromantic interest in either of the boys, and in 1934 he was written out. After a few more years of globetrotting, Tim and Spud grew into young adults. They settled in Africa, joined the Ivory Patrol (a sort of paramilitary police force for white colonizers), and spent many decades hunting down poachers, finding lost civilizations, being captured by cannibals, and squashing tribal rebellions, all the while ignoring the occasional savage princess or girl reporter. They endured through 1996, the last of the old-style teenage homoromances hidden away in the comics sections of a dwindling number of small-town newspapers.

The movie serial version of *Tim Tyler's Luck* appeared two days after Christmas in 1937. Sixteen-year-old Frankie Thomas plays Tim Tyler, but partner Spud, played by twenty-year-old Billy Benedict, is virtually absent, appearing only in the first chapter. Instead, Tim travels through darkest Africa alone. He is heavily feminized by the camera, jaunting through the bush with a sweater tied around his neck as if he just stepped off a tennis court; he seems a scrappy sissy like Freddie

Bartholomew rather than a heroic football star like Jack Armstrong. He is rescued more often than rescuing, participating in the vague euphemisms for sexual assault usually reserved for damsels in distress: He is carried off, kicking and screaming, twice. When he strips down to his underwear to swim in a lagoon, a movie convention usually intended to divest young ladies of their clothes, a crocodile attacks, but lest the homoerotic implication become too obvious, a friendly panther, not Tarzan, rushes to the rescue.

Tim eventually meets a girl, who provides the standard hetero-romantic Chapter Thirteen by falling in love with Sergeant Gates of the Ivory Patrol, but Tim's own romance comes with a man. Early in the series a burly French-accented pirate, Lazarre (Earle Douglas, who selected the name to "de-ethnicize" his original Louis Yaconelli), carries him off into the bush, screaming and flailing his arms like the young ladies who are always being abducted out of their bedchambers by gorillas with rapine on their minds. Tim talks Lazarre out of his dastardly plan and rehabilitates him into an ally. For the rest of the serial, Lazarre provides comic relief with pretensions of cowardice while risking his life to save Tim over and over (the boy needs a lot of saving).

One wonders why director Ford Beebe didn't let Spud tag along on the adventure and take charge of the comic relief instead of Lazarre. Allowing Tim to meet and rehabilitate the pirate certainly adds to the dramatic potential of the series; however, it also inadvertently reflects the sudden intensity of love at first sight. The bond between the brash, working-class pirate and the fey sophisticate tennis player replicates the tough-sissy gender polarization of Freddie Bartholomew and Jimmy Lydon, but with a more powerful erotic subtext. Tim and Lazarre's scenes are peppered with full-body hugs and sly innuendos: "We can't leave until daybreak. You will stay here with me tonight."[33] And they do not participate in the heteronormative conclusion: Evidently they plan to stay together forever.

BUCK AND BUDDY

In the comic strip (1929), Buck Rogers is a twentieth-century American who is buried by a cave-in and reappears five hundred years in the future, in a society crowded with technological marvels, simplistic good versus evil plotlines, and ladies in full-breasted spacesuits. He gawks at them unabashedly and quickly gets a steady girlfriend, Wilma Deering. He sometimes big-brothers Buddy Deering, Wilma's nephew, but the two never express the subtlest spark of homoromantic interest. They rarely even appear in the same continuity. Buddy is usually on the other side of the galaxy, having his own adventures with gal pal Princess Alura and his own Lazarre, a burly ex-pirate named Barney.

However, the movie serial version, released in February 1939, emphasizes homoromance. Powerfully muscular Buster Crabbe, a former *Tarzan, Kaspa the Lion Man*, and *Flash Gordon*, plays Buck, and the handsome, curly-haired sixteen-year-old Jackie Moran plays Buddy, not Wilma Deering's nephew but a twentieth-century boy with a man-sized crush on the test pilot. One wonders why Buck does not meet Buddy in the future, as in the comic strip; perhaps the erotic subtext of the interaction would only be underscored if the two met suddenly, rather than having an ongoing relationship. Yet they are still portrayed almost obsessively as homoromantic partners.[34]

While the two are testing an experimental dirigible, they crash in the Artic, where they are preserved in an intimate pose, Buddy's head resting on Buck's arm, for five hundred years. Revived, they have not a moment to spare on culture shock: They must join the battle against a space gangster who controls the Earth and is strong-arming his way into the Saturn market. Buddy is considered too young to fight and is constantly being told to "wait here," whereupon he cajoles, pouts, or dissimulates his way to Buck's side.

From the first moment of their resurrection, Buck and Buddy share both an amazing intimacy and a curious reserve. While they are always linking arms, grabbing shoulders, hugging each other, or rushing into terrible danger to rescue each other, Buck slings the injured Buddy over his shoulder like a sack of potatoes instead of carrying him in his arms, and when Buddy awakens in a hospital bed, the hand stroking his hair turns out to belong not to Buck but to Wilma Deering. When Buck is stripping down in their quarters, Buddy tries not to look; he faces the other direction, glances quickly around at Buck's hard, smooth chest and shoulders, and then quickly looks away. The teenager in an adult-teen homoromance is usually oblivious to the beauty of his partner's body, just as the woman in a heteroromance is "supposed" to respond to the man's power, prestige, and personality rather than to his physique: Desire must flow only from man to not-man. But Buddy, not yet a man, is both interested and embarrassed by his interest.

The heteroromance is likewise treated with a curious reserve. Although Buck never flirts with Wilma Deering or treats her as anything but a fellow freedom fighter, he ensures that she and Buddy are never together on the same mission. They are presented as alternatives, and eventually Buck must make a choice. In the final chapter, romantic interest or not, Buddy forces a conventional heteronormative ending by shoving them together and then butting out; the screen fades to black, however, before the kiss.

TERRY AND PAT

Terry and the Pirates (1934) presented the most overt adult-teen homoromance in the comic strips. When fourteen-year-old Terry Lee first set out to search for his missing grandfather, accompanied by soldier of fortune Pat Ryan, he was a wide-eyed innocent who seemed to belong in a humor strip, quite out of place among the jungles, copra plantations, and seedy port cities of the South China Sea, where everybody had an angle, a price, and a lot of secrets. He was even drawn differently from the other characters, with a round face and soft, curvy lines amid Milt Caniff's trademark square-jawed, angular men and women. The plots would have worked just as well without him: Pat Ryan and Connie, his stereotyped Chinese valet, could easily have outwitted the pirates, jewel thieves, and island despots all by themselves. Caniff often used humorously drawn outsider characters, like Dickie Dare and the eye-glassed, golly-gee-spurting Wash Tubbs, to link the preternatural world of adventure with the comfortable, familiar world back home. But Terry was neither boy, like Dickie Dare, nor man, like Wash Tubbs. He was a teenager, and he was growing up.

Most comic strip characters do not age, but Terry aged normally, celebrating his fifteenth birthday in 1935, his sixteenth in 1936, and so on. As he approached manhood, his relationship with Pat Ryan became considerably more intimate than those of the other pairs, the homo-romantic slipping inexorably into the homoerotic. Terry and Pat were sometimes shown sharing a single bed, or showering together, or naked together. In a 1936 strip, the sixteen-year-old Terry has just bathed, and he is toweling off. The towel shields his backside from readers, but his frontside is fully exposed to Pat, who is gazing with obvious appreciation.

Buck Rogers, Flash Gordon, and Don Winslow spent half of their time brawling with men and the other half kissing women, but as long as Terry is not yet a man, Pat Ryan actively avoids the tall, slinky femmes fatales who keep wrapping their arms around him. Usually the adults in adult-teen pairs are simply given no opportunity for heterosexual exploits, but to find the adult half rejecting countless flirtations, propositions, and bald-faced seduction attempts suggests a dynamic less subtle than a mere nod at what the intended audience might want to see or not see. When jewelry fence–kept girl Burma throws herself at Pat for three weeks' worth of strips, he consistently rejects her, consenting to a kiss only after she calls him "yellow," denigrating his masculinity, eight times in three panels. Then, after the kiss, he refuses to accept her purring "darlings."

Pat's masculinity is, indeed, open to question, in spite of his square-jawed stoicism and expertise at fisticuffs. He is denigrated by worse terms than "yellow," including "sissy" and "pansy," but only by women, so he won't have to fight back. Late in 1936, when they are all shipwrecked on another island, Burma throws herself at the colonial administrator (although she is supposedly as hard as nails, she falls for every man she sees). The solicitous Pat gives the administrator's wife makeup and hairstyle tips so she can beat off Burma's competition. One expects that, if World War II had not broken out, Pat could have easily returned to America and opened a hair salon.

The sixteen- and seventeen-year-old Terry is often positioned structurally as a parallel to whatever tall, slinky woman is lusting after Pat this time. The lady strips down to her underwear, and in the next scene Terry strips down to his underwear. Pat is knocked unconscious, and the lady gingerly holds him in her arms. The next time Pat is knocked unconscious, Terry gingerly holds him in his arms, in precisely the same position.

Columbia's adaptation, released on May 5, 1940, is one of the era's few intentionally humorous movie serials (it was directed by James W. Horne, who did the Laurel and Hardy shorts). Terry was played as a squealing teenager by twenty-two-year old William Tracy, a rather stout, likable blond. Pat Ryan, the soldier-of-fortune bodyguard, was miscast with Granville Owen, adequately tall and muscular but only five years older than William Tracy—he had just finished playing a college student in *Start Cheering* (1938), and he would go on to play the eternally teenage Li'l Abner in the adaptation of the Al Capp comic strip (1940).

The two are by far the most physically expressive of homoromantic partners in movie serials, one with hand always firmly placed on the other's arm, shoulder, or back, except when they are walking with their arms wrapped around each other's waists. Terry screams and flails like a damsel in distress when he is terrorized by crocodiles, headhunters, and villains who lob hand grenades, and after Pat swoops down like Tarzan to save him, they embrace, Terry's face pressed against Pat's chest. In an early chapter, they are bedded down for the night when a gorilla breaks into Terry's room and tries to carry him away. Pat rushes to the rescue, getting his shirt ripped off in the process. Afterward Terry stares appreciatively at Pat's bulging muscles and hints, "I'd feel a lot better if I slept with you tonight." Pat consents.

Like the Adventure Boys of the serial novels, everyone seems to accept the two as partners without question. Scientist's daughter Normandie Drake never wonders why Pat expresses no romantic interest in her. There is no Chapter Twelve marriage proposal, just Terry expressing his disappointment that they won't have any more fun now that the adventure is over. One wonders which he found the most fun, the peril or the hugging afterward.

The intensification of intimacy as the boy nears manhood (and especially when the boy is played by a man, as with William Tracy) suggests that the teenager is an object of desire not for his innocence but for his potency, not because he resembles a *child* but because he resembles a *man*. The closer he comes to that moment of maturity without crossing over it, the more he is desired. But why would the movie serials feature adult-teen homoromance when the original comic strips featured peers? Perhaps because comic strips, radio series, and boys' book series can go on forever, with the teen always poised on the brink of adulthood, but movie serials, like feature films, end. That means a marriage proposal or heterosexual embrace. A teenage star obviously cannot express any interest in girls or women, but his adult partner can.

Still, the homoromance proved more significant, perhaps more meaningful, than the need to adhere to heteronormative convention. *Terry and the Pirates* simply gives Pat Ryan no interest in women. *Tim Tyler's Luck* displaced the marriage proposal onto minor characters, leaving the homoromance between Tim and Lazarre unscathed. *Buck Rogers* offered a solution that made less structural sense but fit in most closely with the strategies of Lost Boys in feature films (Frankie Darro and Kane Richmond, Billy Halop and almost everyone): The teenager forces a romance between the stalwart and the girl, then grins approvingly at its consummation. Adventure Boys would be grinning at many stalwarts kissing girls as adult-teen homoromance came to dominate during and after the war.

5

TEENAGERS IN WAR

On the morning of September 1, 1939, Nazi tanks rumbled into Poland and began what would someday be called World War II. The theaters were playing *Angels Wash Their Faces*, with handsome eighteen-year-old Frankie Thomas, lately of *Tim Tyler's Luck*, as a reform school boy who falls in love with a boy.

That night gay poet W. H. Auden, living in exile in New York, wrote:

Waves of anger and fear
Circulate over the bright
And darkened lands of the earth,
Obsessing our private lives;
The unmentionable odor of death
Offends the September night.[1]

For the next six years, the private would be public, the social would be political. The complex geographic, political, and economic systems of the world would be as clearly and jarringly divided into domains of men and demons, into home and hell, as the medieval maps with dragons breathing fire at the four corners. The United States claimed neutrality for a few years, but when it entered the war in December 1941, few doubted that the decision was absolutely necessary. There were few conscientious objectors among the draftees; to harbor the tiniest hesitation was deemed the same as telegraphing military secrets directly to the Reichstag.[2] And the unmentionable odor of death offended many a night. Worldwide, fifty-two million people died, in battle, in accidents, of famine and disease, in the death camps.[3]

In April 1945, the war was ending. The enemy was bunkered, final assaults were being prepared, and no one doubted a speedy Allied victory. Morale was high. Moviegoers were watching *Strange Illusion,* with handsome twenty-one-year-old Jimmy Lydon, lately of *Tom Brown's School Days,* as a prep school boy who falls in love with a girl.

Boys who were just turning thirteen when they saw *Angels Wash Their Faces* were now preparing to graduate from high school. Boys born on the night of September 1, 1939 were now in kindergarten. Five years and seven months had passed, less than a tenth of a human lifespan, a few seconds of human history. Yet in that brief period, the heteroromance once anathema to teenage masculinity had become normal, then expected, and then required, and homoromance largely faded away.

SO LONG, FOLKS, I HAVE A DATE

At the beginning of the war, popular writers still seemed queasy about the possibility of heterosexual desire among boys who were not yet high school graduates. In 1939, *Better Homes and Gardens* published "So Long, Folks, I Have a Date!"—a skewed, Erma Bombeck–like take on this bizarre custom of teenage dating. Seventeen-year-old boys liking girls! What would they do next, open retirement accounts? In 1940, child psychologist James Lee Ellerwood revealed what happens "When a Boy Meets a Girl" for *Parents Magazine,* and eugenics devotee Paul Popenoe investigated the mystery of "Your Son at Seventeen" for *Hygeia.* Both still placed the onset of heterosexual interest at the end of adolescence, not at the beginning.[4]

As late as 1942, "Crushes, and What to Do about Them" in *Good Housekeeping* framed teenage heterosexual desire as a problem to be solved, but more frequent was the approach of James Lee Ellenwood, now insisting that "Boys and Girls *Need* to Like Each Other" or Howard Whitman assuring anxious mothers that "Puppy Love is the Real

Thing." In November 1943, psychologist Winifred Vanderbilt Richmond answered the "Boy-Girl Question" once and for all, with enthusiastic approval of boys and girls liking each other while still in high school.[5] By the spring of 1945, there was no oddity, no strangeness, no bemused disbelief. In articles like "The Awkward Age" and "Adolescence: What Is It?" parents, teachers, and teenagers themselves discovered that the teenage boy's "attraction to the opposite sex" was proof of his masculinity rather than a feminizing threat, a cause for joy rather than concern.[6]

Scholars took a little longer to fall in line. Not until 1944 does Caroline B. Zachery tell us that heterosexual desire is, and always has been, universal among teenage boys. It begins at the start of adolescence rather than at the end, at puberty, and its source is purely biological: "[T]he changing body is accompanied by a quickening of the entire tempo of life, an intensification of feeling responses, even to sensory stimuli, a growing attraction for members of the opposite sex, and the appearance of strange and disturbing erotic sensations."[7]

None of these articles, popular or scholarly, fears that teenage heterosexual desire might lead to sexual behavior. The authors found the idea of boys having sex as horrifying as their colleagues, a decade before, had found the idea of heterosexual desire itself. In a study published in the *American Journal of Psychology* in 1943, G. V. Ramsey finds that 98 percent of high school boys admit to masturbation, nearly half to sex with girls, and "a sizeable percentage" to sex with other boys. He frames all three practices as equally deviant and dangerous, proof that wartime stress and lack of parental supervision makes boys grow up too fast. In 1944, George E. Gardner finds that 77 percent of high school boys have had sex with girls, and slightly more than 10 percent have had sex with other boys. Concerned with this "outburst of unexpected, atypical, asocial, immoral, or even abnormal behavioral expression," he concludes that wartime makes it difficult to repress the sexual instinct, so boys bypass the chaste "pal and gang" stage of sexual development and leap straight into self-destructive sexual experiences.[8]

The wartime discovery that "all" teenage boys were—and always had been—attracted to girls was not an invitation for parents and teachers to ignore petting parties or the cars parked at lovers' lanes. Indeed, they would now have to step up their surveillance. Nor, in all likelihood, was it meant to encourage sixteen- and seventeen-year-olds to marry. What *was* it meant to do?

THE PURPLE AND GOLD

High school yearbooks also changed perceptibly during the war years. In 1939, when the Clarksville, Tennessee, *Purple & Gold* named Johnnie Halliburton "Top Husband to Be," and Josephine O'Neal "Top Wife to Be," class wits were beside themselves with amusement.[9] The "Class Acrostic" suggests that Johnnie is a Mrs., reciting: "H is for O'Neal. Ooops, pardon, Halliburton is the name." In the photo spread, entitled "The Domestic Type," Johnnie looks heavily embarrassed, while Josephine giggles at him. Perhaps he was particularly apprehensive about rumors of heterosexual interest because his famous relative, adventure writer Richard Halliburton, had been lost at sea in March 1939, just as the yearbook photos were being taken. Halliburton was a he-man with no interest in women: He shared his Laguna Beach home with a lifelong male partner and invited a coterie of attractive young men on his travels.[10]

But there are many other boys at Clarksville High who do not care for girls. Billy Stephens is voted "Top Woman-Hater." In the "Senior Class Last Will and Testament," Kenneth Hayes wills his "ability to keep his mind on his studies rather than on the women" to a young pal. "Class Ambitions" reveal that many boys, including football star Thomas Elliott, "spend time" with other boys or with particular boy friends. Sports and girls, war and girls, still do not mix.

On March 29, 1940, Selah High School in Washington celebrated its First Annual Sadie Hawkins Day.[11] Students came dressed like the hillbillies in the *L'il Abner* comic strip, and "manhungry" girls chased "scared" boys down the hallways. Any boy who got caught had to escort his captor to the dance that night. Although no doubt some of the boys ran very slowly to ensure their capture, many were not pretending: They really did hate dancing with girls. In the "Senior Class Will," three boys leave their "bachelor ways" to junior boys. Gayle Perry and Fred Steele leave "their combination of Mutt and Jeff" to a pair of juniors. They were called "Mutt and Jeff" after the comic strip characters not only because they were short and tall, but because they were inseparable, joined at the hip. Even the senior class president and vice president display no untoward interest in girls. They must put off heterosexual desire until after the crisis, until peacetime, when they would have jobs and houses and bank accounts. Heterosexual interest was still a deterrent to masculinity: Mooning over girls made teenage boys weak, cowardly, mollycoddled, effeminate.

Two years later, in 1942, the senior class president of Dora High School in Alabama, a boy named Harry Lee Ellis, is being immortalized as girl-crazy in his yearbook photo tagline: "Harry Lee is always in a whirl, he is always looking for a new girl." In fact, nine of the fourteen senior boys at Dora High have taglines praising their girl-craziness:

> "Harry likes to have his fun, to him every girl is just the one."
> "You'll find Leo is never alone. Every time you see him, he's with Ora Stone."
> "O. T. with his black curly hair, you'll find girls are his only care."

Another punishes its lack:

> "Harold is very bashful and quite [sic], you never see him with a date at night."

The point is well taken. Harold McMurran had been dreaming of flight since he was five years old, when a small plane made an emergency landing in a field near his house. He had plenty of company: A dozen or more mass-media teenagers, including Jackie Cooper, Jimmy Lydon, Billy Halop, and Leo Gorcey, sought freedom from their mollycoddling culture in the all-male preserve of flight. But Harold was no dilettante: After graduation, he would become a mechanic in the air force, and eventually he would own the largest aircraft repair company in the Southeast.[12] Yet, according to the yearbook, he had more important things to think about. He should have been dreaming of girls.

Shortly before V-E Day, Columbus High School in southern Indiana published its 1945 *Log*.[13] A cartoon cherub named Life, wearing a letterman's sweatshirt but no pants, investigates what it means to be a high school student in "today's modern world." He explores the hall-ways, the classrooms, the labs, the crowded bicycle-parking lot, the clubs and sports teams, and he sees an endless parade of tightly hugging boy-girl couples. Life discovers that the *Aidettes Amicales* have been sponsor-ing a dance after every home football and basketball game since 1943: "[T]his dance has become a regular event in the life of every Colum-bus High School Student." For holdouts, there was a "Learn to Dance Night" at the Jive Kennel.

Life pays little attention to Ross Barbour, a handsome but "bashful and quiet" young man who has no sports or student council honors to crow about, just band, orchestra, and Future Farmers of America. Yet Ross would become the most famous graduate of Columbus High. While studying at a music conservatory in Indianapolis, he would found the Four Freshmen, one of the most influential jazz combos of the 1950s and popular for generations thereafter. Their "Graduation Day" was requested so often by audiences of high school and college stu-dents, and covered so often—by the Rover Boys, the Beach Boys, and innumerable local groups—that it became an unofficial alma mater, not so much because it evoked the hallowed halls as because it evoked high school sweethearts:

> At the senior prom
> We danced 'til three
> And there you gave
> Your heart to me
> We'll remember always
> Graduation day.[14]

After graduation day, Ross Barbour married Nancy Sue Carlson, his music conservatory sweetheart, and they had children and grand-children, and finally retired to California.[15] Every teenage boy would henceforth have a sweetheart, declared Life. Every teenage boy would gaze at, long for, and dream of girls. Heterosexual desire could no longer be postponed to adulthood. It was required, now.

FOR THE BOYS

War changes every aspect of life, of course, sometimes for the duration of the crisis, often permanently, and its greatest impact is on the young.[16] But why should it change the way teenage boys were portrayed in journalism, in scholarship, and in yearbooks, and perhaps even the way they perceived themselves? Why should the change be so seemingly arbitrary? Teenagers were not permitted to fight, so their girl-craziness or woman-hating should make no difference on the battlefield. Why should the change occur so quickly in Boys Next Door, while Lost Boys lingered in the homoromantic Arcadia until the war's end and Adventure Boys for a decade or more beyond? An analysis of the everyday life of the teenage boy between 1939 and 1945 reveals that he differs from his mid-1930s counterpart in four significant ways.[17]

First, he rarely sees a manly man. Over sixteen million men are in the service, including 70 percent of the male population aged eighteen to thirty-eight and close to 90 percent of the eighteen- to twenty-five-year-olds.[18] His big brother, older pal, and probably his father are gone; whole towns have been abandoned to women and children, and to the men who are elderly, infirm, or 4-F rejects. There is no one to teach him how to be a man, no one to become the object of adult-teen homoromantic passion. However, all of the teenagers are still about. In an era of isolation, gender-role confusion, and absent or compromised masculinity, one would expect the rejection of the feminine to increase, girl-craziness to become more deviant, and the love of comrades to acquire a staggering significance. Instead, the opposite happened: Teenage boys began to approach each other with suspicion, as potential enemies, as potential traitors.

Second, he is functionally adult. He is not planning for the future as much as living his life today. He works in the factories along with the women. He collects scrap metal for victory, buys war bonds, grows a victory garden, serves as an air raid warden. He wears a man-sized zoot suit until fabric shortages force a style change. With his father and brothers overseas, he is the man of the house, and often Mom and Sis defer to his authority. Indeed, commentators feared that he would be crushed by the responsibility and go wild: In 1942, *Life* magazine published two articles about "The Youth Crime Wave," and the first modern juvenile delinquency films appeared in 1943 and 1944.[19] Since a major part of "growing up" was presumably spouse selection, marriage, and family, heterosexual interest, too, could come early, instead of waiting for the high school diploma. However, the percentage of underaged boys who married actually decreased during the war: They would no doubt be enlisting the moment they turned eighteen, and it made little sense to leave a bride behind. Heterosexual interest was not meant to lead to marriage and family, at least not among teenagers.

Third, he is worried. The enemy poses a threat, certainly, but more significant are the traitors at home. In 1940, 1.2 million Americans had been born in Germany, and there were 127,000 citizens and permanent residents of Japanese ancestry. All of them were potential traitors. Anyone else, even a native-born Anglo-American, could be a spy, fellow traveler, coconspirator, or fifth columnist. The biggest threat, however, came from the loyal Americans who inadvertently abetted the Axis by being indolent, lazy, uncaring, or stupid; by talking too much; by failing to notify the authorities about suspicious activity. The Office of War Information distributed posters with slogans like "A careless word—a needless loss" and "A careless word—another cross [on a grave]." Homoromance necessarily occurs between boys or men who are strangers at first, and during the war, strangers are not to be trusted.

Finally, his heroism is directed entirely at other boys and men. Today wars may be fought to save heteronormative institutions like the nuclear family and heteroromance, and even in 1942 most of the songs that the soldiers sang were about Mom or the Girl Next Door, but the home front was awash with homoerotic imagery. Of 357 World War II posters preserved at Northwestern University, twelve portray women, but not sweater girls (with the exception of one featuring Li'l Abner's Daisy Mae): They are sharply dressed, efficient-looking army officers and nurses, obviously intended to attract female recruits rather than to represent "what we are fighting for." Ten of the posters portray children or families, but again, far from "what we are fighting for," they are busily canning vegetables or gathering up scrap metal, and a child is crying because he is too young to enlist.[20]

Forty-five of the posters sell war bonds, encourage limiting travel, or promote factory work by displaying a brawny, handsome male soldier peering through an artillery sight or launching a hand grenade, with slogans like "Don't let him down!" "His life is in your hands!" "Give him the best you've got!" and "Keep it up, brother!" An agonized older soldier holds his dead or dying young buddy, a visual illustration of homoromantic grief, with the caption "Give 'em the stuff to fight with!" Or else the workers at home are portrayed as brawny, handsome men, often shirtless, with slogans like "Put your muscles on a war basis—sign up for a farm job!" Soldier and hometown patriot, both portrayed as boys or young men, share a physicality, emotional intensity, and dynamic of rescuer-rescued that draws perilously close to a symbolic homoromance.

Some aspects of the teenage boy's life in wartime seem amenable to girl-craziness, others to homoromance, and indeed there was considerable confusion in mass culture portraits of the period. However, another phenomenon eventually tipped the scale and made girl-craziness hegemonic: the fear of the invert.

THE INVERT

The "common knowledge" of the prewar era taught that sometimes men acquired the soul and spirit of the other sex, becoming pansies, Percies, fruits, or, more technically, inverts. They would then forever after mince, skip, wear makeup, call each other "dearie," and cast lascivious eyes at "normal" men. In the Jazz Age and the early years of the Depression, inverts were tolerated as harmless eccentrics, as jokes. The cartoon flapper Betty Boop often encountered laughable Percies and pansies. A hint—or double dose—of androgyny in a Franklin Pangborn or a Jack Benny actually enhanced his popularity. Virtually no articles on "the problem of homosexuality" appeared in the scholarly journals of Britain, the United States, or Germany. There were thriving gay and lesbian communities in Hollywood and Harlem, in Paris and Berlin, with nightspots, private parties, open expressions of romantic interest, open homoromantic unions. As long as they maintained a heteronormative façade, perhaps being seen at parties on the arms of ladies or submitting to a studio marriage, actors like Erroll Flynn and Clark Gable could seek out male partners with abandon.[21]

But the rumors of war brought the era of relative freedom to a close. In 1937, FBI head J. Edgar Hoover declared "War on the Sex Criminal," and psychiatrists began examining the gay inmates of prisons and psychiatric hospitals, assuming that they were representative of the gay population as a whole. They proclaimed, with increasing urgency as they waited out the Blitz in England and awaited the war in the United States, that "inversion" was not an in-joke or a lascivious wink, but a dangerous disease, threatening body, mind, and soul.[22] The "homosexual psychopath" was a danger to himself and others, compelled to commit the most atrocious acts of rape and murder, not to mention seductions to produce more of his kind. Obviously he could not safely live among ordinary people. An alarum had been raised, and the psychosis that dare not speak its name quickly became the most significant factor in dividing the world into good/evil, civilized/uncivilized, masculine/feminine, healthy/depraved, Allied/Axis.[23]

The words "invert" and "homosexual" were rarely written or spoken outside of the technical literature. In ordinary discourse, people used code: weak, girlish, sickly, indolent, aesthetic, sensitive, artistic, even "that way." When op-ed pieces complained about "milquetoasts" or "unmanly men," readers knew that they really meant gay.[24] In 1942, popular novelist Philip Wylie published *Generation of Vipers*, blaming smothering, mollycoddling American mothers on the proliferation of "milksops" among the youth of the day. Everyone knew what he *really* meant, and the book became a bestseller in spite of its cover-full of dull-sounding subtitles: "A Survey of Moral Want & a Philosophical Discourse Suitable Only for the Strong . . . a Signpost on the Two Thoroughfares of Man: the Via Dolorosa and the Descensus Averno."[25]

When the war began, the U.S. Army officially banned inverts, or "homosexuals," from military service, and recruitment offices devised several (completely ineffective) tests to weed them out.[26] However, inverts were presumed equally dangerous on the home front. They were very likely to be fifth columnists. Didn't the Nazi storm troopers worship at the altar of inversion? Wasn't Berlin a famous mecca for inverts?

Even those who did not actually sympathize with the Axis were seen as duplicitous, weak willed, and untrustworthy, very likely to be black-mailed, coerced, or bribed into spying for the enemy.

Speculation about the cause of "inversion" ran rampant. Some scholars suggested estrogen poisoning in the womb and offered as evidence the thin, willowy frames; soft, hairless faces; long fingers; and high-pitched voices of gay asylum inmates.[27] Some suggested that the same-sex atmosphere of the military barracks was itself a cause: A 1943 issue of *Marriage and Family Living* warns that boys in the military may be tempted to indulge in "homosexuality, autoeroticism, miscellaneous sex perversions," and consequently be unable or unwilling to engage in "normal" heterosexual relations upon their return.[28] Others countered with Oedipal fixations, lack of early religious training, absent or smothering mothers, too many male friends, too many female friends, unhappy heteroromance, hetero-debauchery, masturbation, and simple evil.[29] But everyone agreed that once inversion happened, it spread like a disease, through seduction, rape, or even the merest social contacts. A single invert might, intentionally or not, pervert an entire school, church, neighborhood, or military base.[30]

Everyone also agreed that the teenage boy was most susceptible to seduction or perversion, since he was not heterosexual *yet*. Freudians believed that he was still in the "pal and gang" stage, sublimating "homosexual tendencies" into passionate, starry-eyed, yet presumably nonsexual crushes on buddies or older men[31]; but an invert could easily transform something noble and beautiful into something vile, transform David and Jonathan, Damon and Pythias into mincing queens, dooming them to lives of sadness and despair.[32]

KING'S ROW

Several of the bestselling novels of the war years touch on the woeful potential of an adolescent hero falling prey to inversion. In Henry Bellarman's *King's Row* (1940), Boy Next Door Parris gets a girlfriend at age fourteen: They kiss, go skinny-dipping, and have a barely veiled sexual encounter. The premature heterosexual experience weakens his sensibility just enough for him to fall victim to classmate Jamie Wakefield, "too pretty for a boy, prettier than a girl."[33] They hold hands, kiss, and have another barely veiled sexual encounter. Though Parris goes on to a heterosexual adulthood, the moment of same-sex contact has a devastating effect, ruining his relationships with women and compelling him to "tragically" devote his life to his best friend Drake.

In *The Web and the Rock*, one of many effusions of autobiography from the then wildly popular Thomas Wolfe, fifteen-year-old George Weber suffers a barely veiled sexual assault: The other boys try to rip his pants off, like the Dead End Kids accosting a sissy, but here "with eagerness and mirthful cruelty . . . with secret, unclean laughter." Wolfe spends the next hundred pages excoriating them, and all boys everywhere, as "jeering, ugly, unwholesome, smug, complacent," and so on. Then he sends George off to college, where he falls into starstruck, stammering love at first sight with Jim Randolph: "a creature of such magnificence that he seemed to have been created on a different scale and shape for another, more Olympian, Universe . . . he was all the Arrow collar young men one had ever seen in pictures, all the football heroes for the covers of the *Saturday Evening Post,* he was all the young men in the Kuppenheimer clothing ads, he was all of these rolled into one, and he was something more than all that."[34]

That single sexual assault, years ago, caused George to spend a lot of hours staring at handsome young men in advertisements, and he is "saved" only when his new boyfriend takes him to a burlesque show and seduces into the joys of heterosexuality. Wolfe devotes the last five hundred thousand or so words of the novel to answering the question: What do young men want? The answer: a woman.

Billy Wilder's classic film *The Lost Weekend* (1945) conveniently omits the reason for young writer Don Birnam's four-day-long drinking binge. Not so the 1944 novel by Charles Jackson. *What is amiss?* Don asks himself, quoting Shakespeare. *You are, and do not know it.* He ignores his wife and a flirtatious lady friend to obsess over same-sex desire, vaguely describing liaisons of the past and homophobic jokes in the present, wondering if male acquaintances desire him or believe him to be "queer." When he sees a heterosexual couple in a bar, he fantasizes: "[D]id she lay her head on his stomach, feel his chest and thighs, was he big?" If the man were alone, Don asserts, "he would advance and find out a thing or two."[35]

In high school, Don thought he had a boyfriend; they used to meet in an abandoned carriage shed for what Don considered "the most important thing in life." He was devastated to discover that the other boy was just "having fun"; he had been fantasizing about girls the whole time. At seventeen, a college freshman, Don fell in love with an older classmate named Tracey, but not only did Tracey fail to return his affection, he told everyone in the college about it, causing a witch hunt, scandal, and life-long disgrace. Now thirty-three years old, Don gets drunk, but not, as one would expect, to mask his same-sex desire or to assuage his guilt over being "abnormal." Instead, drunkenness and inversion are species of the same sickness, the results of a perversely self-destructive narcissism (he fantasizes about being both Aschenbach and the boy he desired in *Death in Venice*). Don has become one of "the defaulters, the renegers, the backward-lookers, the adolescents, the ungrownups." He is frozen on the brink of adulthood, like the teenagers in the homoromantic Arcadia, but here with tragic consequences: He is unable to finish his novel, hold down a job, or experience the "mature" love of a woman.[36]

The same-sex bond that had once been a sign of manliness now threatened to feminize the teenage boy, or worse. Every same-sex friendship, even the rough-and-tumble camaraderie of the army barracks or the locker room, must henceforth be suspect. It must be accompanied by jokes, put-downs, and protests of disinterest. The response to a rescue must never be a starry-eyed "If it weren't for you . . . ," but instead a shoulder-pounding "I never thought I'd see your ugly mug again!" And every same-sex friendship must be countermanded by wolf-whistling expressions of interest in girls.

6

LOVE FINDS ANDY HARDY

On March 12, 1937, the character of the Boy Next Door changed forever. In a minor subplot in MGM's *A Family Affair*, small town Judge Hardy orders his sixteen-year-old son Andy to escort a girl to a party in order to butter up her bank-president father. "Holy jumping Jerusalem, a party with girls!" Andy yelps, imagining an experience as abhorrently sissified as wearing a Little Lord Fauntleroy costume. Griping, complaining, muttering under his breath, he is deposited on the girl's doorstep for his shotgun date. He knocks timidly, hoping that no one will answer and he can claim that he was stood up. But no such luck: The door opens, and she stands before him. A vision of loveliness in a new party dress. Suddenly the universe has changed. Andy stares, stutters, adjusts his tie, a posture of embarrassment in the face of destiny that would be repeated countless thousands of times in movies and TV shows, evoked countless thousands of times in books and magazines, but was then brand new, at least among sixteen-year-old boys, the first portent of the adolescent hetero-erotic mania that would invade and ultimately conquer Arcadia.

An adaptation of Aurania Rouverol's *Skidding,* which ran for 428 performances on Broadway between 1928 and 1930, *A Family Affair* starred fifty-nine-year-old Lionel Barrymore as crotchety Southern-fried Judge Hardy, who objects to a proposed aqueduct that would allow his small town of Carvel, Idaho, to market its water to a big city downstream. The townsfolk revile him for "pulling down the pillars of civic progress," but he stands his ground, realizing that the aqueduct would allow the big city to monopolize the town's economy. This plot-line seems impossibly obscure today, but in 1937 monopolies were a touchy issue, sure to draw audience interest.[1]

The judge's opponents try to discredit him by spreading the rumor that his daughter and her husband are divorcing: Obviously anyone so debauched as to have a divorce in the family is not fit to evaluate the local economy. More scandals arise when Judge Hardy's other daughter falls in love with one of the aqueduct engineers and the judge's son turns into a girl-crazy kook. Andy Hardy's transformation from woman-hating to girl-crazy is scripted not as a celebration, a joyous rite of pas-sage, but as one of the judge's headaches.

In the original play, Andy Hardy is described as "a handsome but unkempt fellow of sixteen with a ruffled mop of hair that stands on end . . . he looks like a shaggy, overgrown puppy,"[2] and he was played on Broadway by Charles Eaton, a wispy, androgynous sort,[3] but direc-tor George B. Seitz wanted to compete with the Jones family pictures, across town at Twentieth Century Fox: The teenage son there was played by blond, square-jawed, stunningly handsome Kenneth Howell. So Seitz cast blond, square-jawed, stunningly handsome Frankie Thomas, the veteran of seven Broadway plays and the weeper *A Dog of Flanders.* But at the last minute MGM mogul Leo B. Mayer stepped in, sent Frankie Thomas off to do the serial version of *Tim Tyler's Luck,* and insisted on Mickey Rooney for the part. Mickey was not a logical choice: He gen-erally played Lost Boys, rough-and-tumble rapscallions, Irish-Catholic street kids with names like Snapper, Freckles, and Gig, but not Boys Next Door, not small-town middle-class Protestants, not Andrew Hardy. And he was hardly qualified for heartthrob status, frozen a nonheroic 5'3", with a scrunched-up face and a roundish Santa Claus nose; he was reviled by a critic of the day as "that gnomish prodigy, that half human, half goblin man child, who is as old in cinema ways as Wallace Beery and twice as cute."[4] Yet he looked *real,* like someone who actually could be growing up in Carvel, Idaho, and gripe about being forced to dance with girls.

A Family Affair ends, like nearly every movie ever made, with an as-surance of heterosexual destiny: Judge Hardy and his wife, adult daughters with reconciled husband and engineer-boyfriend, respectively, embrace. The teenage boy has heretofore been excused: He either gazes approvingly at the adults or shuffles off in disgust to seek out his girl-hating chums. But now, when the adults are finished embracing, a moment before the final fade-out, Andy Hardy makes movie history again by grabbing his girl. The original play bids farewell to Andy as he is ruminating over his new real-estate business. Scriptwriter Kay Van Ripper changed the emblem of his maturation from the economic, a move from idleness to meaningful employment, to the hetero-erotic, a move from woman-hating to girl-crazy.[5]

Though critics generally praised *A Family Affair*, audiences seemed unable to conjure much enthusiasm. Through the remainder of 1937 and into 1938, there was no indication that Andy Hardy would soon become the archetype of youthful America. Mickey Rooney continued to play teenage boys who like boys: He refuses to dance with girls and trounces a snively snob who does; he goes wild over Ronald Sinclair; he helps his sister snare a man without romancing anyone of his own; he has an Irish street kid–aristocratic snob romance with Freddie Bartholomew; he finds love and belonging with Spencer Tracey.[6] Two more segments of the Judge Hardy series appeared, *You're Only Young Once* and *Judge Hardy's Children,* still with Andy's adolescent girl-craziness presented as an odd quirk, one of the judge's headaches.

ANDY HARDY FINDS AN AUDIENCE

Love Finds Andy Hardy premiered on July 22, 1938, with Andy the undisputed star. The *New York Times* called it "[e]asily the best of the Hardy series, with Mickey Rooney, America's kid brother, in the tragi-comic ecstasies of puppy love," but the aesthetic quality of the film is not as relevant as its symbolic function.[7] The plot has become an archetype, replaced a thousand times in movies, radio shows, television shows, and comic books, but then it was brand-new, reflecting brand-new teenage customs, like boy-girl dates.[8] At Christmastime, Andy needs $8 to buy a car, so he takes a job keeping the wolves from "sweater girl" Cynthia (Lana Turner) while her boyfriend is away. Cynthia turns out to be a wolf herself, disgusting Andy with her constant groping and fondling, but he can't drop her until after the big Christmas dance. Meanwhile, Betsy Booth (Judy Garland), the daughter of a famous actress who happens to be spending the holidays with her grandparents in Carvel, offers to lend Andy the $8, but only if he "dates" her for the same dance. Then Andy's regular girlfriend Polly Benedict (Ann Rutherford) returns early from her family's vacation and insists on being "dated" as well. Now Andy has three dates, each impossible to break!

Foregrounding Andy's plight and relegating the rest of the Hardy family to the background tripled the box office of *Love Finds Andy Hardy* and transformed the series from B-list ephemera into a hot A-list property. The next few years were crowded with Hardys (all but one directed by George B. Seitz). Andy Hardy became so recognizable that he and the judge appeared in *Andy Hardy's Dilemma* (1938), a short about the importance of contributing to the Community Chest (without any character exposition), and in December 1939 the family offered filmgoers a separate Christmas greeting. Mickey Rooney was the number one box office draw in the United States three years running, in 1939, 1940, and 1941, mostly for the Andy Hardy series. He shared a special Oscar with Paramount warbler Deanna Durbin for "bringing to the screen the spirit and personification of youth," and an Oscar certificate went to MGM to honor the series' excellence in "representing the American way of life."[9] Andy Hardy had become "typical American teenager," his life the model for what teenage boys' life should be: old-fogy yet endlessly permissive parents, authoritarian yet somehow caring teachers, tiger-striped jalopies, crazy money-making schemes, malteds at the drug store, Saturday-night dances, pals, and gals. Especially gals.

Film historians today tend to ignore the Andy Hardy series altogether or to make it emblematic of a lost golden age, seductive yet trite and banal.[10] Even a celebration of B movies critiques the series as "drenched in an almost insufferable sentimentality."[11] But this is no Disney nostalgia with kids and dogs. Levy comes closer to the point when he notes that the inhabitants of Andy's world pursue "a vision of happiness which eludes them."[12] Everywhere in Carvel one sees sadness, disappointment, a sort of bleak resolve to tow the mark. Judge Hardy is no font of pragmatic wisdom or small-town content: Roiled by the success of his classmates at Ivy League Wainwright College, now governors, Supreme Court justices, and college presidents, he constantly falls prey to con artists and get-rich-quick schemes. Mrs. Hardy is timid, sickly, often an invalid, not infrequently on her deathbed. Aunt Milly is a sad, lonely schoolteacher, never quite fitting into the family and yet never quite acquiring her own identity. Sister Marian dates a succession of drunkards, cads, and scoundrels. Girlfriend Polly Benedict is rather a cad herself, dropping Andy without hesitation whenever she spies a man who is older, taller, richer, or wearing a uniform. And Andy's friends are always sad or quirky wise guys, too tall or too short, too rich or too poor, failures.

Within this scandal- and despair-ridden prototypical Peyton Place, Andy Hardy ages from sixteen to nineteen, from adolescence to young adulthood, each installment adding new experiences and new growth. Though he is as fallible as the other characters, as likely to jump to conclusions, act without thinking, betray friends by accident or design, he is as absurdly attractive as a boys' book hero. Every girl he encounters wants to kiss him. He comes home from a party with a phone number scrawled across his chest. He is mobbed at a school dance. He asks his sister for advice on how to *diminish* girls' admiration sufficiently to make it through high school without marrying. He complains, "I'm a nervous wreck! Do you think there's anything wrong with a guy if he *doesn't* want a girl kissing him all the time?" The awestricken judge asks, "Man to man, how do you do it?" Andy has no explanation: He is not handsome, not a gridiron star, not wealthy, not sophisticated, not talented, not particularly smart. He is good-natured and fun-loving, but these are hardly qualities that set hearts to fluttering.

Yet still the girls mob him, and not only the girls: Boys, children, men, and women, everyone he encounters seems to fall in love with him. In *Andy Hardy Gets Spring Fever*, Andy's crush on the young drama teacher is partially requited: They will be milestones in each others' lives, she says. Meanwhile, a classmate oddly named Stickin' Plaster gets a blatant, doe-eyed crush on Andy, and during the school play manipulates the prop moon to "accidentally" sabotage his big love scene.

Though beset-upon by the adoring glances of everyone he encounters, girls and boys, men and women, Andy has no sidekick like Henry Aldrich's Dizzy or Archie Andrews's Jughead. His male friends come in packs—perhaps the adoring glances of a constant companion would suggest romantic interest too blatantly. Instead, Andy devotes all of his emotional and erotic energy to chasing girls or, rather, to choosing from among his droves of female suitors (after all, it's *Love Finds Andy Hardy*, not *Andy Hardy Finds Love*). This single-minded obsession with the feminine would imitated and expanded in uncounted thousands of mass-culture texts through the next fifty years, and even today it is sold to millions of men as what they once were, to young boys as what they will become, and to teenage boys as what they are, or should be, today.

Andy's girl-craziness seems so "normal" to modern depictions of teenage boys that it is difficult to remember how problematic MGM found it. Was it a winning quality or a distracting flaw? Was the character successful *because of* or *in spite of* it? Penrod, Alfalfa, and Peck's Bad Boy could express "cute" heterosexual puppy-love because their immaturity presumably made physical expression impossible. But how would audiences react to a teenager, sexually mature, aggressively physical, expressing heterosexual desire when he was five to ten years from the possibility of consummating that desire in the socially respectable institution of marriage? Would he be taken as a sex maniac or one of the bug-eyed drug addicts from *Assassin of Youth* (1940), who kiss only because they're high? Early in the series, Louis B. Mayer complained, "If you let Andy get too crazy about girls, you'll lose your audience!"[13] Some early installments eliminate Andy's girl-craziness altogether. In *Out West with the Hardys* (1938), Andy is humorously pursued by an eight-year-old tomboy instead of a teenage girl. In *Judge Hardy and Son* (1939), he is too busy dealing with his mother's near-fatal bout of influenza to worry much about girls.

Often Andy finds his superheroic attractiveness a headache. He complains that sweater girl Cynthia doesn't want to "do anything fun," like go swimming or ice skating; all she wants to do is hug and kiss. On vacation on Catalina Island, his new girlfriend lures him onto her family's boat. He suggests that they visit a tourist attraction called the Bird Farm, but she exclaims "Kid stuff!" and tries to pull him down onto the couch. He literally fights her off and runs away, behaving precisely like a girl who has been subject to an inappropriate advance.[14]

When Andy does exhibit girl-craziness, it is coded as a childish affectation, something to be overcome in manhood, like Willie Baxter's infatuation with baby-talking Lola in the Booth Tarkington novel *Seventeen* (1918). In *Love Finds Andy Hardy*, Andy invites Polly Benedict to a dance at the country club:

> Andy: [Looks away coyly.] There's a lot of swell places where you can sneak out between the dances.
>
> Polly: Really! I think we're getting much too old for that sort of thing—hugging and kissing!
>
> Andy: [In a little boy voice.] Aw, I ain't ever gonna get too old for huggin' and kissin'!

His voice, his mannerisms, even his grammar becomes infantilized (he says "huggin' and kissin'" instead of "hugging and kissing," though elsewhere his diction is flawless). Andy often becomes the passive victim of experienced older women, vamps, and gold diggers, but even his flirtations with girls his own age are conducted in an oddly infantile manner: He wrings his hands, shrugs his shoulders, averts his eyes, the very picture of a shy, timid schoolboy.

Likewise, Andy's girl-craziness is a sign of effeminacy, the antithesis of the aggressive, tough self-confidence that Boys Next Door expected of themselves and others in the 1930s. Rudolph Valentino and Jackie Cooper's interest in women was ridiculed as effeminacy and possibly perversion.[15] Even Mickey Rooney's adopted Irish ethnicity was presumed a feminizing trait.[16] Irishness was coded as debauched and dangerous, and though the character of Andy Hardy was about as small-town, native-born, Protestant respectable as the scriptwriters could produce, having him played by "Mickey Rooney" immediately added a question of failed or inadequate masculinity.

The implication that a girl-crazy boy is feminine, gender-transgressive, and potentially gay is not lost on either Andy or contemporary audiences: In his memoirs, Mickey Rooney reprints the complete text of a love letter that "Andy Hardy" received from a smitten gay fan in 1940.[17] Andy calls himself "the sensitive type," code for pansy. He is photographed ironing a lacy nightgown, and then blackmailed. His friends parade around with a sign reading: "Miss Andy Hardy, Ladies' Laundress. Linjeree washed and ironed by my own dainty hands!" In *Andy Hardy Meets Debutante* (1940), Andy deflects his concerns over lack of manliness onto a toddler named Francis, whom he encounters at an orphanage:

> Andy: Hello, little girl.
> Francis: [In a tough-guy pose.] I'm a boy, see?
> Andy: You talk like a little girl. How do you ever expect to
>   grow up to be a big he-man?
> Francis: [Sarcastically.] Like you?

To remedy the association of girl-craziness and childishness or effeminacy, Andy's body is on constant display. Those who know Mickey Rooney only as the stout hobbit-like grandfather of his later roles would be surprised that as a young man, he was extremely athletic, with a tight, toned physique. This was the beginning of the "age of the chest," a time in which the chest was being fetishized in both men and women.[18] In 1941, Bob Hoffman published the first edition of *The Big Chest Book*, advising that "Big Chested Men are strong and healthy" and "Every man should seek a better chest."[19] Yet the chests of Boys Next Door were rarely displayed on film: In all of their dozens of Boy Next Door roles, Jackie Cooper takes his shirt off three times, Jackie Moran twice, Jimmy Lydon only once, and Dickie Moore not at all.[20] But Mickey Rooney spent an amazing amount of screen time in every picture half-naked, bounding down the stairs in his undershirt, stripping down for bed or to bathe. In the 1930s topless men were still barred from most beaches, and in *You're Only Young Once*, Marian's lifeguard beau wears a sleeveless top, but the seventeen-year-old Andy goes swimming bare-chested.[21]

For someone who lives in a northern climate (Carvel starts out in Idaho, then shifts to upstate New York), Andy spends an inordinate amount of time in swimming pools, again shirtless, and wearing extremely revealing Speedo-style swim trunks instead of the baggy trousers then in style.[22] *Love Finds Andy Hardy* has two five-minute pool scenes, and *Andy Hardy's Double Life* keeps the teenager in a swimsuit for about a quarter of the total running time. Of course, there are also girls in those scenes, but usually in the background while the camera remains firmly fixed upon Andy. The practice became so well-known that *Girl Crazy* (1943), which is not in the Andy Hardy series, contains an interesting tease: Upon arriving at his new college in the New Mexico desert, a tired, dusty Danny Churchill (Mickey Rooney) announces that he's going to take a shower. Then he pauses a beat for audience laughter at the intertextual joke. The obsessive display of Andy's body seems to affiliate him with the superb physiques of the boys' book heroes, defining him as a strong, powerful, masculine Boy Next Door in spite of his feminizing girl-craziness.

The most interesting evocation of girl-craziness as effeminacy occurs in *The Hardys Ride High* (1939), which, not coincidentally, marks the shift from peer-peer to adult-teen homoromance during the war. Andy becomes infatuated with an older man who pretends to return his interest but actually has a sinister ulterior motive.[23] Thus adult interest in teenagers, which heretofore had always been presented in mass media as an unmitigated good, acquires an aura of suspicion, even of dread.

Claimants to a fortune of $2 million, the Hardys move to a mansion in Detroit, where Andy becomes infatuated with a fellow claimant, strikingly handsome man-about-town Phil Wescott (thirty-year-old John King).[24] To no one's surprise, Phil seems to return his interest. On a "private" tour of the family automobile factory, the eagerly horny Phil can't seem to keep his hands off Andy, constantly hugging him, patting his shoulder, guiding him with a hand to his back. Andy is noticeably flattered by the young man's attention. That night, they go out on a more formal date to the Paradise Club, a sort of 1930s version of the Playboy Club—an odd choice for Phil, who has described himself as a "woman hater." Phil ignores the scantily clad female dancers to gaze at Andy with undisguised desire; Andy does not ignore the dancers, but he continues to respond to Phil like a bashful schoolboy who has just received his first valentine.

However, Phil is not really interested in romancing Andy or in sleeping with him. His nefarious plot involves a chorus girl–accomplice, who will invite Andy to her apartment for "a late supper." Phil will then "accidentally" stumble upon the seventeen-year-old in an act of heterosexual congress and squeal to Judge Hardy, who will be disgraced and forced to abandon his claim to the fortune. The plot is ruined when Andy agrees to the dinner but insists that Phil come along, thus ruining any opportunity for an "accidental" discovery and feigned indignation.

Since Andy does not realize that he is being conned, his insistence on Phil's participation seems odd: Traditionally, heterosexual boys abandon same-sex chums the moment a girl smiles at them. No doubt his request is innocent of sexual intent, but Phil certainly behaves as if he has been asked to participate in a ménage à trois; he becomes increasingly nervous on the way to the apartment, and shortly after they enter he makes an excuse and says goodnight. Andy, now alone with a chorus girl making eyes at him and speaking in double entendres, bolts for the door. Today the scene looks very much like a gay teenager's ineffectual attempt to maintain a heterosexual façade, and indeed later Andy worries that a "real man" would have stayed. Judge Hardy reassures him: It is perfectly normal for teenagers to be appalled by the prospect of a sleazy one-night stand; thirty years ago, he himself bolted for the door of a gilded age cathouse.

Still, the fear that something is "not right" about Andy lingers, unstated or barely stated, through the summer of 1940, through *Andy Hardy Gets Spring Fever* and *Judge Hardy and Son*. Not surprisingly, Mickey Rooney's other film roles in 1939 and 1940 are strictly traditional: He has a postadolescent heterosexual romance in *Babes in Arms*, and playing *Young Tom Edison* at the age of sixteen, he never once mentions or looks at a girl.

LOVE AND MARRIAGE AND MOTHER

As World War II began, Andy Hardy's girl-craziness had to be revised; it could no longer point toward the past, toward childish infatuations, effeminacy, or perversion. It had to lead directly to adult responsibility, to "the sanctity of the home, love and marriage and mother," to the "American Way of Life."[25] The change is foregrounded in *Andy Hardy Meets Debutante*, which, significantly, premiered on the Fourth of July weekend, 1940.

In the frame story, Judge Hardy and family go to New York to work on the case of an orphanage threatened with closure because its administrator "lost faith in his own country" and deposited its funds in a European bank that defaulted. As if that were not patriotic enough, the judge takes Andy on a tour of the Statue of Liberty and the busts of "Mighty Men of Old" in the NYU Hall of Fame, meanwhile pontificating about fighting for freedom, all men being created equal, life, liberty, and all that jazz. Immersed in scene after scene of jingoistic oration, scripted not by the liberal Kay Van Ripper but by conservative Thomas Seller, Andy's girl-craziness seems even more infantile and effeminate than before, and his peers are not shy about punishing him. In an early scene, Polly Benedict and buddy Beezy (George P. Breakston) lambaste Andy for keeping a scrapbook of newspaper and magazine photos of debutante Daphne Fowler (Diana Lewis).[26]

> Polly: Of all the ridiculous little boy exhibitions! Collecting
>   pictures of a perfectly awful girl that he's never seen!
> Beezy: [In a childish singsong.] Andy's got a crush on Daphne
>   Fowler!

Andy angrily replies that it's no puppy-love crush, desire without the intention of fulfillment: He actually knows Daphne Fowler and she is interested in him, so they would be dating but for the distance—he's too young to travel to New York by himself. Then Judge Hardy announces the family's upcoming three weeks in New York for the orphanage case, and Andy's friends goad him into agreeing to bring back a photo "proving" that he has a debutante girlfriend. If he fails, they will disgrace him by printing a humiliating photo in the Carvel High *Olympian*.

Andy hatches several schemes to meet the debutante, but he only succeeds in charging up $36.50 for a fancy dinner and losing an expensive pearl tie stud. Despairing, he tells Judge Hardy, "I just realized today that some people are better than me." The judge criticizes Andy for "sniveling over class, money, social position" when he has the ability to accomplish anything he wants. He proves his point by winning the orphanage case, even though he is a paltry small-town judge and his opponent a famous attorney. Reenergized, Andy finds a deus ex machina in regular foil Betsy Booth, who happens to be a Manhattan sub-deb herself and a close friend of "Daph." He gets his introduction and his photograph (it shows Miss Fowler clinging hopefully to his shoulders), and returns triumphantly to Carvel High. For some reason he has Francis the Orphan in tow, and his friends assume that he has become a father, that he has channeled his girl-craziness into marriage and family. Though he quickly corrects them, his girl-craziness has become a positive trait: active, masculine, connected with fighting for liberty, connected with the American Way of Life. Andy's girl-craziness has made him a man.

> Beezy: I should have known better than to trifle with a man like Andy!
>
> Polly: [To Andy.] Are you engaged to Daphne Fowler?
>
> Andy: No. [She's] just another milestone in my career . . . can I help it if I have irresistible charm?
>
> Polly: That's not charm, that's polygamy! [Melts into his arms.] But, oh Andy, how we women love it!

When Andy's girl-craziness is associated with masculinity, the fear of perversion is deflected onto the older generation. Lewis Stone looks like a grandfather rather than a father, and he always plays Judge Hardy as thoughtful, slow-moving, and crotchety, lacking in the robustness of youth. But in this movie he deliberately takes on a feminine pose. Andy comes home in the last scene to find Judge Hardy wearing a mink stole, mincing and limp-wristing about the drawing room. As Andy gapes in amazement at this evidence of "inversion," we learn the truth: The Judge is modeling a gift to his wife. Still, it would be more logical for him to ask Mrs. Hardy to try on the stole rather than to pose as a drag queen. Immediately afterward, Andy goes up to his room and arranges large photos of the girls he has dated during the series so far. "How one's women do add up!" he exclaims, correlating youthful masculinity with girl-craziness for perhaps the first time in mass culture.

JUDGE HARDY'S BOYFRIEND

The next two installments of the series return the eighteen-year-old Andy to the homoromantic Arcadia of the 1930s, but briefly, tentatively, and with increasing dread. *Andy Hardy's Private Secretary* (1941) was scripted by novelist Katharine Brush, who wrote the Freddie Bartholomew vehicle *Listen Darling,* and Jane Murfin, who cowrote the camp classic *The Women* (1939), so we might expect a minimum of heterosexual hijinks. Instead we find parallel stories of homoromantic courtship. Judge Hardy insists that the snobbish Andy give jobs in his upcoming high school graduation festivities to two poor kids: Kathryn Land (opera-singing Kathryn Landis) and her brother Harry (Todd Karns, best known as George Bailey's little brother in *It's a Wonderful Life*). He even drives out to the wrong-side-of-the-tracks hovel with Andy to make sure that his boy behaves honorably.

Andy agrees to hire Kathryn as the private secretary of the title and, intuiting that the sensitive, artistic Harry would make a good interior designer, puts him in charge of decorating the school gym. Meanwhile, the judge spies their handsome dad (Ian Hunter) painting something in the backyard and, barely able to contain his glee, announces that he "has some business to attend to" and joins him. During the flirtation he discovers that, though down on his luck and working at an auto garage, Mr. Land is superbly educated. Among his other accomplishments, he is fluent in Portuguese.

The rest of the movie barely touches on the private secretary angle, and Judge Hardy's wife and Andy's girlfriend barely appear: Homoromance and girl-craziness do not and perhaps cannot occur in the same movie, since one is emblematic of the old-style Boy Next Door and the other of the new. Instead, the judge eagerly pursues a friendship with Mr. Land. We see the two riding cozily in a convertible; when they are caught in the rain and seek refuge in the auto garage where Mr. Land works, they must change out of their wet clothes into mechanic uniforms. The sequence allows the judge to demonstrate that he is no snob, but it also gives the two men a moment of intimacy unusual among adults during the period. Judge Hardy is amazingly concerned with Mr. Land's welfare; he pulls strings in Washington to get him a job with the State Department, and when Andy botches it, he calls in a favor from the governor to get him a new job. At the end of the movie, Andy and Polly Benedict are parked at a lovers' lane when the judge and Mr. Land pull up in their convertible. They "explain" that they are looking for Andy, but it's a strange, muted explanation, as if they were on their way to park at a lovers' lane for another reason entirely.

Meanwhile, after some sullen bitchiness, Harry falls hard for Andy. He's the first to comfort Andy when he is distraught over failing a vital English exam, and he stays up all night (along with Kathryn and Polly Benedict) to help him study for a re-test. Andy, used to being the object of everyone's attention, is oblivious to his interest. Then, distraught over botching things yet again, Andy decides to leave town. Harry follows, risking his life to hop onto the speeding train. In an eye-gleaming moment, Harry convinces Andy that there are people in town who care for him regardless of his shortcomings. He has family, he has friends, he has a "particular friend." They return to Carvel together. At the end of the movie, instead of going to college, Harry takes a job in Carvel (a decidedly feminine-coded job as a window dresser in a department store), so they will not be parting. At least as long as Katherine Brush and Jane Murfin are scripting their story. But in later installments, with other scriptwriters, neither Harry nor the particular friendship is mentioned again.[27]

On August 15, 1941, the most somber of the Andy Hardy movies, *Life Begins for Andy Hardy*, premiered, again foregrounding a peer homoromance but placing it in a grim, threatening night world instead of Arcadia. According to a contemporary *New York Times* review, Andy is "still is a long way from man's estate," but there is "greater effort to reach mature audiences with Andy's future escapades, for the dialogue in the current chapter is rather on the smart side."[28] The summer after his high school graduation, the eighteen-year-old Andy moves to Manhattan to strike it rich as an office boy. But New York is a topsy-turvy looking-glass world. Betsy Booth, a quiet, lost waif in Carvel, is smart and savvy on her home turf. In Carvel, Andy is constantly mobbed by girls, but in New York, he is constantly being hit on by boys. He takes a room at the City House for Boys, where young men lounge around in their undershirts. One of them, off camera, issues Andy an invitation in a nasal "sissy" voice: "Hi, tenderfoot, drop in sometime." The effeminate intonation of rough-and-tumble cowboy slang is jarring and somewhat disquieting. What sort of world has Andy stumbled into?

Andy still has girl trouble, negotiating the admiration of Betsy Booth and the salacious advances of an older woman, Miss Hicks (Patricia Dane), but most of the plot involves his relationship with Jimmy Frobisher (twenty-one-year-old Ray McDonald), a flamboyantly feminine aspiring dancer. Male dancers were automatically coded as gay, but Jimmy is so excessively flamboyant, theatrical, and tragic that he might as well be wearing a sign. Gigs are hard to find, and he was fired from his job as an office boy, so now he is . . . um, living in Central Park. He makes no overt allusion to prostitution, of course—he might if the movie were filmed today—but he advertises his wares with surprising candor. Andy "feels sorry for him" and sneaks him back to his room at the City House.

They are both penniless, Andy because he is too proud to accept aid from his well-moneyed family and friends, and Jimmy because he is alone in the world—until now. There are scenes of the two chatting cozily, Jimmy lying in his underwear on the single bed while Andy gets dressed. But one day Andy gets a job at Miss Hicks's office, followed by an invitation to dinner and dancing, and when he returns to the room late that night, he finds that Jimmy, feeling betrayed and abandoned, has committed suicide.[29] It is a jarring scene, unprecedented in the Andy Hardy series, and the censors required a tacked-on ending that reveals that Jimmy didn't kill himself after all, he died of a heart attack. Andy concludes that "a fella should go ahead and do what he should do in this world, and not the things that are the biggest, most fun, and exciting." The message is clear: homoromance may be big, fun, and exciting, but it can only lead to tragedy. A fella should do what he should do in this world, reject Arcadia (or rather, the tawdry New York night world) for Carvel, and college, and a heteronormative future.

ANDY HARDY'S BLONDE TROUBLE

Once Andy Hardy set foot on the campus of Wainwright College as a beanie-wearing frosh, he would no longer be America's Kid Brother, and his girl-craziness would no longer be fun, unique, or amusing: Collegians had been acquiring girlfriends ever since *The Rover Boys*. Therefore, the next two Andy Hardy installments, *The Courtship of Andy Hardy* (March 1942) and *Andy Hardy's Double Life* (December 1942), take place immediately after Andy's return from New York, during the summer before he leaves for college. *Double Life* is primarily concerned with the judge's mollycoddling plan to accompany his son to Wainwright, and it ends with Andy boarding the train (alone).

Andy Hardy's Blonde Trouble premiered in May 1944, with Andy still on that train, but it was obvious that a very difficult year and a half had passed. Series regulars were absent or relegated to brief, uncomfortable cameos. Mickey Rooney looked tired and sickly. There were no swimming pool or changing-clothes scenes, no seminudity at all except for a standard bounding-down-the-stairs in his undershirt shot. The double plotline returned to the contrast of the Boy Next Door and the effeminate older man.

In the first plotline, a father reads in a child psychology book that allowing his twin daughters to spend too much time together is unhealthy, so he sends one to Wainwright College and the other to an aunt's house in Vermont. They rebel and show up at the college together, but pretend to be a single person, causing freshman Andy headaches when one flirts with him and the other rejects him. Meanwhile, coed Kay (Bonita Granville) rejects Andy in favor of the suave, fiftyish Dr. M. J. Standish (Herbert Marshall), who seems to be a professor of literature: He recites lugubrious love poetry to classes full of bored, fidgeting young men and sighing, doe-eyed young ladies.[30] Andy can't understand why Kay would prefer an oldster: "That's an insult to young American manhood!" But Standish gloats over his victory: "This was a case in which you were *not* irresistible."

Many movies of the period, including *Her First Beau* (1941), *A Very Young Lady* (1942), and, most famously, *The Bachelor and the Bobby-Soxer* (1947), feature teenage girls preferring handsome, sophisticated men to gawky, goofy Boys Next Door, a problem that first received notice when Judy Garland sang the puppy-love song "Dear Mr. Gable" to a picture of Clark in *Broadway Melody of 1938*. On Broadway, there was a fad of comedies about bobby-soxers falling for older men while their boyfriends fume with indignation: *Janie* (1942), *Kiss and Tell* (1943), *Dear Ruth* (1944). Even the first issue of *Archie Comics* in 1941 has Betty Cooper torn between dweeb-next-door Archie and dashing screen star Tyrone Power: She "can't make up her mind whether to go after the one that's handsome and she'll *never* get, or the one she *can* get, that's Archie." In real life, girls were ten times more likely than boys to be married at high school age.[31] If desire could flow only between men and *not-men,* then teenage boys, *not-yet* men, could be appropriate objects of adult male but not teenage female desire. Besides, their "youthful muscles" were presumably of no interest whatever to girls, who selected romantic partners on the basis of social standing, sophistication, or money in the bank. However much the new awareness of inversion might make teenage boys "seen with" other boys or men suspect, there had to be a paradigm shift before teenage boys could be "seen with" girls effectively, without ridicule.

The shift happens for Andy Hardy when Kay rethinks her interest in the oldster. "I guess I was younger than I thought," she confesses, as she agrees to date Andy in spite of his deficiency in status, charm, and bankroll. Later, Dr. Standish tells the whole story to his old friend, Judge Hardy ("My successful rival for the young lady is your own son"), and the judge bursts into laughter. Girl-craziness has become the defining characteristic of adolescence; when it appears in men, it is silly. But even more significantly, when it appears in men, it is fruitless: Teenage girls are (or should be) interested only in teenage boys.

Three years passed before the next installment in the Andy Hardy series, *Love Laughs at Andy Hardy* (January 1947). Mickey Rooney was now twenty-six years old, survivor of a well-publicized divorce and remarriage, with a newborn son and a hardened, worry-worn face. Longtime director George Seitz refused the project, so Willis Goldbeck, best known for writing the Doctor Kildare weepers, took over. This would not be a lighthearted comedy. The original title, *Uncle Andy Hardy,* referred to the fad (either very short-lived or invented for the movie) of coeds calling their male classmates "uncle," but it also underscores Andy's age: He is now a young adult. He returns to Wainwright College after three years of military service, a twenty-one-year-old freshman. He looks up Kay, his girlfriend in *Blonde Trouble,* in order to propose marriage. But she treats him as a buddy, even calls him "pal," and exudes excitement over her romance with another oldster, a thirtyish business-man. Later Andy is set up on a humiliation date with a six-foot-tall girl, a startling contrast to his 5'3". Again she treats him as a pal rather than a potential boyfriend, and he teaches her to capitalize on her dancing ability to attract men.

Now we see another meaning of "uncle": Andy has become the male equivalent of spinster Aunt Milly, safely asexual, a trusted confi-dant, a warm and caring friend, but never an object of desire. No girls or boys mob him at parties. As if in protest, the camera seems positively obsessed with Andy's nude body. He is fully clothed for only about 30 percent of the running time; elsewhere he is wearing only an under-shirt, stripped down for a bath, or in the swimming pool (even though it's December). Yet even his nudity has become a source of feminizing humiliation. While taking his bath, Andy hears a noise and throws on a woman's flowery bathrobe to investigate; he is promptly locked out-side the house and questioned by the police as a possible transvestite prowler.

Bosley Crowther of the *New York Times* assures audiences that "the same beanie-wearing puppy lover who was having blonde trouble three years ago . . . is now having similar juvenile languish over a sadly mis-taken romance."[32] But Andy no longer has the dilemma of choosing from among three or more potential girlfriends and a passel of male admirers; now he must deal with rejection and loneliness. In the final scene, he tries to return to the woman-hating of prewar teenagers: He discards all of the photographs of girls that he's accumulated during the series and vows to devote himself henceforth to "mature" adult pursuits. But it's too late. A portrait of George Washington on the wall comes crashing down behind him, signifying that he is fibbing.

THE LAST OF ANDY HARDY

Even after *Love Laughs at Andy Hardy* demonstrated that girl-craziness was no longer unique or cute, Mickey Rooney was not ready to give up on the successful Andy Hardy franchise. In 1949 the entire cast moved to radio for the syndicated *Hardy Family*, with Andy as a recent high school graduate working at a series of demeaning jobs (evidently office boys were no longer assured of instant wealth). There was no Polly Benedict, and occasional classmate Beazy was promoted to sidekick status. A few years later, Mickey Rooney pitched a TV sitcom about a young adult Andy Hardy living in Los Angeles with his parents while trying to break into show business. The character's name was changed to Mickey Mulligan at the last minute, and the show, *Hey Mulligan*, ran for only a single season (1954–1955). Mickey was thirty-four years old, bald and prematurely wrinkled, and when he behaved like a teenager, especially when compared with the real teenage actors on *Ozzie and Harriet* and *Father Knows Best,* he seemed uncomfortably like a developmentally challenged middle-aged man.[33]

The last gasp of Andy Hardy appeared in theaters on December 22, 1958. *Andy Hardy Comes Home* had the middle-aged Andy returning to Carvel with wife and son (real-life son Teddy Rooney, who displayed a second-generation Andy Hardy physique six years later in *The Village of the Giants*). The plot was nearly precisely opposite that of *A Family Affair*, where it all began: Andy as a representative of progressive, benevolent big business defeats the short-sighted small-town fogies. The box office was dismal. Fans of the series, teenagers in 1937 but now as chunky and graying as Mickey Rooney himself, preferred to stay home with *I Love Lucy*, and the new crop of teenagers had no idea who Andy Hardy was. They preferred *Frankenstein's Daughter* or *Monster on the Campus*, teen-oriented horror flicks designed to encourage teenage boys and girls to cling to each other. No doubt they never realized that the idea that teenage boys and girls should *want* to cling to each other was only twenty years old, born when a grousing, complaining Andy Hardy first knocked on Polly Benedict's door.[34]

7

WHAT A LIFE!

During the war, awkward, bumbling teenage boys, many with strong heterosexual interests, began to proliferate in radio sitcoms and in comic books. They all ultimately derived from Henry Aldrich, the shy sissy-boy in the Broadway melodrama *What a Life* (1938), who spun off into fourteen years of radio (1939), four years of television (1949), nine movies, and an uncountable number of comic books, musical scores, pin-backs, and toys.[1] The voice-cracking "Coming, Mother!" Henry's milquetoast response to his battle-ax mom's summons, became a famous catchphrase, endlessly parodied by comedians. In 1941 alone, it appeared in three Warner Brothers cartoons: An ant says it in *Farm Frolics*, a gorilla in *Goofy Groceries*, and Henry Fonda in *Hollywood Steps Out*. Henry Aldrich began his career in the old-style homoromantic Arcadia, forming intimate bonds with peers or older men and ignoring girls. He was assigned heterosexual interest to underscore his status as an underdog, as a humorously passive, feminine "namby-pamby."[2] But gradually he redeemed himself, demonstrating wartime strength and courage in spite of his girl-craziness; thus, he represents a transitional stage between the homoromantic and the hetero-obsessed Boy Next Door.

A portly, somewhat feminine nineteen-year-old with a pronounced New England accent, Ezra Stone had been chugging around Broadway for several years, singing, dancing, and clowning unmercifully, when his scenery-chomping role as Misto Bottome in the military-school comedy *Brother Rat* led to his casting as Henry Aldrich in Clifford Goldsmith's new play. He was not the star: The "life" in *What a Life* belonged to Mr. Nelson, a hip, caring high school teacher, who managed to handle a number of teen crises and fall in love with the school secretary, all on a single set (the principal's office), all in the course of a single day. Henry Aldrich was his pet project, a shy, sensitive boy who was constantly getting into trouble: He was caught cheating on his Roman history test, falsely accused of stealing band instruments, and expelled for hitting a teacher. Once again Ezra Stone stole the show, and soon he was appearing in character on *The Kate Smith Show* and on *The Fleishman's Yeast Musical Variety Hour* with Rudy Vallee. In the play, Henry had only a domineering mother, but Clifford Goldsmith quickly wrote new sketches to give him a father, a sister, and an aunt, an entire family in the Andy Hardy mold.

The Aldrich Family appeared as a replacement for *The Jack Benny Program* in the summer of 1939, and it found a permanent place on Tuesday nights that October. It stayed on the air for fourteen years, the only radio sitcom to regularly top the charts, achieving the extremely high Crossley rating of 33.3 (one third of people telephoned the next day said they had listened).[3] Ezra Stone played Henry throughout except for 1943 to 1945, when he was in the military, and for a few months in 1953, as the series was winding down.[4] Afterward the pudgy thirty-six-year-old with the pronounced New England accent found himself unable to get jobs in movies or on television: Though no one knew what he looked like, his voice was instantly recognizable. So he moved into directing, putting his name on episodes of *My Living Doll*, *Lost in Space*, *The Flying Nun*, and *Julia*.

The first regular episode of *The Aldrich Family,* on October 3, 1939, made hapless Henry the object of man-hungry competition between a nice girl and a "necktie straightener," that is, an outrageous flirt who baby-talks at boys. But later episodes shy away from presenting the "typical American boy" as even passively interested in girls, instead emphasizing bumbling but well-intentioned mishaps: Henry keeps pigeons and rabbits in the house to raise money for his mother's birthday present (February 20, 1940) or he saves up cereal boxtops to buy an outboard motor (April 24, 1940).

However, the series also shies away from giving Henry a traditional Boys Next Door homoromance. He does have a series of best friends, Tommy, Toby, Jimmy, and finally Homer. They are exclusive and permanent partners, recognized as a "couple" by parents and peers alike, but they rarely express any significant degree of emotional intensity or intimacy. For instance, in the second season Halloween episode (October 31, 1940), the two are out pranking when Toby falls down a well. Henry goes through absurd machinations to rescue his pal, but he is not frantic with worry, even by the standards of a sitcom—his main concern is how his parents will react—and the incident does not result in a recognized or renewed emotional commitment.

As the series progresses, Henry does occasionally date or have a girlfriend, but the scripts carefully deflect attention away from adolescent sexual potency, framing him as an innocent scamp, as a little boy. On January 22, 1942, for instance, Henry takes a girl to the big dance and thinks that she has ditched him for rich snob George Bigelow (she's actually trapped in the bathroom). The introductory voice-over to the episode compares Henry to the prepubescent characters Huck Finn, Tom Sawyer, and Penrod Scofield (from the Booth Tarkington novels): "They're more than boys in books because the things they say and do are things real boys say and do. And now Henry Aldrich joins the ranks of these typical American youngsters. A boy from your town, perhaps from your home." He is being described as a boy and a youngster to infantilize his heterosexual interest, just as Mickey Rooney's early portrayals of Andy Hardy called for infantilized speech and stage mannerisms to distinguish his "cute" girl-craziness from hetero-erotic desire.

JACKIE COOPER AS HENRY ALDRICH

While the radio series was still in development, Paramount scripted a movie adaptation of *What a Life*. In the original play, Henry is characterized as delicate and somewhat pretty: "Although his features are not fully defined, he might easily develop into a rather attractive young man."[5] But in the spring of 1939, teenage beefcake was bursting from every screen,[6] and director Theodore Reed thought that he needed someone with pinup potential, so he cast Jackie Cooper, seventeen years old, with a solid, athletic physique more appropriate to a teenage Tarzan than to a Dagwood-in-training. Ironically, muscles do not enhance this Henry's manliness; indeed, rumors that Jackie Cooper might be a "pansy" add a degree of disquiet to a character already something of a sissy: shy, sensitive, artistic, Freddie Bartholomew transferred from costume dramas to a modern urban high school. Sneering bullies call him "honey-boy," and teachers, somewhat more tactfully, say, "He's kind of a gentle kid." Henry faces the abuse with sardonic resignation; he has been beaten down so many times by a hostile world that he dare not hope for more than sheer survival. He spends most of his time retreating into his notebook, drawing caricatures of the faculty—but even his artwork is dismissed as a "silly habit," subject to derision at home and detention at school.

In 1939, many on-screen Boys Next Door were imitating Andy Hardy's girl-craziness, even some at Henry's school, but Henry remains steadfastly uninterested. Barbara (Betty Field, reprising her Broadway role) bribes him with cake, but still he refuses to ask her to the dance. Tickets are only sixty cents; asked if there isn't any girl worth that amount, Henry replies, "Not to me!" Eventually she gets a glamour-girl makeover and vamps him into asking, but still, his most significant bond is with a man.

John Howard, who played Mr. Nelson, was twenty-six years old and looked nothing like an experienced teacher, not even a young, hip one, not even with a mustache to add sophistication.[7] He has the superficial charm of someone everyone likes and no one loves, and a hearty but entirely untested self-confidence; one imagines that he has never in his life had a problem more serious than a girl saying "maybe" when he asks her for a date. Then the young Henry Aldrich gets sent to the principal's office, and a man who is not his teacher, advisor, or counselor, who has no job-related reason for taking an interest, finds something inspiring in him. By the end of the day Henry will be an integral part of his life, perhaps more important even than the secretary with whom he has been playfully flirting. Nelson and Henry do not flirt, and they are not playful. Instead, they share a gradually increasing physical intimacy to signify their increasing emotional investment. In their first scene alone together, Henry sits on a window ledge and agonizes over the insurmountable task of reading *Hamlet* while Nelson sits in a chair below, confident, even complacent: He knows how to handle a student struggling with Shakespeare. In the second scene, Henry denies cheating on his Roman history test. They stand face to face, and Nelson confesses that he once cheated on a test, out of fear of failure. It is a touching moment of emotional connection between teacher and student.

In their third scene, Henry has been expelled after punching an abusive teacher, and he intends to run away instead of facing his equally abusive father at home. As he sits on the floor in the locker room to pack his things, Nelson enters and sits on a bench, slightly above him. Their positions have been reversed: Now Nelson is the one agonizing over an insoluble problem. His teacher-college training in establishing rapport with students cannot help him now. The rules of academic interaction no longer apply. He cares about Henry not as a project, not as a student. They stand, face each other, and instead of a buddying hand on shoulder, Nelson shyly reaches out and caresses Henry's arm.

Nelson has arranged for Henry to transfer to the Southside Art School in lieu of an expulsion, but Henry doesn't think that he is talented enough to study art; no one has considered his drawings more than juvenile mischief before. "You can't believe anything good about yourself, can you?" Nelson exclaims in frustration, blaming Mom, Dad, teachers, and principal for his friend's low self-esteem. Soon Henry warms up and excitedly describes the caricatures in his portfolio, though he tries to hide his favorite, Mr. Nelson as a snake charmer. Other faculty members become animals or skeletons, but a snake charmer is a romantic character, magically able to control monsters, and by definition *charming*.

Simultaneously charmed and protected, Henry rushes out to the gymnasium, where the big dance is taking place, and throttles the low-life who framed him for the band instrument theft. Then, for a heteronormative conclusion, he consents to jitterbug with Barbara. But as Mr. Nelson dances nearby, Henry leans over and asks, "Will you come visit me at art school?" In the original play, he asks Nelson for a date:

"Would you mind if I take you out sometime and buy you a milkshake or something?" The roles have reversed: Now Henry is charming, confident, and aggressive, easily taking charge of the relationship. Though it is diffused to a degree by scenes of heterosexual interest, a homoromance is key to both Henry and Nelson's salvation.

What a Life was so popular that Jackie Cooper spent the rest of 1939 and 1940 trying to distance himself from Henry Aldrich with raw, gritty roles, riding the range with Henry Fonda in *The Return of Frank James* and solving a murder mystery in *Gallant Sons*.[8] But he also starred in an adaptation of the Booth Tarkington novel *Seventeen* (February 1940), as wet-behind-the-ears William Sylvanus Baxter III acting goofy over another baby-talking necktie straightener. Eventually he realizes that real men have more important things to think about than women, so he drops her to study for his college entrance exams. But in real life Jackie would continue to be typecast as "sort of a sweet kid," a scrappy sissy rather than a "real man."

The second Henry Aldrich installment, *Life with Henry*, premiered in January 1941 with a script that closely matched the radio series, giving Henry a home life and a fully realized family modeled on the Andy Hardy series: cool, uncaring Dad; imperious Mom; sad maiden aunt; and cad-attracting sister. Though director Theodore Reed failed to copy the most blatant of Andy Hardy's beefcake shots, Jackie Cooper still proved more of a pinup model than in the last picture, squeezing a magnificent physique into a black T-shirt and tight chinos and then expecting the audience to laugh at his slapstick lunacy.

In this movie, Henry displays no heterosexual interest whatever. He pals around with a Polly Benedict clone, but they never jitterbug at any dances. He has a best buddy, Dizzy (Eddie Bracken, who had an unrelated part in the original Broadway play), but he continues to form his primary emotional bonds with older men, one from the upper and one from the lower class. However, these bonds occur beyond the boundaries of ordinary teenage life, far from home and school, in the chaotic slums of the inner city or the pristine wilderness of Alaska. Instead of merging roles, the distinction between teen and adult becomes vivid, exaggerated. Instead of eye-moistening moments with violins playing in the background, there are hints of salacious motives, even of sex.

Though only a year has passed since *What a Life*, adult-teen relationships have become noticeably suspicious.

Two scenes are set in a sleazy one-room flat, where tall, muscular train conductor Bill Van Dusen (Rod Cameron[9]) pastes pictures of pinup girls into a scrapbook and talks about the mail-order brides that he nearly married, while Henry lies cozily on the bed, his shirt half undone. Why must Van Dusen demonstrate his heterosexual interests so obsessively? What precisely have they been up to? Whatever it is, Henry must deceive his parents about his afternoon activities and venture into the world of the "disorganized" lower classes to find it, just as Andy Hardy encountered a rent boy not in Carvel but in Manhattan.

Meanwhile, Henry enters a contest to win a trip to Alaska; he has to come up with $100 for the "entry fee," so about half of the movie consists of crazy money-making schemes. Mr. Aldrich insists that it's a scam, but it turns out to be on the level (sort of): Every year a richster named Sylvanus Q. Satterwaite handpicks a group of boys to tour Alaska with him. Satterwaite is played by fifty-one-year-old Moroni Olsen, the voice of the Magic Mirror in *Snow White and the Seven Dwarfs* (1937) and otherwise usually cast as icily sophisticated villains or no-nonsense authority figures, an odd choice to play someone warm and benevolent. Audiences both then and now might feel a frisson of dread over a middle-aged man desiring that much intimate contact with high school boys, especially when he apparently has no romantic ties with anyone his own age. The camera zooms in for a close-up of a line on the application form: "Don't forget to enclose a *photograph*," suggesting that the boys are selected for their attractiveness as well as (or instead of) their moral character. Halfway through the movie, Satterwaite stops being a tour director for a gang of twenty and seems to be planning a voyage with one special boy: "Henry and I will probably be spending the summer together," he announces.

By this point, Mr. Aldrich realizes that Henry will not be grifted out of his money, but his misgivings increase as he considers something else, something unspeakable but yet terribly salient to the parents of 1941. He rushes to Satterwaite's hotel room with the intention of beating him up and must be forcibly restrained. He knows that the bond between teenage boys and adults might not always be "innocent" homoromance, passionate and intimate yet lacking in sexual expression. He knows of a more disturbing possibility, that Henry, already coded as a sissy by constitution and family structure, could be ruined.

After *Life with Henry*, Jackie Cooper was eighteen years old and ready for adult roles. Yet he spent the rest of 1941 being cast as "sweet kid," especially in *Her First Beau*, an early entry in the "older man competing with Boy Next Door" genre. Though the tagline promises "It's wonderful to be a woman, going on sixteen, and have two men fighting over you!" no one actually fights over anyone. Fifteen-year-old Penny (former child star Jane Withers) acts all "swacky" over visiting college boy Roger Van Vleck (Kenneth Howell), mistaking his polite small talk for romantic overtures, assuming that the flowers he ordered are for her, and so on. But it is all a series of misunderstandings: Van Vleck has no romantic or wolfish interest in the high school girl. Meanwhile, Boy Next Door Chuck (Jackie Cooper) wants to attend Tech next fall and study to become an inventor—he's already working on a human-powered glider. But his father will have none of this inventing nonsense and insists on Princeton and then law school (the same career path that Mr. Aldrich has mapped out for Henry). Chuck must sneak out with yet another lower-class male friend (Edgar Buchanan) to work on the project in secret. On the night of the big party, he sneaks away for a test flight and crashes into the lake, breaking his arm. But an act that would seem foolhardy today only serves to impress upon Dad that he's serious, and he is allowed to apply to Tech after all.

Jackie Cooper's Chuck is far more masculine than his Henry Aldrich, far more mechanically minded, stoic, and adventurous. He even takes off his shirt to display his physique on-camera for the first time. Moreover, flight was conceived of as an explicitly male domain. Many teenage boys in mass media used flight to escape from the circumscript world of heteronormative expectation into masculine adventure.

To further emphasize his masculinity, Chuck displays no romantic interest in girls, not even Girl Next Door Penny. He asks her to reserve the "first, last, and supper dance" for him at the upcoming party, just so he won't have to be polite to some other girl, and when she refuses, flaunting her imaginary romance with Van Vleck and expecting him to be jealous, he exclaims, "You don't have to make a song out of it!"

In the last scene, after father-son and mother-daughter reconciliations, Chuck sees Penny in her new party dress. He gulps, ogles, and stammers, "Gee whiz, but you look slick!"—a moment of heterosexual discovery paralleling Andy Hardy's, but seemingly thrown in as an afterthought. Most of the movie contrasts sissy stuff, like dancing and noticing girls, with the dark, masculine, intensely seductive world of flight.

After a few more adventure roles and the child-star spoof *Glamour Boy*, which would have been more popular had it not premiered the weekend of Pearl Harbor, Jackie Cooper enlisted in the army. When he returned to Hollywood in 1947, his early fame was all but forgotten, but he managed to carve a niche for himself playing befuddled, mishap-prone sorts: a returning GI mistaken for the fictional Kilroy (as in "Kilroy was here"), a newlywed with a pregnant wife in an apartment with a "no kids allowed" policy, a young sailor saddled with a talking duck, a junior politician saddled with a talking dog; then middle-aged businessmen, fathers deficient in hipness, and finally cantankerous oldsters, like *Daily Planet* editor Perry White in the Superman movies. He won Emmies for directing episodes of *M*A*S*H* (1974) and *The White Shadow* (1979). He also ensured that his four children received "normal childhoods": They were not allowed to perform.

COMING, MOTHER!

When Jackie Cooper bowed out of future Henry Aldrich movies, the series would probably have ended if it weren't for the Henry Aldriches multiplying elsewhere. "Mirth of a Nation" Archie Andrews premiered in *Pep* comics in December 1941 and gave the superheroes who dominated the comic book industry some strong competition. The *Aldrich Family* radio series always got top ratings, and it spawned a dozen imitators, including *The Barton Family* (1939), *The Parker Family* (1939), and *That Brewster Boy* (1940). The most famous took a girl's point of view: *A Date with Judy* (1941), about a man-hungry bobby-soxer and her squeaky-voiced boyfriend Oogie, became a popular-culture phenomenon in its own right, spawning a movie, a comic book series, teen fads, and its own host of imitators, notably the long-running *Meet Corliss Archer* (1943). So Paramount producer Sol C. Siegel decided to try a new Henry Aldrich movie, with a full roster of recognizable young adult stars, including June Preisser from Mickey Rooney's movies, Kenneth Howell from the *Jones Family* series, Frank Coghlan Junior from the *Captain Marvel* serial, and Buddy Pepper, a perennial teen movie best buddy. Two actors from *Tom Brown's School Days*, Jimmy Lydon and Charles Smith, would play the leads, Henry Aldrich and his sidekick Dizzy.

Jimmy Lydon was an unusual choice for the milquetoast Henry Aldrich: eighteen years old, only nine months younger than Jackie Cooper, and just as athletic, in fact becoming typecast as a sullen, tough street kid who romances Freddie Bartholomew's sissies. But to create Henry Aldrich he managed an astonishing transformation: Not only did he crack and nasalize his voice, like Ezra Stone on the radio, but somehow he created the illusion of an awkward, string-bean physique, a turkey neck with a bobbing Adams' apple, and limp, greasy hair that hung lifelessly over his brow. That is, he presented the teenager as neither cute (like a child) nor handsome (like an adult), but as uniquely *unattractive*.

The heteronormative paradigm has desire flowing between subject and object, between one who is desirous and one who is desirable. As long as the teenage boy experiences no heterosexual desire of his own, he can be fetishized, the object of homoerotic desire that the adults dare not express or acknowledge for each other. But evidently, when the boy begins to express heterosexual desire, he can no longer be an appropriate object of homoerotic desire. He may be exasperating, perplexing, an object of confinement and constraint, perhaps a juvenile delinquent, but never attractive. This convention was already becoming problematic, as teenage girls were expected to prefer teenage boys to adult men, in spite of their gawkiness.

The first Jimmy Lydon entry, *Henry Aldrich for President* (dir. Hugh Bennett), premiered on October 24, 1941, amid a flurry of teen-themed movies, including Universal's *Flying Cadets* and Monogram's *Spooks Run Wild*. Although the tagline squeals that Henry would be "elected by a *laugh*slide!" and contemporary critic Bosley Crowther calls it "a pleasantly diverting comedy suited to the nether end of a double feature program," it is really a melodrama.[10] Accused of ballot-box stuffing, disgraced, expelled from school, and kicked out of his house, Henry waivers tentatively between misunderstood good boy and unapologetic juvenile delinquent. Mr. Aldrich is a blustering, insensitive martinet, a polar opposite of the benevolent, easygoing Judge Hardy. Mrs. Aldrich is clinging and mousy, unwilling or unable to stand up to her husband.[11] Teachers are portrayed positively in the Andy Hardy series, but here they are hostile, sarcastic, stuffy, and elitist. The high school big shots who try to frame Henry are played by two has-been child stars, Frank Coghlan Junior and Kenneth Howell, their antipathy fueled (at least in audience expectation) by their envy over hot property Jimmy Lydon. An adult-teen friendship has carried over from Jackie Cooper's *Life with Henry*, but now it has a symbolic significance even more sinister than the disrespectable Bill Van Dusen and Sylvanus Q. Satterwaite.

Again deceiving his parents and friends about his after-school activities, Henry has been sneaking off for rendezvous with hunky pilot turned gas station attendant Ed Calkins (Rod Cameron again). Ed cautions Henry to keep their relationship secret, lest they get in trouble with the authorities. What precisely would they be accused of? It turns out that Henry has been taking illegal flying lessons from the grounded pilot, but the secrecy, danger, and legal implications stray uncomfortably close to the new fear of adult-teen sexual contact. It is significant that the forbidden activity is flying an airplane, the exclusively masculine realm that wooed Jackie Cooper in *Her First Beau*. Outsider Ed offers Henry an alternative to his mapped-out future of Princeton, law school, marriage, and children, a site of freedom as untainted by heteronormative expectation as Arcadia itself.

When we actually see the inside of a cockpit, it is presented as an eroticized and potentially sexual space. Henry is forced to pilot Mr. McCloskey, the printer who can clear him of the ballot-stuffing charges, to Centerville. En route, a mouse crawls up Henry's pants leg, and he concludes that Mr. McCloskey is getting fresh. "Stop that!" he cries. "It's very dangerous to tickle someone when he's flying an airplane!" *Tickling* seems entirely too innocent for the action he perceives, which certainly involves an intimate intrusion. But Mr. McCloskey does more than tickle: He grabs and paws at Henry in a scene that suggests passion, even though it "really" signifies terror at the bumpy flight, and finally he faints dead away, his head lolled against Henry's shoulder. This seems to be a way to suggest a danger in the homoerotic night world while at the same time defusing any real accusation with slapstick.

HENRY AND DIZZY

Jimmy Lydon appeared as Henry Aldrich in eight more movies (all directed by Hugh Bennett). They never made the top of the box-office charts, and critics of the era usually ignored them or dismissed them as larks, juvenile fun in opposition to Andy Hardy's lofty symbolic status as "the Stars and Stripes," as "America!" But in spite of the exploding vacuum cleaners, stalled jalopies, and sinking rowboats, Henry Aldrich's Centerville is more grim and foreboding than Andy Hardy's Carvel. Henry is never a big man on campus, never popular with his peers; his strained relationship with Mr. Aldrich lacks the easy intimacy of Andy and Judge Hardy; and his dilemmas are always deadly serious. Andy Hardy may make mistakes, but no one ever doubts his good intentions. However, when Henry is accused of theft, illicit sexual behavior, or clinical insanity, his friends and family turn against him. Andy may be fined for driving without a license, but Henry is threatened with prison, juvenile hall, and a mental hospital; he is disgraced and forced to leave town. Andy is never in a life-threatening situation, but Henry is trapped in a burning warehouse, hangs from a cliff, and is nearly murdered by smugglers.

The war does not exist in postcard-perfect Carvel; but war bonds, war relief funds, rationing, and air-raid drills are ubiquitous in Centerville, adding another undertow of threat.[12] Jimmy Lydon appears as Henry or a similar character in two home-front patriotism shorts: *A Letter from Bataan* (1942) and *The Aldrich Family Gets in the Scrap* (1943). He keeps most of his Henry Aldrich mannerisms, no doubt intentionally, during his dramatic turn as a teenage air force enlistee in *Aerial Gunner* (1943), so when he is mortally wounded, viewers must endure the uncomfortable sight of a boy who worries about chemistry tests and being sent to the principal's office, who rides around in a jalopy tagged with "The Squeezeroo Kids" and babysits to earn extra money, on his deathbed.

After *Henry Aldrich for President*, Henry has no more adult friends:

The adults in his world are at best indifferent, and more likely torment-ing, threatening, and mean-spirited. In *Henry and Dizzy* (1942), Henry borrows a rowboat, which promptly sinks. Mr. Weeks, the boatshop owner, makes him sign a "confession" that he stole it and will pay $135 for a replacement or go to jail. Mr. Aldrich, as abusive and tyrannical as ever, orders Henry to earn the money himself, so Henry and Dizzy start a housecleaning service. Of course, things go terribly wrong, resulting in more damage. Now Henry imagines that he will spend the next thirty-five years in prison. In a fantasy sequence, Mr. Weeks is transformed into a leering prison guard who chases Henry around, graphically licking his lips in anticipation of his (unspecified) abuse.

There is a single bright spot in Henry's world: his sidekick Dizzy. They are not homoromantic partners—their interaction usually lacks intensity and intimacy, they rarely indicate a plan to stay together for-ever, and they are not exclusive. In the earliest episodes, Dizzy is ex-tremely enthusiastic about girls and Henry constantly seeks out older male companions; later, they are usually accompanied by Henry's cur-rent girlfriend or gal pal. Nonromantic best buddies were rare among Boys Next Door of the period; they either formed homoromantic bonds or else traveled in a pack of buddies. Perhaps Dizzy was a carry-over from radio, where solitary actors are hard to script (no one to talk to), but his effect is to destabilize homoromance, forcing the reevalua-tion of every same-sex partnership from the Great Marvel series to the present as "really" a cordial, dispassionate pair of chums.

Jimmy Lydon's Henry does not exhibit Andy Hardy–style girl-craziness. He is never shown kissing a girl anywhere in the series.[13] In *Henry Aldrich for President*, he yells "Yahoo!" and collapses in ecstasy when a girl accepts a date with him, but in *Henry and Dizzy*, he goes out on a date only to please his sidekick, and in several installments he does not date at all. He falls for an older woman, an unrequited puppy love of the sort one might expect of Skeezix or Penrod; he runs in a panic from the attentions of another. Recurring foil Phyllis (Mary An-derson, Diana Lynn) appears variously as his girlfriend, a girl with an unrequited crush on him, and a buddy.

Should Henry Aldrich overcome his sissyhood by embracing or shunning girls? At first the series fails to display a stable attitude toward teenage heterosexual desire. In *Henry Aldrich Gets Glamour* (April 1943), the girls at the malt shop ridicule Phyllis for wasting her time on Henry when he is obviously "a lost cause." Sophisticated Virginia takes on the challenge and lures Henry to a late-night rendezvous, but he is oblivious to her vamping, and when she moves in for a kiss, he abruptly turns away. "What a heartbreaker you turned out to be!" she snarls. "Take me home!" Yet only two months later, in *Henry Aldrich Swings It* (June 1943), Henry is no longer a lost cause: He falls for the new music teacher. But now his friends complain that he's "getting goofy" again.

In the pivotal *Henry Aldrich Haunts a House* (November 1943), Henry has been enduring more abuse than usual. Boys at school call him "milksop" and "pantywaist," and a bully played by Jackie Moran challenges him to a fight. When he refuses, Mr. Aldrich upbraids him as a "sissy" and then chastises his wife for mollycoddling him. Understandably discouraged, Henry seeks out the final adult friend of the series, chemistry teacher Mr. Towers. But tonight Mr. Towers is conveniently absent. His daughter Elise offers herself as a heterosexual substitute, luring Henry into a mad-scientist-style chemistry lab and vamping him:

> Elise: Put your arms around me. Hug me tight, Henry. [Henry complies.] Tighter! Tighter!
> Henry: [Terrified.] Holy smoke!
> Elise: Are you using all of your strength?
> Henry: I'm afraid to!

Sighing with frustration, Elise releases him. She concludes that he is "weak," but she doesn't mean physical strength, since his muscles have been adequately referenced in many episodes.[14] She means cowardly, too frightened to display heterosexual interest, which she connects with Henry's ineffectual handling of the school bully earlier: "Why don't you just admit that you were scared to death?" She shows Henry one of her father's experiments, a potion that will provide the strength of three men. Mr. Towers has been testing it on himself. "That's the kind of courage I admire!" she says. Then she invites Henry to the kitchen for pie, like the child she perceives him to be. Irate, Henry determines to acquire strength/courage; he begins to sip the potion, but a sudden clap of thunder frightens him into drinking the whole bottle. Such a large dose will cause unpredictable side effects, Elise tells him, and may even prove fatal.

Stumbling home past an old haunted house, Henry blacks out. The next morning he hears that Principal Bradley was attacked there. Naturally, Henry assumes that he is the culprit. When he brings Elise and Dizzy to the house to look for clues, he blacks out again, and a moment later they are attacked by the same monster. They conclude that Henry has been transmuting from boy to maniac in Jekyll-Hyde fashion. "Ordinarily you're a very sweet guy," Dizzy squeals, "But now I'm afraid of you." It is interesting that Dizzy uses the term "sweet," a complimentary turn on the same lack of strength/courage that elsewhere gets Henry called "honey boy" and "pantywaist." But when they return to the house for a third time, they discover that the real culprits are counterfeiters, and Henry demonstrates his strength/courage, his manliness, by rescuing Mr. Bradley and his friends.[15]

The next installment, *Henry Aldrich, Boy Scout* (1944), addresses the question of Henry's heterosexual interest in the first scene. Henry sits on a bench in the backyard talking to Elise, now his girlfriend:

> Henry: You know, Elise, since your father gave me more responsibility [in the chemistry lab], I've been blossoming into manhood. I know what I want.
> Elise: [Turns her face up hopefully.] You do, Henry?
> Henry: Sure. I want to win the [Boy Scout] inspection this afternoon.

While the gender-transgressive "blossoming into manhood" still characterizes Henry as something of a sissy, he is only pretending ignorance of Elise's desire for heterosexual practice: He realizes that she wants a kiss. They begin (off camera), while Dizzy and Mr. Aldrich peer through binoculars from an upstairs window:

> Mr. Aldrich: Any action yet, Dizzy?
> Dizzy: [Thrilled.] Oh, boy! He's rising to the occasion, sir!

A few episodes earlier, they would have been mystified and perhaps disgusted by the idea of a teenage boy kissing a girl, but now they heartily desire it.

Elise vanishes from the rest of the movie and appears only in the final fade-out, waving as Henry marches by with his scout troop. Henry goes on to demonstrate his strength/courage through buddy-bonding with the bratty, wise-cracking Peter (Darryl Hickman). Though there is a significant age difference between them—Darryl Hickman is twelve years old and prepubescent, Jimmy Lydon no longer a teenager—they are scripted as near-peers. Their fathers push them into being chums, reasoning that Henry, a reformed "problem child," might be a good role model for Peter. But Henry always had good intentions, in spite of the doubts of the adults—he was a "sweet kid"—whereas Peter is deliberately conniving and malicious: He puts Tabasco sauce in the soup, sabotages the central pole so the tent collapses, and feigns a twisted ankle so the other hikers will carry him; besides, he thinks Henry is a "pantywaist."

At the Camperol (a weeklong wilderness contest), Henry takes the blame for one of Peter's misdeeds and Peter is mystified: Homosocial altruism does not fit into his conception of a pantywaist. But in a late night heart-to-heart, Henry explains, "Stronger scouts have to help out the weaker." He means not only physically stronger but emotionally stronger. It is a powerfully symbolic moment: Henry's eyes glaze over, and his smile becomes positively beatific. Peter approaches Henry's cot on his knees, a penitent seeking absolution. Both Jimmy Lydon and Darryl Hickman were devout Roman Catholics, so they invest the image with powerful symbolism.[16] Converted, saved, Peter becomes a model scout, coincidentally with a strong case of hero worship or puppy love: He is always grabbing at Henry's arm or trying to hug him, he squeezes between Henry and Dizzy at dinner, and at bedtime he insists on pushing their bunks together.

Henry has already demonstrated team spirit, but he still has to demonstrate strength/courage, to prove that he isn't a pantywaist. When he angrily refuses to believe that Peter is innocent of sabotaging another team's project, the boy runs away from camp. Dizzy and Henry search for him all night; finally they find him trapped on a crumbling ledge overlooking a canyon. Dizzy lowers Henry on a rope, but his extra weight causes the ledge to crumble away. Peter jumps onto Henry's back, but Dizzy is too weak to pull them both to safety. *And* the rope is starting to unravel. In a harrowing moment, Henry orders Peter to go up alone; he plans to sacrifice his own life for the boy. Fortunately, the other scouts arrive and lower a new rope just in time.

The bond between Henry and Peter is the most intense and intimate of any in the series since *What a Life*, but it lacks the exclusivity and permanence of homoromance.[17] Indeed, the movie is structured around threats to exclusivity: Peter competes with Dizzy for the role of Henry's best friend, and Henry believes that Dizzy is having an affair with Elise. In the last scene, Henry, Peter, and the other scouts march into a superimposed American flag before an audience of beaming parents—and girlfriends. Buddy-bonding does not have the homoromantic potential that it once had, but neither has it vanished altogether. Girl-craziness is acknowledged, but not triumphant.

The two final installments of the series (in April and June 1944) oddly eliminate girl-craziness from the scripts, turning Henry into an all-around do-gooder who facilitates adult romances but never dates girls of his own and is not expected to. He appears with a babe in arms without anyone suggesting that he might have married and become a father. And Dizzy seems considerably more emotionally invested in the relationship than usual. He even tells Henry that he loves him. They have become homoromantic partners in intensity, intimacy, exclusivity, and even, possibly, permanence: Apprised of the details of a wild scheme, he says, "I'll help you—I always do," implying that he *always will*. The director and cast remained the same; the writing staff remained the same, with the addition of Aleen Leslie, protofeminist creator of *A Date with Judy*. Perhaps in the hardest months of World War II, Henry Aldrich was already becoming a nostalgic pleasure, a memory of the old, "innocent" Boy Next Door homoromance.

CADETS ON PARADE

In the midst of the mollycoddling Henry Aldrich series, Jimmy Lydon tried to maintain his tough-guy image in a number of homoromantic melodramas and comedies. During the war, many teen stars were sent to military school to ignore girls; bully, brawl, and bond with each other; and otherwise prove their manhood. Most could play rich or poor, sissy or tough, as necessary: Bobby Jordan played an arrogant, sissified headmaster's son in *Military Academy* (1940) but a masculine regular fella in *Junior Army* (1942). However, Jimmy Lydon always tried to distance himself from Henry Aldrich by playing tough, usually against the sissy of Freddie Bartholomew, his costar in *Tom Brown's School Days* (1940).

In *Cadets on Parade* (Columbia, January 1942, dir. Lew Landers), rich kid Austin Shannon (Freddie Bartholomew), an eighteen-year-old military cadet, is bad at sports and reviled as a "sissy" by his self-made-man father, so he runs away and encounters street tough Joe Novak (Jimmy Lydon). Explicitly marked as masculine-feminine partners, the two set up housekeeping together (in a flat with only one bed). Joe never mocks his partner for being effeminate, but he does gently suggest that success at school and later in business may depend on an increased manliness. Thus, Austin's salvation, his return to middle-class society, comes through learning to box and play football, not through heterosexual experience: No girls appear or are mentioned in the movie. But he, in turn, draws Joe into civilization through the same rubric that girls use with jungle boys, by teaching him to read and use proper table manners. In the end they both enroll in the military academy. The tagline is: "The Story of Two American Boys . . . On the Road to Being Men!"

The last of the Jimmy Lydon–Freddie Bartholomew pairings, *The Town Went Wild* (December 1944, dir. Ralph Murphy), came from Poverty Row PRC rather than Paramount or Columbia. Tall, gangly sophisticate David Conway (Freddie Bartholomew) and blue-collar Bob Harrison (Jimmy Lydon) were born on the same day and are next-door neighbors and best friends, but they do not share a homoromantic bond. They do not express any significant level of intensity, intimacy, or exclusivity. David is dating Bob's sister, but there is no hint at triangulation: He really does spend all of his time with her, while Bob is relegated to the status of third wheel. It is interesting that the sissy gets engaged while the he-man never expresses any interest in girls, but still, one must wonder why the scripted homoromances between Freddie and Jimmy ended so abruptly. Perhaps they were too old, well beyond eighteen, scripted as young adults rather than high schoolers.

The film flopped, and Freddie Bartholomew's film career was in decline. Even a contractual marriage with a studio publicist failed to re-kindle Hollywood's interest. His last movie role was in *St. Benny the Dip* (1951), as a Catholic seminarian with a prissy, affected manner reminis-cent of Roddy McDowall; placing him in seminary excused him from the mandate of expressing heterosexual desire but did not make audi-ences desperate to see more of him. Later he dabbled in advertising, produced television soap operas, and married twice more. He died in 1992.[18]

STRANGE ILLUSION

There wasn't much mass culture available in the spring of 1945, with all eyes trained on Europe and most of the teen stars overseas. It seemed that only Jimmy Lydon was still working, but he was tired of boyhood: He was twenty-one years old, handsome, mature, ready to become "James" and move into serious adult roles. His first "James Lydon" bill-ing was the film noir *Strange Illusion*, again from PRC (1945, dir. Edgar G. Ulmer): a *Hamlet* redux about a prep school boy who suspects that his mother's suave new boyfriend murdered his father, or perhaps he's suffering from paranoid delusions.

At first *Strange Illusion* seems an unabashed return to the homo-romantic Arcadia. Paul Cartwright (Jimmy Lydon) learns that his be-reaved mother is dating again just as he and his friend Dr. Vincent (forty-six-year-old Regis Toomey) are returning from a month-long fishing trip. A month of togetherness seems a bit much for adult-teen chums, and Vincent never mentions a wife or girlfriend (he carefully specifies that he wants to get home to his *sister*). Could this be an adult-teen homoromance? But no, their relationship is decidedly lacking in meaningful glances and hands tenderly grasping shoulders.

Back home, Paul reunites with a best buddy, George (a young-looking Jimmy Clark), with whom he does share meaningful glances and hands grasping shoulders. They walk down to dinner together in matching ties, and when Paul faints from nervous exhaustion, he awakens to George by his bedside. Perhaps this is a peer homoromance? No—as the story progresses, Paul becomes increasingly uninterested in George and increasingly smitten with his sister Lydia (Mary McCleod). They even kiss after a pool party. When Paul is confined to a mental hospital through the machinations of his mother's evil boyfriend, the first person he calls is Lydia, not George. In the climactic scene, the three friends go together to confront the murderer; but when Paul is shot, it is Lydia, not George, who rushes to him—his true love, not a mere buddy. The teasing introductory scenes only reinforce the conclusion that two boys together are (and always have been) mere buddies; to find homoromantic passion and intimacy in some of them is (and always has been) misreading. The movie ends with Paul dreaming that he takes Lydia's hand and leads her into the future. George does not appear in the dream, the potential for homoromance faded away as a hint of the distant past.[19]

Jackie Cooper showing all that the censors would allow. (Movie Star News).

Jimmy Lydon and Charles Smith courting disaster, *Henry Aldrich, Editor* (1942).
(Photofest).

Jimmy Lydon and Charles Smith, proud parents, *Henry Aldrich's Little Secret*. (Ohlinger).

Jimmy Lydon hugs Freddie Bartholomew for the last time (sort of), *The Town Went Wild* (1944). (Photofest).

Dickie Moore, less Valentino-esque in adulthood. (Movie Star News).

Teen sleuth Frankie Darro, with Mantan Moreland taking up the rear, *On the Spot* (1940). (Photofest).

The Dead End Kids in 1937. (Movie Star News).

Billy Halop and Kenneth Howell getting roughed up, *Junior G-Men* (1940). (Photofest).

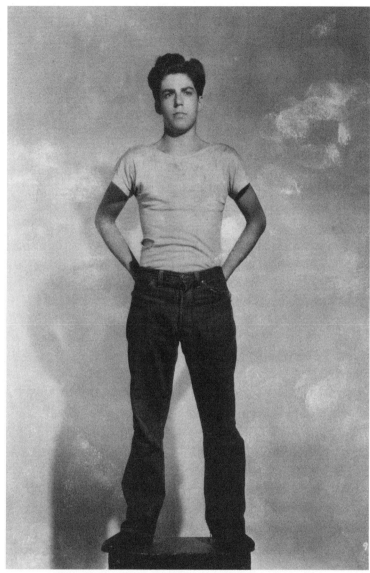

Billy Halop, diamond in the rough. (Movie Star News).

Bobby Jordan tries to calm an obsessed Leo Gorcey,
That Gang of Mine (1940). (Ohlingers).

Leo Gorcey and Bobby Jordan share a melancholy moment, *Flying Wild* (1941). (Everett Collection).

"Should I hit him or kiss him?" Leo Gorcey and Huntz Hall,
Dead End (1937). (Ohlingers).

The Boy has surpassed the Man. Johnny Sheffield and Johnny Weissmuller, *Tarzan and the Huntress* (1947). (Photofest).

Superhero and sidekick, *Tarzan and the Huntress* (1947). (Ohlingers).

Sabu struggling to find the right words, *Thief of Bagdad* (1940). (Photofest).

Sabu demonstrates that he is a boy. (Movie Star News)

8

MEET ME IN ST. LOUIS

In April 1939, a few weeks after it wrapped up *The Wizard of Oz*, Arthur Freed's musical unit at MGM (known as "Freed's Fairies" because of its profusion of gay talent) began work on what was probably the first Boy Next Door musical, *Babes in Arms* (dir. Busby Berkeley, October 1939). Rodgers and Hart's summer stock players became children of down-and-out vaudevillians trying to avoid being sent to a state work farm. *Strike Up the Band* (September 1940) followed, transforming George and Ira Gershwin's cheese factory workers into a high school swing band, and then *Babes on Broadway* (December 1941), with an original story about young adult song-and-dancesters in New York City. Soon the roles of Central Casting were depleted as studios all over town grabbed all of the young women and undrafted young men they could find, shoved them into sorority sweaters and lettermen's jackets, and began filming "barn musicals" about teenagers saving or winning things by putting on amateur shows.

The musical has always had a queer sensibility, with frequent gender transgressions and a subtle, almost closeted legitimization of same-sex desire. Of course, it is at heart a comedy, where journeys end with lovers' meetings. The stories exhaustively and repeatedly validate starry-eyed loves of guys and dolls, their humorous or earnest quarrels, misunderstandings, break-ups, and reconciliations, and even the most ornery of woman-haters, such as Henry Higgins in *My Fair Lady*, will be exclaiming "Liza, where the devil are my slippers?" as the curtain drops. Same-sex desire appears in the form of a joke or aside, but it never troubles any character's dreams: To argue that Jud is in love with Curly in *Oklahoma!*, or Bill Calhoun with Fred Graham in *Kiss Me, Kate*, requires more than a little audacity.

But the musical is not a story, it is a show. Spectacle triumphs over plot, singing and dancing over dialogue, broad, flamboyant, silly display over naturalism.[1] Even the Hollywood film musical, with its realistic-looking sets and intimate close-ups, features characters who find nothing unusual in stopping on a busy street to break into song, with a full orchestra in the background and passersby chiming in.[2] There are dream sequences, fantasy sequences, shows within shows. Same-sex desire is articulated in the clash between the stringent heteronormativity required by the plot and the patent artifice of the spectacle, in songs where Henry Higgins asks "roommate" Colonel Pickering, "Would you complain if I took out another fellow?" (in *My Fair Lady*), or a group of beefy sailors hang all over each other while ironically proclaiming that "There's Nothing Like a Dame" (in *South Pacific*). During the war, evaluations, expulsions, and demonizations of same-sex desire appeared across the universe of mass culture, and the Hollywood musical was no exception, yet glimpses of the homoromantic Arcadia still appeared in the interstitial spaces, in the spectacle.

MICKEY AND JUDY

Strangely, the least-telling evocation of same-sex desire in the Boy Next Door musicals comes in *Babes in Arms*; perhaps the gay playwright Lorenz Hart's terror of being outed resulted in an aversion to scripting same-sex friendships of any sort. Mickey Rooney gives Judy Garland his music school pin in the first scene, and kisses her in the last, and in between is vamped by a squealing necktie straightener (June Preisser), while other boys appear in an unvariegated mass, as if not worthy of his notice.[3] *Babes on Broadway* (not a sequel) is nearly as squeamish about potential teenage homoerotics. Though Mickey Rooney begins as part of a musical trio, he does not express any significant emotional attachment to either of his partners, and soon he drops out to pursue Judy Garland.

The amateur shows in these musicals do tread the boundaries of gender transgression, but very gingerly, by displacing the spectacle onto the nonwhite and the nostalgic. In *Babes in Arms*, the teenagers perform a "dear old minstrel show," a salute to the blackface performances of yesteryear.[4] Mickey Rooney and Judy Garland (in blackface and male drag) riff on the old "That was no lady, that was my wife" gag. But in a moment of gender instability, Judy plays the man who was with "a lady last night." The gender instability is heightened because she was currently being masculinized as unattractive in mass media discourse and black men were traditionally feminized.

Babes on Broadway features another minstrel show, with Judy Garland again in black male drag singing "Franklin Delano Jones," about the first black president of the United States. This time Mickey Rooney participates in the gender instability: He appears onstage dressed as Carmen Miranda, in a fruit-laden headdress and an outfit bare at the shoulders and belly, his muscles strangely accentuated. He sings "Mamãe Eu Quero" (1940), which Miranda borrowed from a Brazilian performer, Vicente Paiva e Jararaca. The singer is an adult, yet he begs his mother to let him breastfeed:

> Mamãe eu quero, Mamãe eu quero, Mamãe eu quero, Mamá
> Dá a chupeta, dá a chupeta, dá a chupeta pro bebê não chorá
> [Mama I want you . . . She gives the breast so baby doesn't cry.][5]

That is, a man dressed as a woman sings about a woman pretending to be a man, and conflates filial and erotic desire in the bargain. It is a heady mixture, especially when juxtaposed with the sappily sentimental main plot, Mickey singing to Judy "I like New York in June, how about you?"

Strike Up the Band is more obviously about teenagers than the *Babes* musicals. The characters are high school students rather than young adults or kids of all ages. There are many scenes set in the school and frequent references to contemporary teen fads and customs. The plot involves a standard teen-adult generation gap: Jimmy Connors (Mickey Rooney) wants to become a drummer, while his mother insists that he go to college and on to medical school. But the girl-craziness he expresses in the Andy Hardy series is absent. Heteroromance occurs only in parallel stories of unrequited love: Willie Brewster (fifteen-year-old

Larry Nunn) has an unrequited crush on Mary Holden (eighteen-year-old Judy Garland); meanwhile, she has a crush on Jimmy Connors, but he's an old-style Boy Next Door, interested in boys rather than girls. Both learn to see the value of nonromantic friendship; the crisis, about the gang rallying around Willie when he becomes desperately ill, makes agonizing over who wants to kiss whom seem rather silly.

Jimmy has an unrequited crush of his own, on classmate and band member Phil (William Tracy, star of the *Terry and the Pirates* serial and Mickey Rooney's real-life brothel buddy). Phil ignores frequent hints at homoromantic intent, so Jimmy tries to defuse his heterosexual interest, dragging him from the arms of his girlfriend, scheduling practices during their dates, and arguing that girls are a trivial distraction to the important work of their swing band: "You gonna play the saxophone or you gonna keep your mind on the girls?" Phil still doesn't get it, so Jimmy invites him to his room to "discuss money-making strategies" and places his hand atop Phil's for a good thirty seconds. This explicitly romantic gesture appears among same-sex partners nowhere else in the hundreds of cultural objects analyzed for this study. Phil doesn't respond; they must remain friends, not even best friends of the Henry Aldrich and Dizzy sort. But again, friendship is sufficient.

The amateur musical in *Strike Up the Band* is no knee-jerk nostalgia, but *Nell of New Rochelle*, a twenty-minute-long spoof of old cliffhangers that carefully mirrors the unrequited romances of the main plot. Mary plays a "fallen woman" (she made "one mistake," evidently sex outside of marriage), and Jimmy plays a foppish gadabout in heavy makeup that is meant to reflect silent film practice but actually makes him look like a stereotypic 1930s "pansy." Phil plays a mustache-twirling villain who leers at them both, perhaps attracted by their hints of sexual deviance. He tries to force Mary to marry him, and then he lures Jimmy into a bar (thirty years later, they're still drinking). Finally Phil realizes that one can't acquire boyfriends and girlfriends by bullying (a lesson that Jimmy might have learned in the main plot), and he decides to do them both in: He ties Mary to a log about to be buzz-sawed and Jimmy to railroad tracks with a train fast approaching. Jimmy is rescued by Willie Brewster, his dead son turned angel (an eerie precursor of his upcoming medical crisis), and then he rushes off to rescue Mary. Boy-girl romance wins out, barely. Desire remains ambiguous in the "apparently gay, ab-horrently gay, Gay Nineties."

Back in the main plot, Jimmy starts noticing Mary, in a gruff he-man fashion (he asks, "Couldn't you be my girl without us getting silly about it?"), and in a sort of playful retaliation, Phil starts dragging *him* away. In the musical finale, as Jimmy and Mary bend in for a kiss, Phil shoves his saxophone between them, and then with an impish grin he pulls Jimmy into a reprise of his earlier showstopper, "Drummer Boy," but with a none-too-subtle change: The chorus singing about the erotic thrill they get from the Drummer Boy's syncopation is now composed entirely of men. The boy-girl kiss never happens. Both heteroromantic and homoromantic desires remain unfulfilled, but as an American flag unfurls and Jimmy and Mary march, not into marriage but into war, no one seems to notice. Friendship alone is important; friendship alone endures.

TOO MANY GIRLS

College boys, old enough to marry, were never required to shun girls; Freddie the Freshman won the girl along with the football game, and when the boys' book heroes started their careers in college, they usually had girlfriends. But RKO's collegiate musical *Too Many Girls*, though hyped as a festival of never-ending cheesecake ("It's knee-deep in gorgeous gals and gaiety!"), provides a glimpse into Boys Next Door in the last days of the homoromantic Arcadia.

After a six-month run on Broadway, the movie version premiered on October 8, 1940, with most of the stars reprising their original roles. College football star Clint (Richard Carlson, later to specialize in low-budget beefcake horror movies) is spending the summer with Argentine prep-school sensation Manuelito (Desi Arnaz) at an inn in rural Maine, hoping to seduce him into playing for Princeton.[6] Then Jojo (Eddie Bracken) and Al (Hal Le Roy) show up to woo him for Harvard and Yale, respectively.

Manuelito is a "boy" (Manuelito, not Manuel) and from Latin America, currently invested with enormous erotic symbolism as the object of U.S. political and economic desire. Not oblivious to the homoerotic implications of three "older men" competing for his affection, he protests that he prefers women:

> Manuelito: I am very bored with men. I am not interested with
> men.
> Clint: [Dismissively.] You belong at Vassar.
> Manuelito: Yes, I . . . [Suddenly insulted.] If there's a double meaning
> in that, I got it!

The competition ends abruptly when wild-child college freshman Connie Casey (Lucille Ball) sashays into the inn, and all four boys gape in hetero-erotic awe. Mr. Casey, her tycoon father, thinks that she needs a clandestine bodyguard to keep her focused on her studies, and they all volunteer, even though they must abandon the Ivy League for Potawatomie College in Stopgap, New Mexico, they will not be allowed to play football, and they will not even be allowed to date her. The writers probably expected audiences to posit a heteronormative explanation for the sudden decisions to drop long-cherished career plans, that girls are the only worthwhile goals in boys' lives, but a closer look at the scene reveals something else entirely. First Mr. Casey offers Clint the body-guard job. Jojo enters, sees his long-term competitor being snatched away, and instantly petitions to go *with him*. Then Al enters, sees the *two* together, and argues that three bodyguards are better than two. Finally Manuelito, after months of exuberant courting, sees all three of his "suitors" abandoning him to chase a woman, and, with a look of near panic, insists on coming along. They are not expressing heterosexual mania but instead trying any ploy they can think of to stick with their bickering buddies, trying to maintain bonds that are passionate, intense, and physical. At Potawatomie, those bonds may become permanent: Mr. Casey and Mr. Lister, his companion of unspecified status for the last thirty years, sing their alma mater, "Potawato*mine,*" their arms wrapped around each other's waists. This journey will be a fulfillment of mascu-line intimacy, what the bickering signified all along.

Potawatomie College is indeed "knee-deep in gorgeous gals": They outnumber the boys ten to one. But it is also as queer as *La Cage aux Folles.* Most of the girls belong to an antikissing sorority, deferred from the overtly Sapphic only by their initiation question—"What is your goal in life?"—and their whole-hearted approval of plebe Connie's response: "To get a man!" The "no romance" clause in the bodyguard contracts applies only to Connie, yet the four chums spend most of the movie trying to keep each other away from all girls, sometimes dragging each other from heterosexual lip-locks. "Do your duty—be a man!" they exclaim, arguing that boyhood heterosexual interest is a deterrent to the big, important work of adulthood, their bodyguard jobs, their classes, or the football team: The ban on playing football has been forgotten, and when the four superstars pool their talents, they are able to beat all of the big-name schools. Soon they are playing Harvard and Yale.

As in most musicals, there is a gushily romantic primary plot: Clint begins wooing Connie away from her boyfriend, Beverly Waverly, a middle-aged playwright who out-feys Noel Coward (played by Douglas Walton, the over-the-top Percival Priceless in *Dick Tracy vs. Cueball*). But Waverly, far from being upset by the competition, seems unsure exactly who is being wooed: In one scene, Clint sees Connie sitting in the desert, studying her calculus, and calls, "Are we alone?" Waverly sticks his head up from behind a rock and calls back, "No—there's a woman here," thinking (or pretending to think) that Clint wants a rendezvous with him.

Musical comedy usually contrasts heteroromantic plots, one lugubrious and the other humorous: *Oklahoma!* contrasts "People will say we're in love" with "I'm just a girl who cain't say no," and in *Kiss Me, Kate,* "I'm yours 'till I die" shares a stage with "I'd gladly give up coffee for Sanka." But here the humorous secondary plot is a homoromance between Jojo and Manuelito. Their attention parallels the Connie-Clint storyline, but without the risk: Football players who court each other do not jeopardize any big games. The parallel becomes most blatant after Connie and Clint sing a love duet, "I Didn't Know What Time It Was." The scene shifts to Jojo singing the same song to Manuelito, with the same intensity, the same gestures, even holding his hand. Manuelito looks upset, almost enraged. Is he displeased with the news that Jojo is in love with him?

After Jojo sings four excruciating lines about finding the meaning of life in his beloved's eyes, Manuelito asks, "Yeah?" in a tough-guy taunt, as if he has been insulted. Jojo affirms, "Yeah! And then he said. . . ." The viewer is finally off the hook: Jojo is not describing his own romantic interest, but his disgust at eavesdropping on Clint's earlier heterosexual display. Manuelito is upset because Clint has dishonored their contract.

Since the viewer is now wise to the situation, the joke should be over. But Jojo continues, taking Manuelito's hand and singing again. He sings the entire song, compulsively, with only an intermittent "then he said" as a weak assurance that he is not evoking a secret love of his own. It is a disquieting scene, not at all like the joyous gender-bending and double entendre–laced queering of the rest of the movie. Beneath the camaraderie of buddy-bonds lurks a desire that cannot be named, thought of, or envisioned, except in the Freudian moments of jokes that last too long, comparisons that are too apt. The movie ends with heterosexual passion apparently triumphant: Clint and Connie, Jojo and a girl embrace. But Manuelito, who has often mentioned girlfriends but has never been shown with a girl, is left out of the triumph. Dressed in a stereotypic Latin American costume, complete with sombrero, emasculated, he leads the others in a conga.[7]

GIRL-CRAZINESS AND PATRIOTISM

Back in the Arthur Freed unit at MGM, *Best Foot Forward* (dir. Edward N. Buzzell, June 1943) still must contend with queasiness about heterosexual interest in Boys Next Door. Lucille Ball, playing "herself" as a sarong-clad Dorothy Lamour parody, fears that she is past her prime (even though she had played a college freshman only three years before). Her agent insists that "the American boy wants you!" and to prove it, he talks her into accepting a prom date with Bud Hooper, a cadet at the Winsocki Military Academy. Eighteen-year-old Tommy Dix, who also played Bud Hooper on Broadway, is short and slim, with early Technicolor accentuating his soft, pretty features, and his skittishness around girls has become slightly suspect. His classmates are all aggressive, unrepentantly girl-crazy wolves who laud his date with the film star, but the adults are scandalized by this evidence of heterosexual passion, like the townsfolk in *Henry Aldrich Gets Glamour* two months before. When Lucy attends the prom and causes a riot, Bud is expelled from Winsocki for unmanly girl-craziness. To save his career, Lucy visits the general in charge and argues that heterosexual desire actually benefits young soldiers:

> The Flying Tigers were full of Bud Hoopers, and do you know what they used on the field in Chung King to tell which way the wind was blowing? One of my silk stockings! You're a soldier, General . . . it wouldn't hurt your aim any if your rifle butt was resting against your sweetheart's hankie, would it?

Convinced that teenage boys are not too young for girls after all, the general reinstates Bud. In the last scene, the cadets sing "Buckle Down, Winsocki" as they parade across the football field at St. John's Military Academy into a superimposed American flag. Heterosexual interest has become patriotic, girl-crazy boys are nevertheless strong, confident, ready to fight. Many of the cast members apparently marched directly from *Best Foot Forward* into the real-life war: They disappear from the annals of Hollywood and Broadway for several years, or forever.

A few months later, Norman Taurog directed Mickey Rooney and Judy Garland in their last MGM barn musical, *Girl-Crazy* (November 1943). Again, Boy Next Door Mickey Rooney must overcome the "stigma" of girl-craziness. He plays Danny Churchill Jr., a Yale frat boy who scandalizes his newspaper-editor father by cavorting with women in nightclubs. Danny's girl-craziness is decidedly effeminate; he sings that he passively, perhaps masochistically, likes girls who "treat him rough." So Dad ships him out West to Cody College, where there hasn't been a woman since the Civil War, to "make a man out of him."

Since collegiate movies traditionally encourage heterosexual desire, it seems odd that the boys of Cody College display none—Ginger (Judy Garland), the only girl in the county, is not mobbed by dating requests, and even her boyfriend refers to their "meeting of the minds," their intellectual propinquity, rather than her great beauty. The script makes it clear, however, that their lack of girl-craziness has made their lives meaningless. They are bored and listless, singing "I'm Biding My Time" while waiting for the state to shut the college down due to lack of interest.

When Danny tries to court the rough, no-nonsense Ginger with suave sophistication and compliments, she recoils in disgust. She prefers he-men who would rather swing her over their shoulders than describe her eyes, real men who breakfast on "nails and Texaco":

> You're no cowboy! You're soft, and how, boy!
> [Feels his arm.] I feel no muscle—a fist of tussle!
> I must refuse you, I cannot use you!
> [Spoken.] You silly man, you!

"You silly man!" is a reflection of "you nassty man," a lisping pansy catchphrase popularized by radio comedian Joe Penner. It signifies that Ginger finds Danny, and perhaps all girl-crazy boys, soft and effeminate.

Danny proves himself not through a display of strength and courage, nor through taking his shirt off, but through a savvy ability to capitalize on girl-craziness. First he makes Cody College coed to ensure that there are girls around, and then he sponsors a beauty contest to kick-start the boys' heterosexual longing. Now there is no shortage of applications for admission. After a Wild West–themed showstopping number, Ginger and the collegians recognize that girl-craziness can actually save the day. Is not passive and passionless at all; it is exuberant, energetic, powerful—and it leads to home and family and motherhood. Most wartime musicals fade out with the stars marching into American flags, but *Girl-Crazy* ends with a celebration of heteronormative domesticity, a cartoon of housewife Ginger and her child listening to the radio in a middle-class living room while the sun in the window grins its approval.

MEET ME IN ST. LOUIS

In *Girl-Crazy*, a foppish, sissified Boy Next Door is wild about girls; but MGM's *Meet Me in St. Louis* (November 1944) envisions the opposite problem: a strong, masculine Boy Next Door who is not interested in girls at all.[8] The year 1904–1905 in the lives of the Smith Family is set in a St. Louis so Technicolor-bright, so postcard-perfect that it seems to glow, in a mythic Middle America as far removed from contemporary woes as humanly possible, with no World War, no war of any kind, no foreign countries, no poverty, no crime, no racial strife, no ethnic minorities (not even the Irish), no generation gap (the teenagers dance to "Skip to My Lou"), no one who is nasty, mean, or bitter, no conflict at all except for a few sitcom-simple misunderstandings and the threat of being expelled from paradise.

The heavy-handed attempts of Esther Smith (Judy Garland) to woo reticent Boy Next Door John Truett (Tom Drake), bolstered by her sister snaring a man and her brother being snared by a woman, present a paean to heteronormativity, queered only by the curiously gender-bending girl-meets-boy plotline and by backstage gossip about Judy Garland's real-life designs on both Tom Drake and director Vincente Minnelli.[9] Both were gay. Drake proved "a lost cause," unable to perform with a woman when the moment of reckoning arrived (though that didn't stop him from marrying Isabelle Dunne in 1945, and divorcing her in 1946), but Judy managed to elicit a spark of heterosexual interest in Minnelli, drag him to the altar in June 1945, and have a child with him before they divorced.[10]

In the long, slow summer of 1903, Esther spends many weeks gazing at new neighbor John Truett across the yard as he practices for football and basketball and pretends to smoke a pipe, but for some reason he never gazes back. She sings:

> He doesn't know I exist, no matter how I persist
> So it's clear to see, there's no hope for me
> Though I live at 5135 Kensington Avenue
> And he lives at 5133![11]

Strategizing, Esther asks her brother, recent high school graduate Lon (Henry H. Daniels), to invite the Boy Next Door to his off-to-Princeton party. John eagerly accepts; evidently it takes a hunky college man rather than a Girl Next Door to incite his interest.

At the party, Esther descends the staircase with dramatic flourish in a new dress, expecting John to gape in an Andy Hardy–style transformation. But he is ignoring her in favor of an intense conversation with

Lon; there is little doubt about whom he prefers to spend time with. Not yet discouraged, Esther drags John bodily away from his same-sex flirtation, throws herself at him during the "Skip to My Lou" line dance, steals his hat so he'll have to stay behind to search for it, refuses to let go when he offers a good-bye handshake, asks him to help turn off the lights (hint, hint), and as a last resort descends the staircase again (maybe he'll get it this time). But John doesn't take the bait; he extricates himself from one last handshake, exclaims, "You've got a mighty strong grip for a girl!" and leaves Esther stammering with frustration.

In the next scene, John has consented to a trolley ride downtown, but with the gang, not as a date, and he arrives only *after* the famous "Trolley Song" about how he makes Esther's heart pound. He remains oblivious to her heteroromantic overtures until the night of Halloween, when she decks him (due to a misunderstanding) and then returns to apologize. "It's no worse than football practice," he admits, "But it's better with a girl . . . if you're not busy tomorrow night, could you beat me up again?" Like Mickey Rooney's Danny Churchill in *Girl-Crazy*, he likes girls who treat him rough, girls who are strong, powerful, and masculine; heterosexual interest is still a feminizing trait. He then riffs on their first meeting, asking Esther to help him turn off the lights, and when she points out that they're already off, he swoops in for a brief, squeamish kiss. "You've got a mighty strong grip, *for a boy*," she exclaims.

Now that Esther has punched John into a discovery of girls, they are "in love" for the two remaining segments, Winter and Spring, leaving the plot to connect the other Smith children with boys and girls. There are only a few momentary setbacks, again of a gender-bending sort. For instance, in the Winter segment John is distraught: He cannot attend the Christmas ball because he has "nothing to wear." Next he'll be worried about the state of his hair and makeup.

In the springtime conclusion, four hetero-couples gather to view the spectacle of the St. Louis World's Fair. Esther expresses awe that such a magnificent sight can be seen "Right here in our home town! Right here where we live!" But the viewers are watching the reaction shots of the couples—Esther and John, Lon and the girl who snared him, sister and her husband, Mom and Dad—all paired and enclenched, so that the magnificent sight becomes not the World's Fair but heteroromance. Both are artificial structures, empty inside; yet they are so bright and pretty, so symmetrical, with so much attention to trompe l'oeil realism that we can almost forget how much strategizing, deception, sublimation, and lying they require.

DICKIE MOORE

Born on September 25, 1925, Dickie Moore had intense, dark eyes and a pale, sickly appearance that became somewhat sensual in adolescence, like the consumptive glow of Carmen. Though he grew up in the child-star era of the 1930s—he performed in many of the *Our Gang* comedy shorts and worked with Jackie Cooper in *When a Feller Needs a Friend* (1933)—he never became either a scrappy sissy or a he-man in adolescence. His characters never expressed any heterosexual interest, even in the wake of Andy Hardy, yet they smiled at Joe E. Brown in *Gladiator* (1938), Gary Cooper in *Sergeant York* (1941), and Glenn Ford in *The Adventures of Martin Eden* (1942) without any noticeable homo-romantic passion. Even at the age of seventeen, he was playing children, often crippled boys, and his characters were invariably seeking out parents rather than lovers.

Then girl-craziness hit suddenly, in the spring of his seventeenth year (May 1942), in *Miss Annie Rooney* (United Artists, dir. Edward L. Marin). Yet it was still a sickly, passive sort of girl-craziness. Wearing glasses to hide his Valentino-esque sensuality, Dickie plays a poor little rich boy who swoons over sassy wrong-side-of-the-tracks Shirley Temple. "Two weeks ago," he gushes, "I was just Marty White, with practically nothing to live for. And then—bingo! You!" To demonstrate his affection, he busses Miss Temple's cheek, his first boy-girl kiss, he claims, on screen or off.[12]

After playing against Don Ameche in the treacly *Heaven Can Wait* (1943), the eighteen-year-old Dickie moved to Poverty Row PRC for his only musical, *Jive Junction*.[13] Like *Girl-Crazy,* the plot centers on the paradox of the new-style Boy Next Door, whose interest in girls codes him as too effeminate to attract the very girls he longs for. Dickie plays Peter Crane, a music conservatory sissy who returns to the urban high school he left years before. His girl-craziness is ensured from the first scene, when he becomes reacquainted with his old buddy and his sister, formerly a pig-tailed pest, now a beauty. "We do grow up!" Dickie moans in appreciation, as he proceeds to ignore the boy friend and court the sister. She rejects him, preferring he-men like the school bully Grant Saunders (significantly played by an adult, forty-six-year-old Jack Wagner).

In spite of his ogling, moaning, and rejecting of a potential homoromantic bond, Peter is a flamboyantly feminine, nonscrappy sort of sissy. He refuses a fight on the grounds that as a musician he must not injure his hands, and bully Saunders lisps, "Keep 'em pretty, honey!" Recognized throughout the high school as "one of the girls," Peter becomes the conductor for an all-girl jive band. "And will we make the boys jealous!" he exclaims. It is through their shared interest in music, first classical, then jive, that his girl friend warms up enough to kiss him.

But then she is forgotten, as if teenage heteroromance is too heady a topic for a Boy Next Door musical. The last half of the musical gives Peter a homosocial goal: He wants to befriend his sissy-hating classmates. He can't prove that he is a regular fella by dating girls, of course, and he's too young to join the army, but he can do the next best thing, he can entertain the troops. He and the gang transform the old barn into "Jive Junction" and invite the soldiers to dance with the high school girls, including their own girlfriends. Everyone is happy until the boys discover that they're being cuckolded. Not content to leave the girls on the dance floor, the soldiers are asking them out for drives and hamburgers afterward, illustrating the adolescent paradox that Mickey Rooney would face in *Andy Hardy's Blonde Trouble* (1944): Girls prefer older men, but older women do not prefer boys ("You're too little, too late," one quips when she thinks Dickie is asking). So Peter brainstorms a solution—he invites some older women to Jive Junction—and the intergenerational heterosexual practice evens out.

Donny O'Connor

A month older than Dickie Moore, born on August 28, 1925, Donald O'Connor (then called Donny) was never a child star: He spent his childhood prancing and pratfalling in vaudeville with his circusperformer parents. He hit Hollywood as a dancer in 1937, had bit parts in weepers and dramas, and starred in *Tom Sawyer, Detective* (1938) and *Million Dollar Legs* (1939). He was not cute, he was not muscular, but he was lithe and agile. As he grew into adolescence, Donny became a Freddie Bartholomew–style scrappy sissy, seeking love and understanding in the arms of a chum or older man while performing acrobatic stunts that would shame Frankie Darro.

As late as 1942, in *Private Buckaroo* (Universal, dir. Edward F. Kline), the sixteen-year-old Donny, who has fibbed his way into military service (he said that he was "over 18" without lying because "18" was written on the sole of his shoe), buddy-bonds with a handsome older man, a drafted singing cowboy named Lon Prentice (Dick Foran). He even asks, "Do you want to walk back to camp with me?" somewhat suggestively after a USO dance. As a corollary, Donny is actively opposed to heterosexual expression. When he sees a girl and a boy kissing, he sneers, "Vampire!" The big musical number, set to the Andrews Sisters' "Don't Sit under the Apple Tree," consists of a series of boys sitting on benches under an apple tree, ignoring blatant flirtations from girls. The point of the song, that one need not avoid apple trees as a general rule but only to be faithful to a heteroromantic partner back home, is forgotten: These boys are not interested, period.

In the denouement, as Donny prepares to be shipped out to the Pacific, his dance partner from the musical review asks for a good-bye kiss, so he busses her forehead. She exclaims, "Are you kidding?" then grabs him and kisses him on the mouth. He breaks away in disgust and moves on. He is not happy or awestricken; he has not been magically converted to girl-craziness. Foxhole comrades were still deemed essential to military success, girls back home effeminizing detriments.

Between 1942 and 1945, Donny O'Connor and some combination of Gloria Jean, Peggy Ryan, and Anne Blythe became Universal's answer to Mickey Rooney and Judy Garland, starring together in an endless number of Boy Next Door musicals (all directed by Charles Lamont). They were extremely popular: By the time he joined the army and left the series, Donny was receiving forty thousand fan letters per month, more than Mickey Rooney.[14] Yet in spite of the girl-crazy competition, Donny's Boys Next Door maintained a squeamishness about girls. In *Get Hep to Love* (October 1942), Donny's character isn't hep to love: His goal is to find a family for a teenage orphan played by Gloria Jean. *When Johnny Comes Marching Home* (December 1942) has Donny and Gloria as theatrical teens hiding a war hero from his throngs of fans. Not until *It Comes Up Love* (April 1943), in the midst of a plot involving hooking up their widowed parents, does Donny sing "For the First Time" and kiss Gloria without grimacing or pulling away.

After *It Comes Up Love* there was no stopping Donny: His characters were girl-crazy with not a hint of deviance. He is not passive or effeminate, like Danny Churchill in *Girl-Crazy*. He is not subject to sneers and innuendos from the other boys; in fact, they are just as likely to wolf-whistle at passing ladies. The adults do not gape in astonishment at his untoward girl-craziness; they accept it as an unremarkable fact of life, the teenage condition.

More important in marking the decay of the homoromantic Arcadia, Donny's characters vigorously reject any potential for same-sex bonds. In *Top Man* (August 1943), Don is nice enough to his older sister's boyfriend (Noah Beery Jr.), but the two are acquaintances, not friends, and they share not a single eye-glimmering moment. His peers are all wise-guy competitors for the attention of it-girl Connie (Susan Foster). They treat each other with undisguised hostility, agreeing to work together in the aircraft factory or to put on a show only because they are willing to "set aside their differences" during the crisis; one gets the impression that when the war ends, they will be constantly knocking chips off each others' shoulders. Don treats Tommy (Dickie Love), a barely pubescent young teen who hangs around the malt shop, with the same undisguised hostility. When Tommy's older brother is killed in action, Don does comfort him, but very briefly and through a "manly" discussion of vengeance rather than hand-on-shoulder tenderness.

Perhaps the most interesting aspect of *Top Man* is its obsession with demonstrating that Don is indeed an adolescent. In real life he was approaching eighteen, and he could easily have been scripted as a college man, but instead the script leaves no trope unturned in presenting him as still a teenager. He is continuously called a "kid" and a "youngster." He vaults hedges; he climbs through windows; he is uncomfortably inexperienced at driving a car; he grumbles about being too young to enlist in the military (that is, *not yet* eighteen). When his father enlists, he becomes the "man of the house" and ludicrously attempts grown-up activities like shaving, reading the newspaper, and ordering around the maid. He is attending college, but it is a *junior college* that looks exactly like a high school, with locker-lined corridors, a cafeteria, dances in the gym, and a blustering principal lifted directly from the Henry Aldrich series. The term itself was obscure in 1943; there were fewer than four hundred junior colleges in the United States, enrolling less than 1 percent of the college-age population, so audiences would probably be thinking of high school regardless.[15] The effect is to promote Don aggressively as a *teenage boy* for whom liking girls is normal, natural, and expected.

Chip off the Old Block (February 1944) begins as Donny, a young adult, is on his way home from military school. In *This Is the Life* (April 1944), Donny is a young adult soldier in love with a girl who is in love with an older man. But the distinction between teenager and adult no longer matters, at least in the arena of hetero-desire. The title card tells us that "Romeo O'Connor is up to his *necking* in joy," but by 1944, Boy Next Door musicals were asserting that teenage boys have always kissed girls, joyfully and without shame.

9

LITTLE TOUGH GUYS

By 1940, the gritty, desperate world of the Dead End had become a paradise, at least in the mass media, with tiny immigrant flats, open-air groceries, zoot-suited swells in the pool halls and hard-bodied boxers in the gyms. The new Lost Boys were poor yet healthy, starving yet amazingly fit, down-and-out yet deliriously happy. Certainly the war was visible, more visible than in the Carvels and Centervilles of the Boys Next Door: It appeared in war bonds and sugar rationing, and in telegrams in the dark of night with news of fathers and older brothers. But the Lost Boys eagerly desired it: Too young for military service, they tried to bilk, con, or sweet-talk their way into the recruitment office, or they dreamed of the day they would turn eighteen and could join "the toughest gang in the world."

They never, or rarely, turned eighteen. They were perpetually adolescents, too young to enlist, to vote, to drink; they were barely able to drive. They had no homes, or few, but that didn't matter: As Vallant notes, their street was not a transitory site between house and school, but a home in itself, a site of joy and pain, the site where life was lived.[1] They sometimes had mothers, elderly Irish women who groused about their "hoodlum friends" while force-feeding them enormous quantities of corned beef and cabbage. Their fathers were in jail or overseas, or dead, but there were dozens of father figures eager to look after them: older brothers, newspaper reporters, grumpy yet affectionate flatfoots, determined welfare workers, millionaires with straying sons, and grocers who blustered good-naturedly at their shoplifting. They were roughneck sissies, like the grown-up Lost Boys John Garfield and Jimmy Cagney:

tough yet tender, masculine yet not heterosexual, viewing women not as potential lovers but as mothers and sisters.[2] And, indeed, there were few women in their world except mothers, big sisters, and the surrogate big sisters who were dating their older brothers. Throughout the war, as Boys Next Door became increasingly involved with the other sex, Lost Boys continued to ignore girls and form passionate, intimate romances with each other or with men.

FRANKIE AND MANTAN

Twenty-one-year-old Frankie Darro had starred in so many teen melodrama-homoromances that audiences knew what to expect in *Irish Luck* (dir. Howard Bretherton, Monogram, 1939) before they even set foot in the theater: Dashing police detective Steve Lanahan (leading man Dick Purcell)[3] would investigate a murder at a posh hotel, assisted by teenage bellhop Buzzy O'Brien (Frankie); they would share lots of nick-of-time rescues, arms on shoulders, and longing glances before the fade-out, which would involve the teenager grinning approvingly at the detective kissing a girl. But instead, Buzzy ignores the detective he's supposed to be bonding with in favor of hotel janitor Jefferson (Mantan Moreland), an African American character who minimizes the English-mangling drawl, servile shuffle, and eye-bulging timidity of his usual mainstream roles[4]; indeed, in one scene he shows considerable courage, climbing onto a hotel ledge to flag down the police and save Buzzy's life. The palpable chemistry between Frankie Darro and Mantan Moreland stole the show, and during the next two years Monogram partnered them in five more Lost Boy melodramas plus a collegiate comedy.[5] They usually appeared on the same bill with a Boy Next Door romance starring Jackie Moran and Marcia Mae Jones, as if to present contrasting urban/small town settings and homoromantic/heteroromantic bonds.[6] The last two movies brought them all together.

Frankie Darro plays a poor, urban Irish-American teenager (always named Frankie), and Mantan Moreland (named Jeff or Jefferson) his co-worker, assistant, or chum of unspecified status. While working at a series of menial jobs, some of them quite feminizing (assistants at a beauty shop, delivery boys for a flower shop), they stumble upon a crime or a mystery. Jeff wants to leave the matter to the police, but Frankie insists that they get involved—racial stratification makes him the dominant partner, in spite of his age—and the game is afoot.

Like most Lost Boys, Frankie never displays significant heterosexual interest. In *Up in the Air*, he asks a receptionist for a "date" and, when she refuses, so effortlessly offers to manage her singing career that one wonders if he didn't intend a business relationship all along. In *The Gang's All Here*, Frankie and Jeff apply for jobs as truck drivers, and Frankie flirts with the female company manager. Jeff eye-bulges in surprise. Later he angrily exclaims, "I thought you was a woman-hater!" Frankie laughs, reassuring him: He may be a woman-hater, but he is also a "lady-killer," able to use his attractiveness to get them jobs.

In *Chasing Trouble*, Frankie befriends a girl on his flower-delivery route. She admits that she has been ordering flowers to cheer herself up because she doesn't have a job or a boyfriend. Frankie promises to ask his boss to hire her at the flower shop, and, he adds with a wink, "I might even get you a boyfriend!" They are of the same age and socioeconomic class, so surely, the viewer concludes, he plans to *become* that boyfriend. But no, the next scene shows him dutifully making a list of prospects.

Frankie is usually big-brothered by a benevolent, square-jawed reporter or police detective, but these adult-teen relationships are colorless, merely plot devices to give him access to the homicide and bank robbery cases. The emotional heat comes between Frankie and Jeff. Mantan Moreland seems like an odd object of teenage homoromantic desire: He is balding, bug-eyed, and pudgy. No doubt his less-than-Herculean physique coupled with stereotypic African American asexuality allowed the duo to enjoy an exclusivity rare in the homoromances between teenagers and Anglo-white beefcake models, who must always kiss a girl at fade-out.

Many contemporary comedy duos, such as Hope and Crosby and Abbott and Costello, had relationships based on manipulation, bullying, and hostility, and they eagerly betrayed each other whenever a better opportunity arose, but Frankie and Jeff obviously care for each other. They might bicker and complain, but their interactions are intensely passionate and surprisingly intimate. They are holding each other's hands or shoulders for lengthy scenes in all of their movies, and through nearly a third of *You're out of Luck*. When they are disrobing so they can put on disguises, Frankie starts to unbutton Jeff's shirt himself, taking a liberty that one cannot imagine Henry Aldrich taking with his side-kick Dizzy. When the bad guys threaten them with guns, Frankie stands directly in front of Jeff and cradles against him to protect him. When Frankie is knocked out, Jeff forgets his fear and rushes to him, kneels, and holds his head tenderly in his arms. In *The Gang's All Here*, Frankie rests his body cozily against Jeff's leg as they sit on the ground to read the want ads.

Sometimes Frankie and Jeff go beyond physicality to refer to each other in overtly romantic terms. In *Chasing Trouble*, their first attempt to find a boyfriend for the girl on Frankie's flower-delivery route has failed, and Jeff worries that they will have to start the laborious process all over again:

> Jeff: Is we got to go through a telephone book again?
> Frankie: [Preoccupied.] No, no, no, no. Now shut up, honey.

In African American slang of the era, an adult could use the term *honey* to refer to a child of either sex, but Frankie is not African American and Jeff is not a child; for them it can only refer to a romantic part-ner.[7] Frankie calls Jeff "honey" to deflect the harshness of "shut up," unconsciously or consciously foregrounding their romantic bond. In *The Gang's All Here*, truck drivers Frankie and Jeff are captured and held hostage by an evil rival trucking company. Though his hands are tied behind his back, Frankie manages to wrestle a gun from the hulking henchman on guard. A swooning Jeff says, "Superman ain't got noth-ing on you!" and then, sotto voce, "I could get serious about you, Mr. Frankie." In 1941, the expression "get serious" meant the same thing that it means today. It is interesting to speculate on how such lines got by without retakes; of course, B movies rarely got retakes of any sort, but it is also likely that the crew didn't notice, just as they were oblivious to Cary Grant's ad-lib joke about gay identity in *Bringing Up Baby* (1938).[8]

Frankie Darro and Mantan Moreland appeared together for the last time in *Let's Go Collegiate* (1941), not a Lost Boy melodrama but the premiere of a proposed collegiate comedy series. Frankie, Jackie Moran, and Keye Luke, all stars of *The Gang's All Here*, play college buddies, and Moreland plays an employee at the fraternity house, no more chummy with Frankie than with any of the other boys.[9] There is no vestige of their former homoromantic intensity or intimacy, except for a brief tease in the opening scene: Off camera, Frankie is "studying anatomy" on a skittish, uncomfortable Jeff. But the viewer has only a few seconds to speculate on the anatomical region of Frankie's interest before the camera pulls back to reveal that he is fondling Jeff's *head*. To make their heterosexualization complete, they both have girlfriends (though Frankie steadfastly refuses to kiss his). Of course, a college boy could express heterosexual desire with being labeled a sissy, but the question remains: Why was Frankie sent to college, when his teen sleuth series was just starting? Perhaps the homoromantic Arcadia was being sealed more tightly every day.

During the next few years, Monogram partnered Mantan Moreland with several new boys and men: Dick Purcell and John Archer in *King of the Zombies* (1941), Johnny Downs in *Freckles Comes Home* (1942), John King in *Law of the Jungle* (1942), Frank Graham in *Cosmo Jones, Crime Smasher* (1943). Usually he even kept the character name "Jefferson." But the chemistry he shared with Frankie Darro could not be duplicated, and he was relegated to eye-bulging roles as Charlie Chan's chauffeur.

LITTLE TOUGH GUYS

Upon the demise of the Dead End Kids, Billy Halop moved to Universal to star in a knockoff movie called *Little Tough Guy*.[10] Eventually it became a knockoff series, *Little Tough Guys*. Twelve installments appeared on Universal B-tickets between 1938 and 1943, with three stars (Billy Halop, Frankie Thomas, Bobby Jordan), eight directors, and innumerable writers, so it became well-nigh impossible to maintain any sense of unity in theme, character, or situation. Billy Halop's characters are always poor, urban, and eager to show off their muscles, and almost always named Tom or Tommy (because he was Tommy in *Dead End*). But otherwise they have little in common: They may be teenagers or adults, living with parents or living alone, traveling in a gang or with a homoromantic partner, interested in girls or not, depending on the whim of the script.

In *Call a Messenger*, for instance, a teenage Jimmy (Billy Halop), living with his older sister Marge (twenty-four-year-old Mary Carlisle), gets a job at a messenger service. The rest of his gang drools all over the comely receptionist, squealing, "Those lips! Those eyes! Those curves!" but Jimmy ignores her, exclaiming, "Girls are poison!" Instead, he brawl-bonds with his coworker Bob Prichard (Jimmy Butler), who is scripted as significantly older. Jimmy asks him home "for pigs knuckles with the family," ostensibly to fix him up with Marge, but she quickly sees through the charade, saying rather archly, "Tell your *boyfriend* I'm sorry I couldn't stay!" The next date, to Coney Island, involves only Jimmy and Bob. Later Bob is injured in a robbery attempt, and it is Jimmy, not sister Marge, who rushes to his bedside.

In *You're Not So Tough*, Tommy is a young adult, homeless until he ends up at a work camp in California, so it is understandable that the plot might revolve around his attempt to woo young relief worker Millie (Nan Grey). But in *Tough as They Come*, Tommy is a teenager, living with his elderly mother; yet he has two potential girlfriends, a plain Jane who genuinely cares for him and a sophisticate who is using him as lower-class boy toy. *Mug Town* starts with an adult, rail-riding Tommy nevertheless expressing a "love at first sight" enthusiasm for fellow vagrant Steve Bell (Tommy Kelly), but only about ten minutes of screen time into their relationship, Steve is killed in a train accident. The grief-stricken Tommy sets out to notify his family and falls in love with Steve's older brother's girlfriend.

In *Give Us Wings*, Tom is a young adult, living on his own, yet he and sidekick Rap (seventeen-year-old Bobby Jordan, Angel in *Dead End*) share the casual intimacy of homoromance: When they are driving in a car, Rap falls asleep with his head on Tom's shoulder. They go to work for a dishonest crop-dusting company, where Rap flies an unsafe airplane, crashes, and ultimately dies in Tom's arms. The grief-stricken Tom then confronts the evil manager, culminating in an aerial dogfight. Heterosexual interest does occur incidentally, when Tom and Rap both try to cut out from work early to date the same girl in town; but they end up at a fish fry, laughing at the dancing boy-girl couples, making fun of heterosexual practice.

Mob Town, though one of the last in the series, returns to the old-style Dead End Kids plotline of the Lost Boy torn between male admirers from opposite sides of the law. Again a teenager, living with his older sister, Tom is mourning his brother, a criminal recently executed. As in *Angels with Dirty Faces* and practically every other Lost Boy movie, two men are competing for his affection: gangster Monk Bangor (Paul Fix) and policeman Frank Conroy (Dick Foran). When Tom discovers that Officer Conroy arrested his brother and sent him on the road to the electric chair, he makes his decision: Sobbing, he seeks out Monk, who promises that they will "go away together." Instead he uses Tom as the pigeon in a drug-store robbery. Officer Conroy intervenes and is shot, Tom is shot. When they recover, Tom realizes how much he cares for Officer Conroy. They hug, cry, and decide to "go away together," this time for real.

For all its vacillation and confusion, the *Little Tough Guys* series does follow three rules quite stringently. First, homoromance must occur between boys and men, never between boys or between men. In *Give Us Wings*, Rap is scripted as much younger, a teenager in whom young adult Tom has taken an interest; likewise, Steve in *Hit the Road* is a "kid." *Call a Messenger* unconvincingly frames seventeen-year-old Jimmy Butler as an "adult" to nineteen-year-old Billy Halop's teenager. The wartime shift from peer to adult-teen homoromance was practically complete.

Second, homoromance cannot occur simultaneously with heteroromance. A movie can feature one or the other, but not both. In *Hit the Road*, Tommy is first attracted to Steve, but the relationship ends, definitively, before he engages in any heterosexual flirtation. Otherwise he either likes girls and ignores boys, or likes boys and ignores girls. Old and new models of teenage masculinity, woman-hating and girl-crazy, compete but do not intersect.

Third, homoromance ends with tragedy. Any girl that Tommy loves will kiss him at fade-out, but any boy or man that Tommy loves will die in his arms. Even in *Mob Town*, the homoromantic fade-out is preceded by an injury scene that probably was changed from a deathbed scene at the last minute. This is perhaps the most disturbing development, a parallel to Jimmy Frobisher's suicide in *Life Begins for Andy Hardy* (1941). Homoromance has become dark, deadly. Only boys and girls can walk hand in hand into the future.

JUNIOR G-MEN

While Billy Halop was starring in the *Little Tough Guys* series, Universal also placed him in three movie serials that combined the romanticized poverty of the Lost Boys with Adventure Boy globe-trotting.[11] The plots are all about the same: Billy plays a tough teenage gang leader (twice named Billy, once Ace), Huntz Hall his sidekick (Gyp, Toby, or Bolts), and any available roughneck actors his gang. Even though he is a penniless street kid, he somehow becomes involved with spies or subversives threatening to destroy the world, and he grudgingly joins forces with a representative of law and order to fight the common enemy. Amid the explosions, car chases, kidnappings, and threats of torture, the two fall in love, and in a reflection of the film convention of the adult gangster reformed by the love of a woman, Billy decides to abandon his hoodlum lifestyle for a respectable, law-abiding future.

In *Junior G-Men*, Billy's inventor-father has been kidnapped and the FBI believes that he is in danger also, so they assign him a bodyguard, a Junior G-Man (teenage special agent) named Harry Trent (Kenneth Howell).[12] Though playing a teenager, Howell was twenty-seven years old, a handsome, grinning blond with a magnificent physique that he happily displayed in the boxing ring. Perhaps because he was gay in real life, he plays his role with more authenticity than any of Billy's other movie serial suitors, gawking at him in a "love at first sight" moment at their first meeting and courting him above and beyond the demands of his bodyguard job, with invitations to dinner, to a show, for a drive in the country.[13] Gyp (Huntz Hall) is jealous of this new competition, and the two spend the first half of the serial sniping at each other as they maneuver to sit beside Billy at the dinner table or in the car, or to rescue him from danger. But, during the last half, Gyp grudgingly accepts his demotion and goes on to flirt with girls (Huntz Hall's characters frequently like girls, and they are often ridiculed for it).

Trent and Billy share homoromantic intensity, intimacy, and exclusivity without the slightest hesitation; there is no hint of the anxiety that had all but eliminated peer homoromance elsewhere in mass culture. They save each other from various kidnap/murder attempts, burning buildings, and runaway autos, and afterward tenderly embrace, even though Billy offers his rescued father only a desultory handshake. They have quiet discussions with their arms or shoulders casually touching. They plan what they will do together when the crisis is over, and not for an instant does anyone suggest that Trent might move on to other bodyguarding clients: They will be together forever. The last scene shows them having dinner with the gang, or perhaps having the gang *over* for dinner, domesticity replacing the traditional fade-out kiss.

Sea Raiders takes Billy and the gang far from their inner-city habitat to the South Pacific of boys' adventure novels and gives Billy and Toby (Huntz Hall) an unusual degree of emotional intensity and intimacy, as if they are homoromantic partners rather than mere sidekicks. They even triangulate their relationship into a family: Billy's older brother is dating Toby's older sister. Swab, the villain turned "love interest," is played by twenty-year-old Hally Chester, an anonymous member of the gang in several Lost Boy movies, blond like Kenneth Howell but with an unremarkable physique (on display during a nude hazing scene in *The Little Tough Guys in Society*). Here he is a police informant, unprincipled, duplicitous, underhanded, and untrustworthy, a stereotyped "pansy," ridiculed by the gang as a "mama's boy" and a "nancy little thing."[14] Then Billy takes an interest in him and strong-arms him into joining the gang. The arrangement does not sit well with the other gang members, especially Toby, who again resents the competition. Billy treats Swab with a curious disregard, as a possession rather than a potential homoromantic partner; he dangles Swab in front of the others as a trophy, takes liberties with his body to demonstrate not affection, but control. Swab has become his gunsel.

Then, when they are working on a whaling ship in the South Pacific, Swab's foot is caught in a line and he is dragged underwater.[15] Billy dives to the rescue, knocks out the hysterical boy so he will stop struggling, and then cuts the line and swims him back to the ship. Afterward, as they huddle together in blankets, Swab jokes, "You won't get away with this," but he warms up to his role as Billy's companion, allowing himself to be held by the arm or the hand without flinching. Replaced, Toby roils with jealousy. The two snipe at each other constantly, and more than once Billy has to physically restrain them from a brawl.

The competition intensifies when Billy, Toby, and Swab are shipwrecked on a desert island. As they are crawling ashore, Billy is attacked and pulled underwater by a giant octopus. Swab freezes in panic and yells "Billy!" over and over, but Toby, demonstrating a heroism uncharacteristic of the actor's goofball persona, dives into the ocean, wrestles with the octopus, stabs it, and pulls Billy ashore. Billy responds with a noncommittal "Thanks!"

Later, in the jungle, Billy is attacked by a panther. This time it is Toby who freezes, and Swab becomes the rescuer: He shoots the panther and pulls Billy to his feet. Surely wrestling an octopus underwater requires more courage than shooting a panther from several feet away, yet Billy responds to this rescue with a stereotypic gesture of romantic interest:

> Swab: Are you all right, Billy?
> Billy: I think so. I'm too scared to know.
> Swab: It don't look like [the panther] got you.
> Billy: It would have, if it wasn't for you.
> [Looks away, smiling shyly.]

The competition is over; there is no more question about where Billy's affection lies. Swab is no longer a pretty-boy trophy, a symbol of Billy's power, but a permanent homoromantic partner, and Toby is demoted to the status of sidekick. The rest of the adventure shows Swab and Toby learning to work together, as they must, since neither is going anywhere. In the last scene, when the gang and the adults all gather to celebrate their victory over the evil Sea Raiders, Swab is the one framed between Toby's sister and Billy's brother, a new member of the family.

Billy Halop's first two serials were apparently plotted with the sole purpose of getting the young star as naked as possible, as often as possible. He boxes; he strips down for bed or showers; he jumps into rivers;

he is pushed into lakes. In *Junior G-Men*, he teaches Gyp to swim in a lengthy interlude that involves many close-ups of the two bobbing up and down in their underwear. During the underwater fight scene in *Sea Raiders*, the camera zooms in for close-ups of his bare chest, legs, and frontside. Only Mickey Rooney was more thoroughly and blatantly on display. But Billy displays no feminizing girl-craziness requiring a beef-cake remedy; he is himself an object of desire, a street Arab of Alger's myth, a fetishized other—nonwhite, immigrant, forbidden, and power-ful, conceivable only in fantasies and in the homoromantic Arcadia.

In the last of Billy Halop's Universal serials, *Junior G-Men of the Air*, junior pilot Ace (Billy Halop) is scripted as a teenager, still living with his father, but for some reason the kidnapped inventor relative is his *younger* brother (seventeen-year-old Gene Reynolds). Jerry Markham (thirty-three-year-old Frank Albertson), the Junior G-Man assigned to protect him, looks decidedly middle-aged, with a receding hairline and corporate suit and tie. Was Jerry originally scripted as adult, transmuted to teenager at the last minute through a scene at the Junior G-Man Headquarters and a few references to him as a "boy"? Were they both originally young adults? If so, the switch to teenagers didn't help: The peer homoromance is lifeless and unconvincing.

Jerry paws at Ace's arm or shoulder and once even at his butt, in awkward attempts to express homoromantic intimacy, but there are no invitations to dinners or drives, no jostling for position at each oth-er's sides, no embraces after rescues; indeed, Ace is usually rescued by a member of his gang or by an adult while Jerry stands aside, looking worried. Ace and Jerry are alone together in only one chapter, and they never discuss staying together after the crisis. And though Ace is dunked into lakes and rivers frequently, his body is never on display; he is no longer an object of desire. Perhaps we can blame the new directors, Lew D. Collins and Ray Taylor; previous directors Ford Beebe and John Rawlins were considerably more adept at evoking the homoromantic Arcadia.[16] Or perhaps we can blame Pearl Harbor and anxiety about potential inversion that was making every same-sex friendship suspect, even in the nostalgic golden age of the Dead End.

LEO AND BOBBY

When Billy Halop and Huntz Hall moved to Universal in 1940, two of their fellow Dead Enders, twenty-three-year-old Leo Gorcey and seventeen-year-old Bobby Jordan, moved to Monogram to take over the East Side Kids series. Leo played Muggs McGinnis, the diminutive, smart-alecky leader of the East Side Social Improvement Club, and Bobby played Danny, his boyish, innocent-looking sidekick. Eventually Huntz Hall joined the cast as the buffoonish Glimpy, and other gang members were assembled as needed, sometimes with one or two lines, sometimes with no lines at all. They were just background: Leo and Bobby were the undisputed stars.

Not counting the original, thirteen East Side Kids features appeared between 1940 and 1943.[17] Though they had six different directors and were often written and produced in a matter of days, they maintained consistent characters and a strong thematic unity, probably because Leo Gorcey was exercising strong control over the writing and staging. The old model of the teenage boy as a "woman-hater" remains intact. In *'Neath Brooklyn Bridge*, Muggs meets a runaway girl and brings her back to the clubhouse to hide, making an exception to the "No Girls Allowed" rule. At first resentful, the boys warm up to her, but only as a buddy—they link her romantically with an adult friend (Noah Beery Jr., who was only three and a half years older than Leo Gorcey). Nor do they have any knowledge of the heterosexual practice that would enflame the dreams of so many teenagers in later generations. At the end of *Let's Get Tough*, Muggs's big brother gets his military orders just as he leaves the church after his wedding. Muggs tells his forlorn bride that they'll be happy to go on her honeymoon with her instead, and the gang piles into the newlywed car, sublimely unaware of what a honeymoon is for.

Muggs occasionally tries a shy flirtation with a girl, but he is heavily censored by his peers. In *That Gang of Mine*, the boys think that Muggs is receiving love letters from a girl, and they set out to intercept and destroy them (he's actually corresponding with a male jockey). In *Spooks Run Wild*, Muggs sneaks out of their youth camp to visit a girl in town, and the gang tails him, determined to end his transgression into effeminacy.

Boys Next Door often flexed their muscles as a remedy for feminizing girl-craziness, but the East Side Kids, like Billy Halop, revel in physicality for its own sake: "They may be underprivileged," a cop says appreciatively in *Spooks Run Wild*, "But they sure ain't underdeveloped!" The Columbia *Three Stooges* shorts evoke a world similar to the East Side, with pool halls, boxing rings, and boarding houses, with gangsters and molls, detectives and debutantes, but for the Three Stooges, the male body is flabby, malleable, and ridiculous; men take off their shirts and pants to reveal long underwear, and they box fully clothed. The East Side Kids take off their shirts and pants to reveal hard muscle, and they box nearly nude, the male body signifying beauty beneath their dead-end lives. Boxing is particularly important to them, as important as swimming when they were Dead End Kids; they are always participating in boxing contests or settling their differences in the ring. Joyce Carol Oates notes that boxing is a supremely homoerotic sport, an opportunity for men to display and manipulate each other's bodies, using their beauty for a mechanical end yet inviting the spectator to view, to lust.[18]

Early on, Muggs receives the most attention, but the camera quickly switches to Danny. When they go swimming, Danny is the first to climb out of the water, so the camera can linger on his hard-ribbed chest and backside. When they strip down for bed, he is the first one, sometimes the only one, to display his chest and stomach. He sleeps in his underwear, even when the rest wear pajamas. When he is fully clothed, he stands erect with his chest shoved out, as if posing for a muscle magazine. Oddly, his standard costume is a striped shirt and a sailor cap, which Dyer notes was considered both boyish and effeminate, conjuring images of the liminal space of sailors—rootless, anonymous, and overtly sexual.[19]

Even in the days of the Dead End Kids, there were glimpses of a special intimacy between Bobby Jordan and Leo Gorcey. In *Angels Wash Their Faces*, for instance, while the gang is discussing some crisis or other, Bobby sits at the far left of the stage, casually reclining against Leo, who is caressing his chest. But in the East Side Kids series, especially as Leo Gorcey took more creative control over the scripts, their relationship becomes integral to the stories. In *That Gang of Mine*, the gang tries to talk Muggs out of his dream of becoming a jockey, but he ignores them. Then Danny suggests, softly, that he might not be qualified, and he is devastated. In *Bowery Blitzkrieg*, the two break up after a quarrel, but when Muggs hears that Danny has been shot and needs a transfusion, he rushes to the hospital to volunteer to donate blood, even though it means he will miss the Golden Gloves boxing contest.

Even Muggs's heterosexual flirtations are organized around a conflict with Danny. In *Pride of the Bowery*, Muggs makes a date with a girl, and Danny asks if he can go along. When Muggs refuses, he pouts: "We ain't never been separated before." In *Smart Alecks*, Danny is injured again, and as he is recovering in the hospital, Muggs proclaims that he will "oscillate" with the pretty nurse: "Nothing to it, a new experience, that's all." Evidently he doesn't want a kiss for its own sake; he merely wants to entertain his pal. After the kiss, he pours a pitcher of water over himself and "faints" into Danny's lap, leaving open the question of whether he is actually overcome by heterosexual desire or concluding his "act" by designating Danny as his real interest.

Glimpy (Huntz Hall) competes with Danny for Muggs's attention, just as he does with Billy Halop's characters in the concurrent *Junior G-Men* serials. He and Danny are constantly jostling each other for the prized position at Muggs's right side. In *Bowery Blitzkrieg*, after another Muggs-Danny breakup, Glimpy moves in, aggressively paws at Muggs, and offers to take him for a bicycle ride. Riding astride Glimpy's handlebars, Muggs gets a dreamy expression on his face and jokes, "Why don't you sing 'Bicycle Built for Two'?" But Danny always wins in the end. In *Clancy Street Boys*, after the usual jostle for position, Danny puts his arm around Muggs's shoulders and his hand flat against his chest. Not to be rejected so easily, Glimpy tries the same gesture with Danny, but Danny shrugs him off.

All of the East Side Kids hang over each other as if they are a single mass, but Muggs and Danny far surpass the others in intimacy, demonstrating an easy, unself-conscious familiarity with each other's bodies. In *Boys of the City*, they mischievously shove a piece of cake into Scruno's face; as they rub it in, they interweave their fingers, a rather intricate

gesture almost impossible to achieve by chance, subsuming their affection under a façade of playful roughhousing. In *Pride of the Bowery*,
Danny rubs down boxer Muggs between rounds, a standard practice;
but in odd contrast to Glimpy's meager arm massage later that year in
Bowery Blitzkrieg, Danny explores every inch of Muggs' body, vigorously
rubbing his chest, shoulders, arms, and thighs. At one point he pulls
open the top of Muggs's trunks with one hand and slides the other
down his abdomen, as if he intends to reach inside. Desired and desiring, with an explicit acknowledgment of same-sex desire that moved
from the homoromantic squarely into the realm of the homoerotic,
Muggs and Danny so effectively countermand the girl-crazy antics of
Andy Hardy and Henry Aldrich that it is difficult to believe that they
coexisted at precisely the same moment in history. Yet they played in
the same theaters, or in theaters nearby, on the same days in the same
weeks.

It is usually dangerous to look for parallels between fictional characters and the actors who portray them—Frankie Darro's on-screen
chemistry with Mantan Moreland does not answer the question of his
off-camera erotic interest—but since the East Side Kids and especially
Leo Gorcey were notorious for fading in and out of character, it might
be profitable to look at Bobby and Leo off camera. Their biographer
notes that from the beginning they enjoyed a rapport that was "relaxed,
easygoing, and carefree."[20] Their mutual affection was clearly visible and
remains visible in the form of some remarkably intimate candid photos
that survive: They wrap their arms around each other, rest hands against
thighs, rest heads on shoulders, gaze into each other's eyes. They resemble nothing so much as the collections of photos from the Victorian
era, when men who loved men were not yet classified as gay, nor men
who loved women as straight, and hands resting on thighs may or may
not signify homoromantic intimacy. But Leo and Bobby were thirty
years too late for such gestures to signify anything else.

A puzzling out-of-character moment occurs in *Mr. Wise Guy*: While
the gang talks to their reform school headmaster, we glimpse Leo
Gorcey and Bobby Jordan across the room on a large leather couch. It
is unclear whether they are in character; they may believe that they are
not in the shot. Their legs and thighs are pressed together; their hands

drift casually across their knees. They are grinning, delighted in each other's company. If we watch carefully, ignoring the main action of the scene, we can see Leo bring his cupped hand close to Bobby's ear as if to whisper. He remains for only an instant, long enough for only a word or two. Whatever he says—or does—behind the hand, it is not a joke, as Bobby's expression becomes somber; he is embarrassed or upset. Leo has gone too far.

We cannot know if they became real-life lovers since they both died before anyone would admit to such relationships willingly. However, Leo's daughter, Brandy Gorcey Ziesemer, wrote a psychoanalytic master's thesis in which she explains his lifelong history of irrational and self-destructive behavior as the result of a serious psychic conflict between his "sensitive" inner nature and the brashly womanizing, boozing public persona that he adopted "for self-preservation." Preservation from what? "Sensitive," which Ziesemer uses over and over, has long been code for "gay." A more recent biography by Leo's son is equally evasive.[21]

We know that Leo Gorcey was not unfamiliar with Hollywood's gay subculture. Early in his memoirs, he jokes that "most of the sex kings and queens fell in love everyday—the kings fell in love with the kings and the queens fell in love with the queens."[22] He alludes to gay men and lesbians in positive or neutral lights several more times, a remarkable feat of candor before Stonewall (the book was published in 1969). It is also remarkable that as Leo Gorcey takes creative control, the East Side Kids movies become completely free of the gay-baiting "Are you a boy or a goil?" taunts common in the Dead End Kids movies. In fact, a sissy-boy named Algy (Eugene Francis) appears four times as a sort of honorary gang member.[23] With his apparent openness to same-sex desire and "sensitive" inner nature, one can easily imagine that Leo found time among his six marriages for a romance with the obviously smitten Bobby. Perhaps it is significant that Bobby married only once, in the spring of 1946, after he returned from World War II and found his place at Leo's side usurped once and for all by Huntz Hall.

Former Little Rascal Sammy Morrison as Scruno was added to the previously all-white cast to allow for some racist gags (e.g., when the other boys get pie for dessert, he is served a gigantic slab of watermelon), but from the start the gang had continuous, intimate access to his body as a safely "sexless" conduit for homoerotic display. In *Boys of the City*, they consider going fishing, and Scruno remarks, "I love catfish!" Pete (David Gorcey), who has been cradling Scruno in his arms, groans with desire and nuzzles his neck. Is he reacting to the possibility of catfish? When Glimpy enters the series, he uses Scruno for rebounding; that is, whenever Danny jostles himself into position at Muggs's side, Glimpy immediately seeks out Scruno and assuages his frustration by rubbing his back or caressing his face. In *Spooks Run Wild*, when he sees that Muggs and Danny have gone off to explore the haunted house without him, Glimpy insists on holding Scruno's hand, claiming that he is frightened. In *Let's Get Tough*, when he sees Muggs and Danny together in their standard hand-on-chest position, Glimpy quips, "We're having a party. Everybody has to bring something worthless. I'm bringing Scruno." Then he hugs him affectionately. In *'Neath the Brooklyn Bridge*, they dance a jitterbug, dipping and swaying energetically with no hint that they are performing a spoof. Ostensibly they are entertaining a girl visiting the clubhouse, but it never occurs to them to invite her to participate. As the dance ends, Glimpy tries a flying leap into Scruno's arms, but Muggs, who has just entered, catches him instead, thus nicely underscoring Scruno's role as a substitute.

Kid Dynamite (February 1943) is the last East Side movie in which Muggs and Danny's relationship is pivotal; perhaps their off-screen affection was becoming uncomfortably noticeable, or perhaps they were winding down the character in preparation for Danny's entry into the service later that year. In the first scene, Muggs announces that he's going to see Danny with, "I've got a date." Glimpy asks, "Can I come?" just as Danny did when Muggs had a date with a girl. Muggs refuses. Their bond is exclusive.

The characters are now young adults, both over eighteen, so heterosexual practice would seem licit. But when Muggs discovers that Danny has been dating his sister, Ivy (Pamela Blake), he fumes with jealousy. He discovers that they plan to compete in an amateur jitterbug contest, so he decides to compete, too. Not that he is interested in dancing, or in girls:

> Ivy: I can't believe it! Muggs is with a girl!
> Glimpy: I didn't know you went in for dancing!
> Muggs: Sure. I'm ambidextrous.

Certainly Muggs "means" that he can function in either the male environment of the gang or the female environment of the dance floor, but in the context of their surprise, the malapropism strays very close to meaning *bisexual*, that he likes girls as well as boys. At the contest, Muggs dances in an oddly disengaged fashion, gazing goofily at the ceiling but never at his partner (his real-life wife, Kay Marvis), being dipped and tossed over her back like the female partner in a jitterbug. When Danny wins the $50 prize, Muggs strong-arms it away from him. Now Ivy is upset because Danny never stands up to Muggs; he is not an equal partner in a homoromance, but a gangster's gunsel, a subordinate in a relationship built upon the threat of violence.

Soon Ivy is forgotten, but there is a new threat to their relationship: Danny has joined the army. Muggs reacts with inarticulate rage, as if Danny is leaving him on purpose. After completing boot camp, Danny comes home to await his assignment, and the rest of the gang is delighted to see him, but Muggs quips: "I wanna stop this gang before they start kissing him." To maintain his dominance in the relationship, he orders Danny to help them steal tires. When Danny refuses, Muggs insists that they fight. But Danny is a better fighter and "licks" him.

Muggs returns to his flat and sobs into a pillow. Danny is now an adult, tough and strong, making his own life decisions, and their relationship must end. The homoromantic Arcadia endured for awhile in this East Side far removed from the life experience of small-town Anglo-white audiences. However, even here, only two boys or a boy and a man can love each other; two men together can never hope for anything but friendship. Muggs decides to enlist too, but he joins the navy, not the army. He and Danny are not boys' book heroes who pursue military careers as a couple. They are separating for good.

Bobby Jordan appeared in two more East Side Kids movies as an ordinary member of the gang, never hinting that Danny and Muggs once shared a special intimacy. Then he moved on to other projects. He has a poignant cameo in *Bowery Champs* (1944): Home on leave, he searches for Muggs, and Muggs searches for him. But they never find each other again.

After the war, Bobby Jordan returned to the series, exchanging his sailor suit for chinos and a black leather jacket. One wonders what he learned overseas: A returning GI would wear a flight jacket, but Bobby wears a motorcycle jacket without a motorcycle, an early emblem of the postwar gay subculture, not popular among heterosexual urban youth until Marlon Brando started wearing one eight years later.[24] But his early intimacy with Leo Gorcey is gone; he is an anonymous gang member, not even allowed to jostle for position with Huntz Hall. He hung on through 1947, then left the series for good. Afterward he had sporadic film and television roles, but more often he survived on odd jobs: He worked as a bartender, a door-to-door salesman, and an oil driller. He was married for eleven years, had a child, and divorced in 1957. Later he lived with a male friend, but the nature of the relationship remains unknown. He died on September 10, 1965, only forty-two years old.

AFTER BOBBY

With both Bobby Jordan and Sunshine Sammy Morrison gone, Huntz Hall's Glimpy has nothing to stop him from the favored position at Muggs's side.[25] Yet the two display little emotional intensity or intimacy, and no exclusivity. Instead, Muggs is constantly introducing new boys into the gang, as if hoping to fill the gap that Danny left. The extremely athletic David Durand, star of Columbia's humorous "Glove Slingers" shorts, played in back-of-the-gang limbo twice and then suddenly became Muggs's sidekick in *Follow the Leader;* then he was drafted and left the series. In *Block Busters,* Muggs takes an interest in a young, fey French refugee and teaches him to "be an American," slurp sodas, and play baseball. But the boy never appears again.

In *Million Dollar Kid,* Muggs and the gang set out to reform Roy Cortland (Johnny Duncan), son of their wealthy benefactor. Roy is a sissy-boy who has no use for his home gym (he's busy cutting out paper dolls, Glimpy suggests), yet he is so hungry for male companionship that he hangs out in Fink's Pool Hall with "geraniums" (criminals) who talk him into participating in a strong-arm robbery. Muggs doesn't try to modify Roy's softness and passivity. Instead, he demonstrates that he is tougher than the criminals, and therefore a more worthy object of adoration, by trouncing the boy at boxing. Then he offers Roy manly hand-on-shoulder compassion and a place in the gang. In the last scene, Roy has become a rather gender-transgressive "club secretary," happily typing while Muggs dictates.

Leo Gorcey and Johnny Duncan enjoyed a great deal of on-screen chemistry, but Duncan was already committed to playing juvenile delinquents elsewhere (*Teen-Age, Delinquent Daughters, Youth Aflame*), so he had little time for the East Side Kids. He appeared as an ordinary gang member in *Mr. Muggs Rides Again,* and he repeats the Million Dollar Kid plot in *Come Out Fighting*: He plays the police commissioner's sissy son, drawn away from his geranium-gangster pals into Muggs's arms again through the manly sport of boxing. But by that time, the series was ending. It would be reborn in 1946 as the Bowery Boys, the homo-romantic Arcadia replaced by a paradise of girls.

10

BUDDY, BUCKY, AND ROBIN

Young men who dropped into the drugstore in the spring of 1938 on their way home from *Bulldog Drummond's Peril* could browse among long rows of pulp magazines: *Weird Tales*, with a cover illustration of a woman in a red dress tied to a wheel; *Amazing Stories*, with an unconscious woman in a red dress being carried down a ladder; *Astounding Science Fiction*, with a close-up of Mars from the bridge of a space ship; or *Action Comics* 1, with a square-jawed, muscular man in a red-white-and-blue costume lifting an automobile over his head.[1] If they chose the muscleman over cheesecake or Mars, they could read for the first time of Superman, a benevolent alien who was space-wrecked as a baby, grew up among the primitive Earthlings like Tarzan among the savages, and now has "sworn to devote his existence to helping those in need."[2] Born of high school science-fiction buffs Joe Schuster and Jerry Siegel in 1932, Superman had been making the rounds for six years, unsold, in a comic book marketplace devoted mostly to reprints of newspaper comic strips, and the publishers still didn't realize that the Man of Steel was about to revolutionize the industry. That first issue of *Action Comics* also featured stories about reporter Scoop Scanlon and boxer Sticky-Mitt Simpson, and Superman did not appear on the cover again until issue 7. But even early in the series he seemed destined for greatness, with a little help from the Siegel and Schuster spin doctors. A display ad in issue 2 catches the readers' eyes with a shirtless, flexing Superman and asks that they petition their hometown newspapers to join the thousands of newspapers around the world that already carried the

Superman comic strip. However, there was no *Superman* comic strip at that time.

In spite of the flippery, Superman was quick to "take off." A daily comic strip did begin in 1939, a radio series in 1940, theatrical cartoons in 1941. *Action Comics* sold 500,000 or more copies every month, when other popular titles might sell 200,000, and the *Superman* title introduced in 1939 sold over 1,300,000, one for every two households in the United States.[3] Live action exploits took a little longer: The first movie serial did not appear for ten years, and the first feature film for forty years (Christopher Reeve's 1978 tour de force). But even without film images, the Man of Steel became a national icon instantly. On February 27, 1940, less than two years after *Action Comics* 1, *Look* magazine published a special comic section, "How Superman Would End the War" (he would transport Hitler and Stalin to a session of the League of Nations). Frankie Darro was compared to Superman without any explanation in *The Gang's All Here* (1941), and a Bugs Bunny parody, *Super-Rabbit*, appeared in 1943.

By Pearl Harbor, the sky was swarming with costumed superheroes. Like Superman, they were the creations of teenagers and young men: Jack Kirby first penned *Captain America* at the age of twenty-four, Bob Kane *Batman* at twenty-three, Carl Burgos *The Human Torch* at nineteen.[4] Children certainly read comics, but a surprisingly number of readers were teenagers and young men (not so many young women). A quarter of all magazines shipped to troops overseas were comic books.[5] For the next seven years, Superman would compete with Andy Hardy, Batman with Henry Aldrich, for the minds and hearts of high schoolers struggling toward adulthood.

Though they acquired their super powers in different ways, by being born on other planets or chosen by Immortals, volunteering for super-secret scientific experiments or accidentally getting zapped with radiation, all superheroes wore skintight muscle-bulging costumes, and they were all staunchly patriotic, fighting Nazi and Japanese monsters much more frequently than gangsters and mad scientists. They rarely worked alone; a few had adult sidekicks, and a few were partnered with preteens, but most shared their lives with teenage Adventure Boys.[6]

SUPERHERO AND SIDEKICK

In an April 1940 episode of the radio *Adventures of Superman*, the Man of Steel helped a young boy named Jimmy Olsen protect his mother's shop from racketeers. Sensing audience identification, the producers soon gave Jimmy a part-time job at the *Daily Planet* so he could follow leads on his own, snoop around abandoned warehouses, get into trouble, and require lots of nick-of-time rescues. But he was a Boy Next Door rather than an Adventure Boy. According to cocreator Allen Ducovny, he was "a typical radio teenager, cut from the same cloth as Henry Aldrich, Andy Hardy, and Archie Andrews," and he was voiced by Jackie Kelk, Henry's screech-voiced best buddy on the radio and TV versions of *The Aldrich Family*.[7]

Jimmy Olsen arrived in the *Superman* comics in November 1941, somewhat older, perhaps seventeen. He was a redhead, like the cliché sidekicks in the serial novels, and his v-shaped torso suggested muscleman potential.[8] Yet he was still portrayed as a Henry Aldrich, a tagalong annoyance rather than a valued partner. He never learned Superman's true identity, never shared the crime-fighting missions except incidentally, never appeared on any comic book covers. Not until 1954 did he receive a secret signal-watch and the designation "boy pal."

The same month that Jimmy Olsen made his first radio appearance, the Bat-man, who had been brooding morosely over Gotham City for about a year, introduced readers to his new sidekick, Robin the Boy Wonder (*Detective Comics* 38, April 1940). As Don Markstein comments, "[I]t was like flipping a light switch."[9] The juxtaposition of innocence and experience, agility and strength, exuberance and solemnity, seized readers' imaginations, and within a few years nearly every superhero in the business had a teenager at his side: The Eagle teamed up with Buddy, Uncle Sam with another Buddy, the Human Torch with Toro, the Wasp with Wasplet, the Shield with Dusty, Captain America with Bucky, the Defender with Rusty, the Green Arrow with Speedy, the American Eagle with Eaglet.[10]

The teenage sidekick may have originated in the Boys Next Door of radio sitcoms, but he was definitely an Adventure Boy, courageous and resourceful, with a physique as absurdly muscular as that of the superhero himself. For the men in the service and the high schoolers who would soon join them, the superheroes and teen sidekicks became beefcake alternatives to the pinup girls featured in *Male Call* and *Jungle Comics*. Robin the Boy Wonder was originally drawn as short, skinny, and barely pubescent, but by the time he celebrated his fourteenth birthday in *Batman* 10 (April–May 1942), he had the body of a very athletic young adult, displayed in a costume considerably more revealing than its inspiration in *The Adventures of Robin Hood* (1938): a red vest tight enough to highlight "ripped" pecs and abs, green sleeves open at impressive biceps, and extremely short green trunks. His legs were bare, to facilitate his high-kicking fighting style.[11] The Human Torch's Toro was a black-haired teenage bodybuilder, naked except for another pair of extremely short green trunks. The Eaglet's sidekick Buddy wore a white muscle shirt and extremely short blue trunks.

Superheroes and sidekicks were never biological father and son, nor were they adopted father and son.[12] Even more distant kinship was rare. They met as strangers: Either the superhero was attracted to the teen's spunk, ingenuity, and athletic prowess, or else the teen importuned his way into the superhero's life. Magno the Mystery Man simply took an interest in neighborhood kid Davey. After Batman helped Dick Grayson capture his parents' murderers, he suggested that the boy return to his job as a circus acrobat, but Dick pleaded: "[T]ake me with you." Delivery boy Tim Roland just happened to be at the drugstore when Bob Benton was transformed into the Black Terror, and he talked his way into sidekick status.[13]

The Adventure Boy sidekicks had no interest in girls, of course, but it is curious that the adult superheroes had no interest in women. Sometimes their foppish alter egos had girlfriends to escort to the opera or discuss fripperies with, but once they donned their skintight muscle-bulging costumes, they sought out the wild freedom of men. More often, however, they preferred men in both public and private life, actively rejecting heterosexual involvement even as a normative façade. When Captain America's alter ego, Steve, is cast in a play and finds that he must do a love scene, he stammers and sweats: "Huh? Love scene? Who, me?" Sidekick Bucky giggles from offstage, aware that Steve is not the girl-kissing kind.[14]

We might explain the lack of heterosexual interest in the adult super-heroes as a convention reflecting the "innocence" of the preteen readers of the 1940s era, except that many readers were teenagers and young adults, and the superheroes who were partnered with men or went solo usually had girlfriends (e.g., *Dollman*) or avidly romanced women (*The Spirit*) or had origin stories involving the woman they loved (*Hawk-man*). The superhero-teenager bond simply precluded heterosexual in-terest. It is not only that the superheroes disdained women: They were shown with their sidekicks in precisely the same situations in which other superheroes and their pulp predecessors were shown with girl-friends. They shared domestic space, but not as father and son or legal guardian and ward: The superhero rarely handed out allowances or pun-ishments, or chided the sidekick for coming home after curfew. Instead, they dined together, lounged around the parlor, chatted in bedrooms, as if they never wanted or needed anyone else. They went out on "dates," to restaurants, to movies, to the theater; they took vacations together. They were adult-teen homoromantic partners, like Terry Lee and Pat Ryan, except that their intimacy and exclusivity exceeded anything in the newspaper comics.

When not actually fighting crime, the superhero kept his hand firmly attached to the shoulder or back of his sidekick, a gesture that signifies both protection and sensual engagement. The Eagle flew with Buddy riding piggyback, a curious spectacle since they wore identi-cal costumes, blue shirts and shorts with red-and-white striped capes. The American Eagle carried Eaglet in his arms. Captain America and Magno walked with their arms around their sidekicks' waists. A cri-sis averted meant a full-body hug. A story's conclusion meant an arm across the shoulders and a whispered "Let's go home."

Pulp magazine covers often featured a woman drawn in the style collectors called GGA or Good Girl Art (because of her breasts, not because she was a "good girl"), tied to something and about to be mur-dered or violated by a drooling villain while the hero rushes to the res-cue. But in superhero comics, the teenage sidekick was either tied next to the GGA woman, or else tied up all alone, and while GBA (Good Boy Art) is not an official collectors' designation, the sidekick's muscles were displayed quite as prominently as GGA girls' breasts. Three of the first ten covers of *Detective Comics* after the introduction of Robin, and nine of the first thirty, feature a surprisingly fit Boy Wonder tied up and about to stabbed, shot, drowned, or otherwise violated while Batman rushes to the rescue. Captain America rescues Bucky in eight of the first ten covers of his comic book, and fully half of the first thirty. Bucky is often (but not always) drawn in GBA form, and his green-skinned, fairy-tale ogre captors have devised extremely creative means of execution: He is strapped to an operating table next to a monster while a leering Nazi doctor prepares an injection; mummified and threatened with an Iron Maiden; threatened with hot coals while hanging from his wrists; in a cemetery, about to be buried alive; thrown overboard with a five-hundred-pound weight around his neck; strapped to a table while a bed of spikes lowers onto him.[15]

As the war progressed, many other superhero comics followed suit. The magazine racks of every drugstore were overflowing with images of superheroes rushing to the rescue of bound-and-threatened GBA sidekicks. The Human Torch's sidekick Toro, nearly naked, muscles straining, chest heaving, is tied spread-eagle in the path of a tank, tied to the barrel of a cannon, or lowered into a buzz-saw machine. Roy the Super Boy, his massive chest jutting out of his red-and-white striped shirt, is tied to a rocket about to be launched into space or is about to be doused with nitroglycerin and ignited. Dusty the Boy Detective, in a skintight blue costume, is about to be stabbed or tied to a runaway jeep. The Black Terror starts out rescuing GGA girls along with sidekick Tim, but soon Tim is tied up alone, muscles straining in GBA form, about to be run over by a jeep, eviscerated by a buzz saw, executed by a Nazi firing squad, or used for archery practice by a weird cult. For a change of pace, it is superhero Mr. Scarlett rather than sidekick Pinky who is strapped to a makeshift electric chair.[16]

Comic books and pulps were not alone in featuring attractive people tied to things and about to be violated in sexually symbolic ways. Such scenes were common everywhere—in movies, radio plays, boys' books, on Broadway. They were used to create suspense and clarify the emotional investment of rescuer and rescued, who finally realize how much they care for each other. The rescued generally reacts to the narrow escape by melting into the rescuer's arms or else stammering, "If it wasn't for you, I . . . I'd be. . . ." But superhero comics usually presented GBA instead of GGA bondage threats, identifying the teen sidekick as an alternative to the spunky girl reporter as an object of erotic fulfillment. The superhero and sidekick lingered in a homoromantic Arcadia for several years longer than the Boys Next Door and Lost Boys; not until after the war would Robin, Buddy, and Bucky either surrender to girl-craziness or retire.

WORLDS OF IF

Depression-era pulps often included ray gun–wielding spacemen among their stables of barbarians, detectives, cowboys, and soldiers, but science fiction as a distinct genre arguably began in the spring of 1938, when John Campbell took over the editorship of *Astounding Stories* and changed the title and focus to *Astounding Science Fiction*.[17] Dozens of pulps specializing in science fiction soon appeared, five in 1939 alone (*Dynamic Science Stories, Fantastic Adventures, Future Science Fiction, Planet Stories,* and *Unknown*), but *Astounding* was the most popular, with a circulation of 150,000, and the most influential, with a group of regular contributors—Isaac Asimov, Robert Heinlein, L. Sprague de Camp—who defined the field for generations. It is still being published under the name *Analog Science Fiction & Fact*.

Science fiction readers were mostly teenagers and young men, and the authors were even younger than comic book artists: Jack Williamson was publishing professionally at age twenty, James Blish at nineteen, Isaac Asimov at eighteen, and C. M. Kornbluth at a seasoned sixteen. They considered themselves a new breed, finding wonder not in the moldy, labyrinthine cities of Atlantis and Hyperborea, or jungles just a few weeks away by boat, but in the distant future or in the vastness of space. Their heroes were rarely literal teenagers—there were no frame stories with homework assignments or the "big game," no Uncle Jims to chaperone—but they were nevertheless Adventure Boys, described as youngsters and kids, under adult supervision or guardianship as they explored new worlds free from the social and technological constrictions of adulthood.[18]

When the stories starred adults, they usually concluded with a marriage proposal, like Chapter Thirteen of a movie serial. In Jack Williamson's "The Legion of Time" (1938), a college boy is drawn into adventure by "a girl . . . beautiful!" who materializes in his dorm room; later they marry. In his "Darker than You Think" (1940), a reporter is drawn into adventure by a girl with "a million dollars worth of flamered hair"; again, they marry. Shorter stories made do with frequent references to heterosexual desire: Theodore Sturgeon's "It" (1940) is set on a bucolic modern-day farm, where a man lets his unrequited love for his brother's wife "eat at him quiet and unmentioned," even though it is irrelevant to the plot about fighting off an animated corpse.[19] But when the stories starred Adventure Boys, heteroromance was absent. The heat of passion came from men and "youngsters" gleaming at each other.

Isaac Asimov's first published story, "Marooned off Vesta" (1939), presents a survival dilemma: A spaceship is destroyed by meteors, leaving three survivors in an orbit around Vesta (a moon of Jupiter), with their engine and communications equipment gone and only three days' worth of oxygen. Crewman Mike O'Shea, an Irish stereotype, just wants to die drunk. One would expect Mark Brandon, a teenager like the author, to whiz-kid a rescue plan, but he veers between morose inertia and hysterics, and instead the other surviving passenger, "adult" Warren Moore, brainstorms a way to propel them to safety on the moon's inhabited surface. He also takes an interest in Brandon, chumming with him, comforting him, but more, framing the boy as the reason they must survive. As Moore crawls slowly along the outside hull of the spaceship, exhausted and almost in despair, he comes to a porthole:

> Behind it was Brandon. A deep breath and he felt better, his mind cleared. . . . Brandon slept on the couch. His face was worn and lined but a smile passed over it now and then. Moore raised his fist to knock. He felt the urgent desire to talk with someone, if only by sign language; yet at the last instant he refrained. Perhaps the kid was dreaming of home. He was young and sensitive and had suffered much. Let him sleep.[20]

The vision of Brandon sleeping, a powerful symbol of innocence and trust, compels Moore to finish the rescue. Twenty years later, in

"Anniversary" (1959), Asimov imagines that Moore has been hosting an annual reunion for the survivors. O'Shea usually bows out, but Brandon comes religiously. Asimov mentions Mrs. Moore in the very first sentence (he packs her off to spend the night at her mother's), but "the kid," now middle aged, mentions neither a Mrs. Brandon nor any ladies' man conquests.[21] Even after twenty years, the adolescent is free from heterosexual desire, with the accompanying openness to homoerotic potential (perhaps for that reason, Mrs. Moore is asked to stay away *all night*).

Foundation

During the war, science fiction magazines continued to juxtapose stories about men and women with stories about men and Adventure Boys. Though it is seven thousand years hence in A. E. Van Vogt's "The Weapon Shop" (1942), protagonist Fara Clark lives in a bucolic village not much different from Andy Hardy's Carvel: He has a motor-repair shop, a subservient wife ("she had had a pleasing habit of obedience that had made cohabitation a wonderful thing"), and a surly juvenile-delinquent son who hangs around on street corners. Robert Heinlein's "The Unpleasant Profession of Jonathan Hoag" (1942) has Nick and Nora Charles–type married sleuths discovering a horrible secret about the nature of reality (it's not real) and finding surcease in each other's arms.[22] However, the far-future gay ghetto of Ross Rocklynne's "Backfire" (1943) is inhabited entirely by teenagers (aging stops at eighteen), evidently all male, and all deliriously happy, until a time traveler from the twentieth century threatens to ruin things by accusing them of being "weak, sniveling, snobbish degenerates!" Charles S. Geier's "Environment" (1944) is a lyrical tale of homoromantic freedom as two young men land on a far-off planet to explore a deserted alien city, and find world enough with each other.[23]

In March 1943, *Astounding Science Fiction* published two stories set in the sultry swamps of Venus. "Clash by Night" begins in a tavern where men and women dance together, and gives the protagonist a "free marriage" (i.e., an open marriage) to the beautiful Ilene; there is a lot of pillow talk about how heterosexual romance makes life worthwhile:

"[I]t's something more than love. Separately we're halves. Together we may be a complete whole." "Q.U.R." begins in a tavern occupied exclusively by men and has the protagonist taking an interest in a youngster named Quimby. They set up housekeeping as well: They entertain friends together, and the company man awakens with the "young blond giant" beside him. We are not apprised of their pillow talk. The difference between the two stories is not in setting or year, but in two possible sources of domestic fulfillment for men: Ilene or Quimby, woman or boy.[24]

In May 1942, *Astounding Science Fiction* published "Foundation," twenty-one-year-old Isaac Asimov's account of far-future "psycho-historians" trying to stanch a Galactic Empire's slow but inevitable fall into the Dark Ages. He published five more installments during the war, and three afterward, all collected with introductory materials as *The Foundation Trilogy*.[25] To the modern palate it is deadly dull stuff, with no character development, no technological marvels, no intriguing far-future societies, just innumerable junior politicos with names that sound like anagrams (Sef Sermak, Poly Verisof, Limmar Ponyets) having discussions in boardrooms. Even Asimov, returning to the books after thirty years, complained: "[A]ll three volumes, all the nearly quarter of a million words, consisted of thoughts and of conversations. No action. No physical suspense."[26] But *Foundation* was extremely popular at the time, and it is still lauded as a masterpiece of science fiction. There are no literal teenagers (except for the nyak-hunting fifteen-year-old King Leopold), but there are many structural teenagers, "youngsters," whom the adults approach with a mixture of fear and desire.

In the wartime *Foundation* stories, women simply do not exist. A governor's wife gets half a page, a dowager duchess and a female secretary get a sentence each, and that's it. No doubt some of the absence of women stems from 1940's sexism: Asimov presumes that in the far future, men will run the galaxy and therefore conduct the interminable boardroom discussions, with women present only to take dictation and fetch coffee. But even in their off-hours, the men seek out exclusively male companions. Sef Sermak hosts a clandestine meeting at his house, with no hint of a wife hovering in the background or any wives waiting for his coconspirators back home. Salvor Hardin finishes up his political strategizing with Poly Verisof and says, "Let's get out and make a night of it. I want some relaxation." The next scene does not involve looking for girls or at girls; evidently Verisof will provide Hardin with relaxation enough. Hober Mallow, who rates one of the few physical descriptions in the stories (he is "superbly muscular"), reclines naked while Ankor Jael, lying next to him, places a cigar in his mouth and then one in his own, a surprisingly romantic gesture, surely a reflection of Paul Henreid lighting two cigarettes and passing one to Bette Davis in *Now, Voyager* (1942). The reader is not informed what they were doing prior to the scene, but it is not difficult to imagine something that requires nudity and culminates with a desire to smoke.

TERRY AND THE PIRATES

Though *Terry and the Pirates* once evoked an intense, intimate, and exclusive relationship between adult Pat Ryan and teenage Terry Lee, as the war began Milt Caniff gave Pat a more overt interest in heteroromance. At first Terry tried to "rescue" Pat from women's clutches, or he sat home alone, jealous, while Pat was out on a date, but toward the end of 1940, the seventeen-year-old began grinning at the spectacle of Milt Caniff's trademark shapely, alluring, dangerous women.[27] In the spring of 1941, Terry was eighteen, a young adult, and therefore old enough for his first heterosexual date and his first kiss (not with the same girl).

However, Terry's same-sex interests remain, curiously confused amid the plethora of heterosexualizing. A summer 1941 continuity without Pat, set in a refugee camp in China, immerses him in a gender-bending love quadrangle. Terry is in love with longtime friend and ally Burma, but she insists on treating him like a little brother. He is also interested in Raven, the elderly American woman who runs the camp (drawn inexplicably as a stern, square-jawed man in drag), but she prefers the dashing British pilot Dude Hennick. Meanwhile Dude romances all three, glamour girl, elderly drag queen, *and* Terry, using the same jovial, wisecracking tone. On July 29, 1941, a new shipment of phonograph records arrives from the United States, and Dude asks Terry, "How you fixed for hot licks? Like to rip a rug?" Terry points out that Burma has a sprained knee, so he has no female partner. Dude exclaims, "That's an angle ... but we'll take a chance!" hinting that *he* might be a partner before relenting: "A musical heat treatment will help Burma's leg."

Terry is understandably confused by his attraction to Dude, whom he wants to dislike as competition. So he acts out. He escorts Burma to a party, then has a temper tantrum and storms off when Dude dances with her. He kisses Raven during a blackout and is mortified to find Dude taking credit. But then he ends up bunking down with Dude, listening to his tales of adventure just as he once listened to Pat's, and eventually accepting his attention. When Raven dies during a mission, they console each other with earnest intensity, and the reader expects that Dude will become Terry's permanent partner. But then the "real" Pat returns, and Dude makes a hasty, uncomfortable exit.

The reunion between Terry and Pat is short-lived. Evidently their friendship was too overtly romantic to withstand the compulsory heterosexuality of two adults, so they were separated for weeks of independent adventures, and finally Pat vanished from the strip altogether (although he continued to star in the radio series). In 1942, Terry joined the air force, where he met with wisecracking fighter-pilot Flip Corkin. They fought together in the Pacific theater during the war and stayed together afterward, swashbuckling around Southeast Asia for thirty years before retiring. Though they were permanent partners, their bond lacked the intensity and intimacy of homoromance, and they both fell in love with women, frequently. Only in the 1947 comic book version, with Terry recast as a teenager, could he fall in love with a man again.

BOY

World War II comics featured nearly as many jungle heroes as superheroes—full-muscled, loincloth-clad Tarzans with names like Ka'anga and Lo-Zar, who swooped down on vines to rescue immaculately coiffed, bikini-clad scientists' daughters. Or else immaculately coiffed, bikini-clad jungle ladies with names like Nyoka and Sheena swooped down on vines to rescue hapless male explorers in pith helmets. But none had teenage sidekicks. A minor adult-teen homoromance occurs in a backstory in *Captain America* comics, when "Cave Boy" Tuk (actually an exiled prince of ancient Atlantis) is rescued and carried to safety by the blond, muscular Tanir.[28] But after a few stories and a few more rescues, they part, and the Cave Boy wanders the Paleolithic alone.

Jungle Teens likewise failed to establish peer homoromance. The "Man-Boy" Beebo has only a talking horse for company. Wambi, a South Asian in dhoti and turban (even though he lives in Africa), travels with a menagerie of animal friends. The superbly muscled jungle teen Zudo travels alone.[29] Their stories involved the standard headhunters, leopard cultists, witch doctors, and ivory poachers, sometimes with a rescue of GGA ladies or pith-helmeted milquetoasts, but no one falls into anyone's arms afterward, and at the end of the story the teenager wanders off alone.[30] The psychosexual metaphor of the strong rescuing—and then falling in love with—the weak might work with same-sex pairs in Gotham City, but not in the jungle. The colonial world was too savage, its passions too visible, for a homoromance to masquerade as a sexless friendship.

At the movies, Tarzan practically monopolized the field of Jungle Men, and while preteen Jungle Tots appeared occasionally, Jungle Teens were vanishingly rare.[31] Only one of any significance appeared between 1935 and 1948: Tarzan's son Boy, who became a teenager only by "accident" as his franchise was extended.

When MGM executives wanted to expand the audience of their extremely successful Tarzan series by giving the Ape Man and his Mate (Johnny Weissmuller, Maureen O'Sullivan) a child, they faced a quandary: Since the couple was not married, Jane could hardly give birth to Korak.[32] Instead, *Tarzan Finds a Son!* (1939) envisions an airplane crash in the jungle with a sole survivor, a cooing infant whom Tarzan names Boy. It is an odd name, and evidently a last-minute change—the trailers call him Tarzan Jr. One wonders why Jane did not insist on Tarzan Jr. or John Clayton Jr., particularly if she expected the child to one day survive hazing at Eton. But if Tarzan and Jane are the primal Man and Woman of a sexless heterosexual Eden, then their Boy must be the primal Boy, the archetype of all Boys everywhere.

The primal Boy was cast with seven-year-old Johnny Sheffield, son of character actor Reginald Sheffield and already a Broadway veteran, handpicked by Johnny Weissmuller from the hundreds of hopefuls roused by a cattle call in the *Hollywood Reporter*. Perhaps Weissmuller was shopping for a surrogate son of his own: At the time he was childless. On September 23, 1940, his third wife, Beryl Scott, gave birth to Johnny Weissmuller Jr., but the couple soon separated, and between 1943 and 1953 the elder Weissmuller was forbidden by court injunction from seeing or contacting his son.[33] A cursory perusal of Hollywood gossip magazines of the period reveals the intensity of Weissmuller's custodial investment in his Boy. He taught Johnny to swim and wrestle, and often took him places off camera. They were a common sight at premieres and Hollywood hotspots.

Johnny Sheffield played Boy in eight pictures,[34] a rather limited repertoire for the 1940s; yet he became so famous that his presence in a Cisco Kid Western or a boy-dog tearjerker proved too distracting to audiences, and roles outside the jungle quickly dried up—he was only and always the primal Boy. As he entered adolescence, the camera fell in love with him, giving him the lion's share of close-ups and some full-body shots that seem embarrassingly intimate today.[35] Like his movie dad, he wore only a skimpy loincloth, so viewers could watch his physical development year by year more intimately than the real children of their own neighborhood. Watching a boy negotiate adolescence must have been an odd experience for viewers used to seeing movie teenagers played by full-grown adults, but Johnny was no ordinary Boy. Like his pulp predecessor Korak, he had the body of an adult when he was barely pubescent. In *Tarzan and the Amazons* (filmed September-October 1944), Johnny at thirteen could easily pass for a high school athlete. In *Tarzan and the Leopard Woman* (filmed July-September 1945), he is nearly fifteen, but he already sports the thick, heavy chest, flat belly, and deepened voice of young adulthood. In *Tarzan and the Huntress* (filmed September-November 1946), he is nearly sixteen years old and nearly six feet tall, with a chiseled torso that makes forty-two-year-old Weissmuller look flabby and out of shape, a middle-aged businessman ludicrously enacting a Tarzan fantasy. The Boy has surpassed the Man, and Johnny Sheffield must retire from the series.

Although the teenage Boy is handsome enough to compel most of his classmates at Randini High School to write his name amid hearts in their notebooks or scramble to ask him to the Spring Fling, he is paradoxically forbidden contact beyond the Escarpment (the Tarzan family's treetop playland). As a child, he often had friends: In *Tarzan's Secret Treasure* (1941), the ten-year-old shares his adventure with native boy Tumba (Cordell Hickman), who stands next to the family at fade-out as if he has every intention of joining the cast. But as a teenager, Boy is entirely alone. He has few opportunities for jitterbugging with girls: The women he encounters are always older and usually evil; indeed, a half-hour walk in any direction seems to lead to lost civilizations full of evil women, marking as sinister and threatening the girl-craziness that would be merely silly for teenagers back in New York.

Boy's chances of homoromance are equally limited. In *Tarzan and the Leopard Woman*, a boy named Kimba (sixteen-year-old Tommy Cook) appears one day at the Escarpment, claiming that he got lost in the jungle. The Tarzan family takes him in, but Boy is suspicious of his motives and jealous of Jane's overenthusiastic mothering. It turns out that Kimba belongs to an evil leopard cult and plans to prove his manhood by murdering them all. Many jungle-story scripts would have Boy befriend and ultimately rehabilitate the troubled teen, but not here: The two boys never express any sentiment but seething contempt, and the unrepentant Kimba is shot to death while trying to carve out a man's heart.

More often, Boy's homoromantic potential is not stymied by the innate evil of everyone who tromps through the jungle, but by Daddy Tarzan himself. In *Tarzan and the Amazons*, Boy drops a broad hint: "Tarzan, weren't you lonely in the jungle all by yourself, before Jane came?"[36] The Jungle Man denies that he was ever lonely—after all, he had many animal friends, and Cheetah should be company enough for anyone! Then a safari arrives full of male scientists of Jane's acquaintance, and Boy can barely contain his excitement; he wiggles up to one, then another, flirting his way into hand-on-shoulder big-brothering, gifts of binoculars and a magnifying glass, and an invitation to "come around anytime." Tarzan passive-aggressively suggests that Boy would be better off hunting with him instead of pestering the strangers. "They're not strangers!" Boy cries, overreacting with teen angst. "They're Jane's friends, and mine. . . . I don't want to go hunting with you! I won't go hunting with you ever again!"

Tarzan is equally passive-aggressive about denying Boy peer companions. In *Tarzan and the Huntress*, the Tarzan family visits the kingdom of Teronga, where Boy befriends the teenage Prince Suli. It is would be difficult to cast a more perfect buddy: The prince is played by Maurice Tauzin, nine days older than Johnny Sheffield and equally athletic (he would win a marathon in 2001, at the age of seventy). However, when Boy asks to stay for a longer visit, Tarzan says no. Later they find Prince Suli in the jungle, left to die by his evil usurper-uncle. Surely the long and dangerous trek back to Teronga would provide many opportunities for buddy-bonding, but Tarzan has other ideas: "Boy, go home, tell Jane!" he barks. "*We* go to Teronga!" Boy protests, but Tarzan stubbornly leads the prince away. They see each other again only once, at the final fade-out: Boy waves forlornly as the reinstated prince is carried away by his joyful subjects.

What is the significance of these denials? Of course the movies are about Tarzan, so he must wrestle all of the crocodiles, carry all of the rescued princesses to safety, and supervise all of the shifts from absolutism to democracy in lost-civilization governments, but surely allowing Boy some friends would not threaten his status as Busybody of the Jungle. Yet perhaps Tarzan is threatened after all. As Boy hardens into adolescence, his role becomes paradoxically soft and passive—his muscles become purely decorative, to be displayed for their beauty just as Jane's curves, and as useless for fending off crocodiles. Indeed, Boy usually takes Jane's place as the object of Tarzan's chest-pounding heroics. The three pre-Boy movies all end with Jane in a GGA-flimsy costume, tied and threatened, and Tarzan swooping down on a vine to carry her to safety. Jane originally died at the end of *Tarzan Finds a Son!*, leaving Tarzan alone in the jungle with his Boy. Fan uproar granted her a reprieve, but still she spends the latter part of her jungle career either absent, "helping the troops," or else housebound, leaving the Escarpment only long enough for shopping trips to Randini, while Tarzan and Boy reinvent themselves as superhero and teenage sidekick. Jane never becomes the sole object of rescue again: She is captured along with Boy in two of the seven movies after *Tarzan Finds a Son!*, and in four, Boy is captured alone, tied to something, muscles straining in GBA fashion, threatened with violation or murder until Tarzan swoops down to the rescue.[37]

During Boy's adolescence, he and Tarzan are constant companions, leaving little time for Jane, who confesses without complaint, "They're used to doing everything together. Why, they often leave me alone for days!" They leap into the lagoon together, enacting the quintessential moment of jungle romance. They are even shown sleeping together, curled up on the same mat, Boy's head pillowed by Tarzan's bicep (Jane's sleeping arrangements are left unseen). If the homoromantic Arcadia is a displaced fantasy of adulthood, then the viewer must desire the sight of the primal Man and Boy diving into the lagoon together as eternally as the primal Man and Woman. Tarzan must contain his paradise against threats to Boy as well as to Jane, and he must guard as jealously against any other love.

Yet Tarzan and Boy share no passion or intimacy that cannot be explained as the love of an adopted father and son, and their bond is not exclusive; Jane waits at home for Tarzan's return, while Boy actively (though fruitlessly) seeks out boys and men beyond the Escarpment. Tarzan's refusal to allow Boy to see or touch others might easily be rooted in the fretting of an overprotective parent rather than the jealousy of a threatened lover. Theirs is merely a reflection of homoromance, an anodyne in the last days of the war, when love between boys or boys and men was increasingly doomed, despairing, or explained away.

THE ELEPHANT BOY

An orphan, son of a mahout, Sabu Dastigir was riding a real elephant around Mysore when he was signed up to star in *Elephant Boy* (1937), an adaptation of the Kipling tale "Toomai of the Jungle." Wearing only a dhoti and turban, his surname eliminated to enhance his wildness, the twelve-year-old Sabu caused a sensation. He became the darling of British colonial do-gooders. He was transplanted to England as a ward of the state and enrolled in school, but he found little time to study when he was receiving almost as much publicity as Johnny Weissmuller, more than any other teenage actor of the era except Mickey Rooney.

Contemporary critics loved Sabu, but they seemed more interested in his body than his talent. "He arrests attention and catches the eye as a star should," notes *Screen Thrills Illustrated*.[38] In 1938, Bosley Crowther lunched with him in the private dining room atop Rockefeller Center and was entranced by his face, "frankly boyish and charming, with white teeth gleaming against brown skin." He seemed somewhat disappointed that Sabu wore a Western-style shirt and pants instead of a loincloth.[39] In 1940, Theodore Strauss interviewed Sabu to determine the toll that two years in the "civilized world" had taken on the "naïve Indian rustic." Though he was surprised that the Elephant Boy did not commonly entertain reporters half-naked, he still found the sixteen-year-old "a handsome and princely fellow ... elegantly attired in a suit with hand-stitched lapels and just the right sash at the waist, his dark brown features richly set off by the cerise turban tightly wrapped around his head." After describing Sabu's costume with the airy precision of a fashion columnist, Strauss goes on paradoxically to adulate the boy's ultramasculine interests in jiujitsu, bowling, swimming, and airplanes.[40]

After a starring role in the procolonial *Drum* (1938), as an Indian prince eager to assist the invading British, Sabu was subject to a bidding war. RKO wanted him for *Gunga Din*, but negotiations fell through when director Alexander Korda insisted on Ginger Rogers in exchange, a girl for a boy.[41] Instead, he was cast in *The Thief of Bagdad* (1940). Though set in the mythical past, the "Arabian fantasy in technicolor" still manages to reify the cultural dynamics of the modern-day British Empire, with a prince who is somehow whiter and more "civilized" than his subjects, and dedicated to replacing his own absolutism with a constitutional democracy.[42]

In the 1924 silent version, Douglas Fairbanks plays a thief who wins the heart of a princess, but Sabu would not win any princesses or express any on-screen heterosexual interest, not until he became a man, so thief and romantic lead were split into separate characters. As the movie begins, Abu (sixteen-year-old Sabu), a spunky, enterprising homeless teenager, steals some food, and while escaping onto a rooftop from a flurry of angry shopkeepers, he spies Prince Ahmad (John Justin) in the street below. He gasps in awe, falling in love at first sight. Shortly thereafter, Abu is captured and thrown into a dungeon, where he encounters

the prince again, his throne usurped by a villainous uncle. The two escape together, steal a boat, and plan to sail downstream from Bagdad to
the ocean, where they might find a safe haven in the wilderness. Then
the prince spies a princess from another kingdom (June Duprez) and
gasps in awe, falling in love at first sight himself. He insists that they
stay in Bagdad. The rest of the movie involves the prince ignoring, en-
dangering, or simply abandoning Abu to make time with the princess,
while Abu follows him slavishly, like a pet dog (and he is actually transformed into a dog at one point). In the throes of unrequited love, Abu
often looks hurt but never complains.

There were Asians in Hollywood—not many, usually relegated
to roles as servants and villains.[43] They were simultaneously objects
of dread and confusion and objects of desire, but Sabu brings desire
alone.[44] Shipwrecked, he lies on his stomach on the beach. He slowly
turns over, a smooth arm outstretched, his lips parted as if in a dream.
The situation does not seem dire at all; he is a model, a pinup boy
in an exotic locale. Sabu complained that he was often mistaken for
a girl in real life because of his long hair and delicate features, but the
camera emphasizes his maleness by often panning out to linger on his
physique.[45] His torso, v-shaped, barrel chested, bronze skinned, sculpted
but softening slightly at the stomach, is often displayed in a bright light
against a black backdrop so every muscle will stand out. He is the Herculean Sorak of the boys' books, the superbly muscled Og Son of Fire,
the adolescent Tarzan.[46] The only problem is, he has no one to desire
him; his love for the prince is unrequited. After he regains his throne
and marries the princess, the prince announces that he is sending Abu
off to school. After he is educated, he will be named vizier of the new
constitutional monarchy. In other words, the prince offers Abu a job.
It is hardly a profession of undying love, but for the colonial subject, it
must suffice.

After starring in a loose adaptation of Kipling's *Jungle Book* (1942),
in which Mowgli befriends both a native girl and a British officer but
falls in love with neither, the eighteen-year-old Sabu moved to Hollywood and signed on with Universal. During the next two years, he
starred as a dhoti-clad colonial Adventure Boy in three Technicolor romances, all set in distant lands where no one had ever heard of Hitler

or Hirohito, with garishly improbable sets, scenery-chomping dialogue, and attractive men and women showing as much skin as the censors would allow.[47] Sabu was in rather an awkward position: Although he (or rather, his body) was the top-billing star of each picture, he was irrelevant to the plotlines, about swarthy adventurer Jon Hall wooing the cool, mysterious Maria Montez. Indeed, after Sabu went off to fight in the war, Hall and Montez kept right on making movies, wooing each other without an Adventure Boy sidekick.[48]

Though heterosexual desire is ubiquitous in his Arabian or South Pacific world, the teenage Sabu expresses no heterosexual interest of his own. In *Arabian Nights*, Ali (Sabu) enters a harem to deliver a message to Sheherazade (Maria Montez), and the sex-starved harem girls engulf him, groping and fondling, intent upon a sexual assault. He screams, "Please stop! Stop it!" with shrieks of terror. They back off, bewildered, as if no man or boy had ever resisted their advances before. The harem guards approach, and Ali must hide. One expects him to don harem-girl drag, a common enough strategy and in fact one used later in the film when the troupe members want to facilitate an escape. But Ali does not. Instead, he swims underwater to the other side of the pool, displaying his muscled backside and buttocks, beefcake in a scene that usually displaces the homoerotic gaze into the burlesque of drag.

Arabian Nights begins with a "love at first sight" moment: During a human-pyramid act, acrobat Ali peers through his own legs (in perhaps the only simultaneous butt, crotch, and face shot in the movies) to gaze upon Caliph Haroun al-Rashid (Jon Hall). In *White Savage* and *Cobra Woman*, the characters are friends from the start. Regardless, the Adventure Boy courts the adult much more aggressively than usual in adult-teen homoromance—hugging him, grabbing him, taking his arm, pressing against his chest in fear or not, unbuttoning his shirt, mussing his hair, offering him flowers, chasing other suitors away with a barking, "Get back, this is [*my*] friend!" Hall's characters respond with amusement and often affection, but not with longing: His heart belongs to Maria Montez.

In the many climactic rescues of the series, Sabu is captured only once, and once he and Hall are captured together, but otherwise Hall is tied, passive, struggling, about to be drowned or fed to cobras, and the teenager comes swinging down on a rope or galloping up on white horse to save him. Structural role reversals were not uncommon in adult-teen homoromances; they minimized the power differential between the partners and thereby distinguished them from the custodial relationships of legal guardians and surrogate fathers. However, in the archetypal moment when a slavering villain threatens torture or murder, the strong nearly always rescues the weak, the man rescues the boy. Sabu's rescues are especially problematic because he is a colonial subject: The White Man's Burden, the European and American custodial imperative, was intimately connected with erotic myth, the colonizer characterized as a seducer and the colonial as seduced, the beautiful harem girl or handsome rent boy.[49] Yet the colonizer's most important myth is that he is desirable, eagerly welcomed by the colonial subject, as Sabu himself welcomed the British invaders in *Drum*, and what better way to demonstrate desirability than to have the subject risk his life for the sake of the colonizer?

Sabu's aggressiveness extends to heteroromance: He practically shoves Hall's characters into the arms of Maria Montez. Then he squeezes between them during their fade-out clench, becoming the "son" in their heteronormative union as if he were seeking a surrogate father all along. It seems absurd to emphasize Sabu's muscular physique, have him approach Jon Hall with blatant and passionate homoerotic desire, and then claim that he is just a little boy, not yet potent, not yet able to experience desire. But such reevaluations were becoming increasingly common during the war, even among Adventure Boys, even in South Pacific fairylands.[50]

11

Unconditional Surrender

On the evening of August 14, 1945, a crowd of 750,000 people gathered in Times Square to await the end of World War II. When the news ticker on the Times building scrolled the words "Official: Truman announces Japanese surrender," they went wild, screaming, cheering, hugging each other, hugging strangers. A young sailor impulsively grabbed the nearest girl, a nursing student named Edith Shain, and dipped and kissed her.[1] Photojournalist Alfred Eisenstaedt happened to snap their public-private moment, and "V-J Day" appeared in the August 27 issue of *Life* magazine. It became one of the most famous photographs in history. It was reprinted in hundreds of books, movies, and television programs, in documentaries and in fiction. It was copied and parodied. A statue entitled "Unconditional Surrender" was erected on the spot where the strangers kissed. The Greatest Generation, and generations to follow, would define the war not so much through the lens of geopolitical change, imperialistic challenges to modernity, authoritarianism, totalitarianism, freedom fighting, or the immeasurable human suffering, but through the lens of heteronormativity. Sixty years later, few non-historians would be able to discuss D-Day, the Battle of the Bulge, the Tripartite Pact, or the Yalta Conference, but almost everyone could envision the boys overseas returning to the girls back home.[2] In a number cut from *Meet Me in St. Louis*, Judy Garland sang:

Songs and kings and many things
Have their day and are gone
But boys and girls like you and me,
We go on and on.[3]

In 1945 and 1946, millions of boys returning from the war were seeking out hometown girls to kiss. By 1950, 72 percent of the men in the United States were married, up from 61 percent in 1940, and the birth rate had doubled, producing a seventy-seven-million-strong Baby Boom that would forever change the way Americans looked at childhood and adolescence, at young adulthood, and, most recently, at old age.[4] But the new husbands and wives did not move into Henry Aldrich small towns. They moved into in cookie-cutter suburbs linked to the city by commuter trains or modern interstate highways. Nor did they have much time to nest. Nearly as soon as rationing ended and the last of the troops returned, it was time to fight again, this time in a Cold War, with opponents more subtle and sinister than the Nazis: Communists, their spies in American grassroots, and, even more perniciously than before, "homosexuals," so easily blackmailed or converted to the cause of evil.

The 1952 Immigration and Nationality Act barred "homosexuals" from U.S. soil because they suffered from "psychopathic personalities," like schizophrenics. But what to do about the ones already here? No one could deny that they existed. Novelists were beginning to write about them (*The City and the Pillar*, *Quatrefoil*), as were poets ("Café: 3 am"; "Howl") and social scientists (*The Homosexual in America*, *Society and the Homosexual*).[5] The popularity of magazines devoted to photographs of muscular men (*Physique Pictorial*, *Body Beautiful*, *Tomorrow's Man*) surely could not be attributed to the handful of bodybuilding enthusiasts. They were even starting to organize, into the Mattachine Society (1951), One, Inc. (1952), the Daughters of Bilitis (1956).

J. Edgar Hoover, Senator McCarthy, and the House Un-American Activities Committee urged Americans to seek out, fire, imprison, or institutionalize these perverts in our midst, not only for their likely communist sympathies and moral depravity, but for their zeal for reproduction. The Kinsey Report's revelation that nearly 10 percent of the adult male population was gay signified not the existence of a previously unacknowledged minority group but how easily "normal" men could be seduced or perverted; unless drastic measures were taken, the percentage would quickly rise to 30 percent, 60 percent, and finally 100 percent—a nation of lisping, mincing communist sympathizers. And, as before, teenage boys faced the greatest danger. Their only hope was to "discover" girls at puberty, to ogle and flirt in middle school, to date openly and voraciously in high school.[6]

In Jerseyville High School in Illinois, the 1949 *Album* asks Carnival Queen Betty Krause, "[W]hose green Chevie is it, that you've been seen riding in?" Maybe Robert Bailey, her dark, pleasant-looking Carnival King? But it is not only the Carnival King and Queen whose heterosexual interests are exuberantly recorded for posterity. Senior Class President James McCoy, though overbrimming with achievements, is given a single ambition: "to be a husband!" Science nerd Robert Krause wants to study chemistry in college so he can make a lot of money, yet the yearbook still manages a lecherous nudge: "[D]oes your longing for wealth have anything to do with a little brown-haired girl?"[7]

Eighteen of the forty-five senior boys are praised for real or imagined heterosexual interest, about the same percentage as at Dora High School a few years earlier, but with more "craziness," more scouring of the countryside for any and all feminine attention:

"His pastime is . . . why, girls, of course."

"His hobby is girls, but not girls with the 'new look'!"

"His hobby is girls in general, and [movie star] Betty Grable in particular!"

"We're wondering if David is still racing to Carrolton, or if he has decided to return to the Jerseyville girls?

Same-sex chums are mentioned only once, but not to worry, homo-erotic potential is dismissed by an implication of heterosexual passion: "He enjoys playing baseball with some of the fellas, but we also noticed that he spends a lot of time with a certain junior [girl]!"

THE TEENAGERS

Frankie Darro and Jackie Moran played college students in *Let's Go Collegiate* (1941), but in May 1946 they returned to high school for *Junior Prom* (Monogram, dir. Arthur Dreifuss). Singer Freddie Stewart (who composed for Frank Sinatra) stars as Freddie Trimble, a strikingly handsome though somewhat feminine Big Man on Campus running for class president on the "so nice it's pathetic" platform, assisted by his gawky, eyeglassed sidekick Lee (Warren Mills). The villains of the picture, rich snob Jimmy (Jackie Moran) and sullen wrong-side-of-the-tracks Roy (Frankie Darro), mount their own presidential campaign, evidently just to stir up trouble. But amid lots of plot complications and annoying patter, the bad guys see the error of their ways, and everyone ends up friendly and singing.

Freddie and Lee, Jimmy and Roy differ considerably from war-time Boys Next Door. First, they use the actual word "teenager." It first appeared in print in 1941 and gained prominence in 1945 when *Life* magazine devoted its June 11 cover story to "Teen-Age Boys." Here it appears everywhere to make sure the audience gets it: The gang is called "the Teenagers," the singing group "Freddie and the Teenagers," and the hangout "The Teenage Canteen." The teens have a vocabulary, customs, musical tastes different from and in opposition to those of the adults, though often their tastes seem odd. For all of the nonstop jitterbugging and exhortations to "get hip," Freddie's big number is a faux Negro spiritual, "It's Me, Oh Lawd."

Second, for probably the first time in a Boy Next Door movie, the possibility of a gay identity is explicitly evoked. Not in a presumably nonsexual homoromance, not in a sinister intrusion from the adult night world, not in an innuendo or aside, but in a boy who might really desire other boys. Dumped by her date shortly before the junior prom, a girl runs crying up the stairs. Lee enters and wants to know what's wrong. Her sister demands: "What if *you* didn't have a boy to take *you* to the prom?"

Startled, Lee thinks about the implication. "What if I *did*?" he exclaims, angry but intrigued, before someone clarifies, "She means if you were a girl!"

Later, at the Teen Canteen, the teenagers pretend to order adult alcoholic drinks, and soda jerk Tiny substitutes teen equivalents: Beer becomes root beer, for instance, and a gin ricky becomes a nonalcoholic lime ricky. Lee flashes a limp wrist and requests a champagne frappé in a nasal sissy voice. There is no such drink; he is simply trying to think of something effeminate to go with his pretense of a gay identity. Tiny's teen equivalent is a "tutti-fruit," a soda named for the ice cream flavor (tutti-frutti) and derogatory slang for gay men.[8]

Eventually Lee "sees the light" and finds himself a girl.[9] Every teenage character in the movie, without exception, becomes heterosexually active and aware by fade-out. One expects Jackie Moran's Jimmy and Frankie Darro's Roy to be a traditional homoromantic couple, polarized into tall/short, light/dark, rich/poor, masculine/feminine partners. However, Jimmy expresses a sleazy, wolfish heterosexual interest from the beginning. Roy starts off with Frankie Darro's usual woman-hater contempt of both girls and the sissy-boys who date them, but suddenly he swoons over eyeglassed bookworm Betty Rogers (Noel Neill, who would play Lois Lane on television). The last holdout has fallen. Heterosexual desire is the new teenage condition.

Junior Prom was so successful that seven new installments were ordered. The gang graduated from high school, attended junior college, and finally became young adults, no longer advertised as "The Teen-Agers."[10] Jackie Moran soon bowed out of the series, but Frankie Darro stayed on without a best buddy through *Freddie Steps Out, High School Hero, Vacation Days, Sarge Goes to College, Smart Politics*, and *Campus Sleuth*—always dark and brooding, but always interested in girls.

Frankie Darro's short stature and baby face allowed him to play teenagers well into his thirties. Afterward he worked sporadically, usually in bit parts, such as the gay pharmacist who examines Cary Grant's injured bum in *Operation Petticoat* (1959) or a pratfalling "little old lady" on *The Red Skelton Show* (1951–1971). He married twice, briefly and unhappily, struggled with alcoholism, and died at the home of a friend on Christmas Day, 1975.[11]

TEENAGE ADVICE

On the radio and TV, clumsy, stuttering Boys Next Door, interested in girls but deficient in manliness, endured for a decade: Oogie on *A Date with Judy* until 1950, Henry Aldrich until 1953, Dexter on *Meet Corliss Archer* until 1954, Walter on *Our Miss Brooks* until 1957. Meanwhile, some of the long-running radio teenagers who had previously been concerned solely with paper routes and bad report cards suddenly began casting longing glances at their female schoolmates: Chester Riley's son Junior on *Life of Riley* in January 1948, The Great Gildersleeve's wisecracking nephew Leroy in March 1949, and Ozzie and Harriet's eldest son David in November 1951. But they had to be nurtured into girl-craziness; it could not be taken for granted.

In the January 1948 episode of *The Life of Riley*, for instance, blustering paterfamilias Chester (William Bendix) is horrified to discover that his fifteen-year-old son, Junior (Scotty Beckett), has invited a *boy* to the New Year's Eve dance. He tries to explain about "the birds and bees," sexual difference, the reason the sailor chose a girl rather than a boy to kiss in Times Square on V-J Day, but Junior insists that he already knows about "that jazz." So Chester puts his foot down: There are "boy people" and "girl people," he argues, and "boy people" should only take "girl people" to dances. "Don't you like girls?" he asks in a timid, hesitant voice, afraid of the possible answer. When Junior admits that he likes girls "sometimes," Chester takes charge, forcing the boy to break his same-sex date and telephone a girl. When the first girl hesitates, Chester forces him to telephone another (resulting, of course, in two dates for the same evening). He is as hysterical in his insistence that Junior *should* like girls as Babbit, thirty years before, was hysterical in his insistence that his teenage son *should not*.

In this age of conformity, when the slightest norm-breaking signified an unhealthy urge toward sexual perversion or communism or both, dozens of teenage advice manuals appeared, penned by journalists, psychiatrists, doctors, educators, and every celebrity with access to a typewriter: Billy Graham *Talks to Teens*, Dear Abby writes *Dear Teenager*, Pat Boone advises those *'Twixt Twelve and Twenty*.[12] They offered guidance on every aspect of the teenager's life, from grooming to dealing with old-fogy parents, but the lion's share of the "advice" involved in-sisting that teenage heterosexual desire was normal, natural, expected, universal, yet paradoxically an accomplishment, something that teens must work hard to achieve. *Teenager's Guide for Living* assures teens that "you can be proud and happy that you are a boy, or a girl, with a healthy sex nature."[13] Not everyone is so blessed.

Teenagers could best assure their elders that they had achieved heterosexual desire by going on boy-girl dates, which the advice books identified as the key to high school success and the sole route to a happy, prosperous future. *Teenager's Guide for Living* offers four chapters on the hows and whys of dating. *Scholastic Magazine* ran a regular col-umn, "Boy Dates Girl," penned by someone named Gay Head. Future *Golden Girl* Betty White chimed in with lessons on *Teen-Age Dance*.[14]

Meanwhile, hundreds of educational films were produced for class-room use, instructing teenagers on the importance of table manners, cleanliness, obeying authority, following the crowd, and, of course, boy-girl dates. *Date Etiquette* (1952), *More Dates for Kay* (1952), *Beginning to Date* (1953), and many others were high school melodramas designed explicitly to introduce teenage boys (and, in one case, a girl) to their heteronormative destiny. The plots involve an older brother or friend pushing the reluctant teen into "taking the plunge" and asking a girl out. Instruction is certainly necessary: There are so many rules, proce-dures, and protocols that dating seems the most complicated ritual ever invented, and one false move is catastrophic. In *Junior Prom* (Simmel-Merservey, 1946), Mike meets his date's parents and tragically forgets his briefing: He tries to shake hands with her mother *before* her father! Everyone rolls their eyes in disgust, and the date is ruined.[15]

Dating: Do's and Don't (Coronet, 1949, dir. Ted Peshak) starts with short, squeaky-voiced Woody (John Lindsay) getting a none-too-subtle hint from a friend that his girl-craziness is overdue: He receives a ticket to the Hi-Teen Carnival in the mail, and it reads emphatically "one couple." "That means a date," he muses. "Just me and a girl ... well, that's all right." After his initial acquiescence, Mom, Dad, and Older Brother spend the next eleven minutes buzzing around him with de-lighted expressions, helping the narrator offer explicit instructions about whom to ask, how to ask, when to arrive at her house, when to take her home, and how to say good-bye (be sure to tell her that you had a good time, but *do not* attempt a kiss). The first date is an entrance into the high school social world, an entrance into heterosexual adulthood, and nothing must be left to chance.

What to Do on a Date (Coronet, 1951, dir. Ted Peshak) introduces a more reluctant dater. Handsome but awkward Nick "has a real dating problem": He doesn't like girls. We can't have that! So his buddy, suave, fast-talking Jeff, bullies him into asking a girl to a group-oriented activity: setting up for a rummage sale at the community center. Nick balks: "Do you suppose I'll have a good time? What am I supposed to do?" But Jeff persists. During the work session, Nick finds a posted list of many other group-oriented activities (a hay ride, a weenie roast) and decides that he might be willing to risk a "real" date with a girl, but only if Jeff will come along. He is not quite ready to abandon same-sex friendships for the uncharted ocean of heterosexual practice, but we are assured that eventually he will be able face a girl all by himself.

Girl-craziness is no longer a symptom of childishness or effeminacy. It is expected of adolescent boys, at least those who are white and middle class. But it is not yet inevitable, an instantaneous, hormone-drenched "discovery" of girls. Boys Next Door must be dragged, willingly or not, out of their homoromantic Arcadia.

TEENAGE COMIC BOOKS

One of Henry Aldrich's most important legacies was the teenage comic book, then read not only by preteens looking for glimpses of their future but by teenagers themselves. The first significant Boy Next Door in comic books, red-headed bumbler Archie Andrews, was introduced in *Pep* 22 (December 1941), getting into mishaps while trying to impress Girl Next Door Betty Cooper. Meanwhile, the cover of the issue showed the Shield and his sidekick Dusty trying to keep a spiked Axis boot from tromping on Europe. The juxtaposition of Boy Next Door and Adventure Boy, both redheads, one frivolous, timid, and girl-crazy, the other serious, stalwart, and committed to a man, would continue for several years. Dusty is slowly being lowered into a vat of acid, and Archie is fumbling a basketball game. Dusty "Fights for the Free French," while Archie runs for president of Riverdale High. Dusty tussles with "The Strangler," and Archie starts an escort service.[16]

Within a few issues, Archie had acquired all the accoutrements of Henry Aldrich–style adolescence: an oddly-named best friend, a class bully, an unassuming girl who carries a torch for him, and a stuck-up sub-deb for whom he carries a torch, plus pedantic teachers, a blustering principal, uncomprehending parents, crazy costumes, weird slang expressions, a malt shop hangout, after-school jobs, sports teams, and Friday night dances, all set in a suburb of New York City called Riverdale. The fads of contemporary teen culture resonated strongly with readers, and Archie quickly got top billing in *Pep*. On the February 1943 cover, Dusty is nowhere in sight, as the Shield and fellow superhero Hangman jubilantly parade Archie on their shoulders. In August 1943, Dusty makes his last cover appearance, tied up by the Nazis in GBA mode while the Shield ignores him to rescue a tied-up GGA nurse.[17] Thereafter Archie appeared on every cover of *Pep*, with the Shield present, if at all, only to proclaim himself a fan. Archie got his own title in 1942 and a masthead proclaiming him "America's Typical Teenager" in 1945. After the war, the Archie comics empire expanded astronomically, into *Laugh* (1946), *Jughead* (1949), *Betty and Veronica* (1950), *Reggie* (1950), *Archie's Joke Book* (1953), and *Archie's Pals N Gals* (1953), all in less than a decade. There would be hundreds of other titles, plus a radio series, a daily comic strip, a feature film, toy tie-ins, and an infinite succession of Saturday morning cartoons.

The early Archie was usually portrayed as the hapless object of competition between two man-hungry girls. But after the war he became undeniably girl-crazy, fainting with a goofy grin whenever a girl smiled at him, melting into a slurry of lust at a kiss. And he was not alone. Newsstands were overwhelmed with comic books set in small-town Centervilles and Midvales, where Boys Next Door drove jalopies, drank chocolate malteds, got into trouble with parents and teachers, sparred with boys, and longed for girls: *Wilbur* (1944), *Buzzy* (1945), *Frankie* (1946), *Oscar* (1947), *A Date with Judy* (1947), *Ozzie and Babs* (1947), *Leave It to Binky* (1948), *Henry Aldrich* (1950), *Stevie* (1952), and many more. Only a few endured through the late 1950s, and only a few were created later. They appeared at a very precise moment in history, at the same moment as the advice books and classroom films, and with a similar purpose: to teach teenage boys and girls that they should (and must) melt into slurries of lust over each other.[18]

Cover gags obsessively demonstrate that teenage boys should think of nothing but girls. In a restaurant, Archie gazes at the many pretty waitresses and claims, "The only reason I eat here is because the food is so good." While cuddling with his girlfriend in a canoe, Binky is so lovestruck that he accidentally paddles with his guitar. In science class, Oogie is attached to a "wish-o-meter" machine; when Judy kisses him, it explodes. Walking past a haunted house, Judy is nervous and frightened, but Oogie is ecstatic because she is clinging to him. Buzzy swoons over the attractive French teacher's conjugation of "aimer . . . to love," while his girlfriend fumes.[19]

A few covers do display the Boy Next Door missing an opportunity for heterosexual practice. Binky and Peggy sit on a sofa. Binky pets his dog and sighs, "A winter night . . . a cozy fire . . . and a dog on your lap. What could be better?" Peggy can think of something and glares at him in consternation. On another sofa, Gabby is casually whistling and playing with a paddleball while his girlfriend vamps him in vain. Oogie and Judy are leaving a Tunnel of Love, a popular carnival ride in which a boat floats through a dark, cavernous space, allowing many opportunities for kissing. Oogie complains, "What a dull ride! I don't see why it's popular—it's so dark in there, you can't see the scenery!" Judy fumes. However, these gags seem to be playing with the boys' stupidity rather than their lack of girl-craziness.[20]

Girl-craziness never implies a desire for sex with girls—the raunchiest of wolves has nothing more on his mind than a kiss, and on the rare occasion that a girl implies that she wants more, the teenager runs away in terror. Nor does it imply that the boy is considering a heteronormative trajectory into marriage and family. Judy and Oogie are gazing at a wedding cake in a bakery window; Judy imagines their future wedding, while Oogie imagines eating cake.[21] Oogie, Archie, and Binky either ignore the possibility of marriage or find it terrifying. They are girl-crazy without thought of physical or social fulfillment, girl-crazy to signify that they are normal, conformist, not gay: Desiring girls is the best way to indicate that they *do not* desire boys.

Lest anyone think that girl-craziness implies sex or marriage, teenage comics nearly always frame heterosexual relationships as tedious, exploitive, and feminizing. Judy exclaims, "Don't you just love hay rides," while Oogie, who is exhausted from pitching all the hay, stares, speechless with frustration. Judy expects to water-ski while being towed behind a row boat, with Oogie furiously rowing. Peggy forces Binky to model a dress while his friend peeks through the window and laughs uproariously. Girls force Howie to play with a beach ball (and pummel him into unconsciousness) while his friends tease, "Dig that Howie, playing those sissy games!"[22]

Most of the Boys Next Door have a pal who is oblivious to girls or even an active "woman-hater" in the Frankie Darro mold. Archie's buddy spies a glamour girl with a dog on a leash and exclaims, "Isn't she a honey?" The gag is, he's talking about the dog. Tommy's buddy tries to pull him away from Ginger, snarling that she "will only make a monkey out of you in ten minutes!" Tommy replies: "But think of those ten minutes!" Wilbur's buddy moans that he has woman trouble—he asked a girl to the dance, and she accepted![23]

However, woman-hating buddies do not mean that the homo-romantic Arcadia endured in Boy Next Door comics. There are few moments of emotional intensity, even of a comedic sort, between the Boy Next Door and his buddy. Also, the boys' book and movie serial emphasis on masculine beauty has vanished: Except for an occasional hunk framed as unwelcome competition, all teenage boys are drawn as skinny, awkward, and unattractive.[24] However, their girlfriends have figures and faces copied directly from glamour-model pinups, suggesting that to desire women is normal, natural, and inevitable, while to desire men is silly.[25] Boy readers would thus believe that if they were not interested in girls "yet," they soon would be, and girl readers would believe that it was their job to bully, seduce, and flirt the recalcitrant boys out of their quiescence.

Gas House Kids

Lost Boys took a little longer to participate in postwar teenage girl-craziness. In October 1946, the twenty-six-year-old Billy Halop became sixteen again for *Gas House Kids* (PRC, dir. Sam Neufield). When Eddie O'Brien (Robert Lowery) returns from the war crippled and therefore unqualified for his old job as a police officer, he decides to retire to a chicken farm in New Jersey. His young pal Tony (Billy Halop) and a gang of unknowns and former Little Rascals (including Carl "Alfalfa" Switzer and Tommy Bond) try to raise the $5,000 down payment. In the midst of the melodrama, we can catch glimpses of an attempt to reinvent the success of Billy Halop's early homoromances. No one in the gang ever expresses the slightest interest in girls. Tony is frequently presented as an object of desire: He delays the plot to work out at the gym and box, evidently just so he can take his shirt off, and otherwise he wears a tight white T-shirt that reveals his physique almost as openly.

But homoromance cannot be sustained in the postwar world. The teen-adult friendship is hasty and underdeveloped. When Tony is kidnapped, his harrowing attempt to escape from a moving car might have come from *Junior G-Men*; the car careens off a cliff, and he crawls from the wreckage and collapses, severely injured, possibly dying. O'Brien rushes off to search for him but does not rescue him; instead, he finds Tony safely in a hospital bed. Perhaps it was too difficult to script a handicapped man conducting the rescue, but still, their subsequent moment of eye-gleaming tenderness makes no sense. The final scene, with the gang happily living at the chicken farm with O'Brien and his new wife, evokes not an escape to Arcadia but a heterosexual nuclear family.

Two more *Gas House Kids* movies appeared in 1947, starring Carl Switzer and Tommy Bond, but not Billy Halop—he had moved on. No longer able to play realistic teenagers, he appeared intermittently in adult roles in movies and on television. He became a salesman and a registered nurse, and started a nightclub act with fellow Dead End Kid Gabriel Dell. Late in life he found new fame on *All in the Family* (1972) as the owner of the taxi company where Archie Bunker worked. He married twice, and died in 1976.[26]

After the Gas House franchise ended, Carl Switzer and Tommy Bond played juvenile gang members again in *Big Town Scandal* (Pine-Thomas Productions, 1948, dir. William C. Thomas), a movie adaptation of the radio-television series *Big Town*. Crusading newspaper editor Steve Wilson (Philip Reed) repeats the old Lost Boy plot of good guy drawing the boys away from their gangster chum through an after-school sports program. But *Angels Wash Their Faces* was nine years ago, and *Big Town* shows the change. Steve's gaze is always moderated by star reporter Lorelei (Hilary Brooke) on his arm, minimizing the homo-erotic potential, and the boys' scenes all but eliminate physicality. They never strip down in locker rooms or for bed; there is none of the grab-bing at crotches or buttocks that defined the 1930s Lost Boys. Indeed, gang leader Tommy (twenty-one-year-old Stanley Clements) is not torn between the gangster and the good guy, but between the gangster and his own girlfriend. At the end of the movie, Tommy goes "straight," rec-onciles with his girl, and kisses her. Steve and Lorelei, eavesdropping, decide to kiss as well. Lorelei quips, "Why should we leave it to the younger generation?" Heterosexual desire has become emblematic of youth, even the lost youth of the Dead End.

BOWERY BOYS

In 1946, Leo Gorcey and Huntz Hall transformed the East Side Kids into a new franchise called the Bowery Boys. The new format would be comedy rather than melodrama, with few life-threatening situations but a lot of pratfalls and malapropisms. No longer tough–tender street kids, the Bowery Boys were postadolescent slackers, several years into adulthood yet still hanging out in Louie Dumbrowski's Sweet Shop all day, "stealing banana splits, applying for jobs and hoping we didn't get them."[27] The plots involved foiling smugglers, thieves, kidnappers, and spies, and occasionally exploring a haunted house, just as on the East Side but with two major differences. First, the main duo, domineering Slip (Leo Gorcey) and dimwitted Satch (Huntz Hall), were a comedic team of the Abbott and Costello school, with hostility and abuse elimi-nating any potential tenderness. Second, they liked girls.

In their first few years, the Bowery Boys remain studiously un-interested: They befriend girls, play matchmaker to older friends, and nothing more. By 1950, however, they are ogling. They are flirting. They moan with longing for the glamour girls they see in magazines or on the street. They have dates and girlfriends. Lobby cards often suggest raunchy burlesque, with Slip and Satch bookended by girls or gazing lustfully at female legs. Of course, no one has sex or even kisses passionately (when a woman invites Satch to her apartment and tries to seduce him, he is terrified and runs away). Of course, no one contemplates marriage. Like the Archies and Oogies of teenage comics, they are girl-crazy with no desire for physical or social fulfillment. Their girl-craziness does not *lead* to something, it *wards off* something.

Leo Gorcey and Huntz Hall kept churning out Bowery Boys features through 1956, though they were increasingly anachronistic among the middle-class juvenile delinquents played by Tony Curtis, John Saxon, and James Dean. Eventually Gorcey, drinking heavily, marrying heavily, and depressed over the death of his father, dropped out of the series, but still it didn't end. Now in charge, Huntz Hall hired Stanley Clements to be the new "straight man" gang leader and kept going for another seven features. He finally announced the end of the franchise in February 1958, a few months shy of his thirty-ninth birthday, having played the same character for over twenty years. His decision was based on fatigue, not on diminished popularity: The Bowery Boys were more popular than ever in their history, making more money on television than they ever had in the theaters. Audiences composed mostly of children and teenagers watched, entranced by this nostalgic urban adolescence: leisure without work, excitement without danger, wisecracks without recrimination, loyal friends, caring adults, and, especially, endless double takes at parades of beautiful girls.

COWBOYS AND SPACEMEN

Between 1946 and 1958, Grossett and Dunlap published thirty-seven volumes of the Teen-Age Library, collections of short stories popular as birthday and Christmas gifts: *Teen-Age Aviation Stories, Teen-Age Dog Stories, Teen-Age Mystery Stories*, and so on. Though there were no recurring characters, they were thematically linked to the serial novels of the 1920s, with Boys Next Door scoring touchdowns or Adventure Boys diving for sunken treasure. The dust jackets seemed particularly given to beefcake. *Teen-Age Sports Stories*, for instance, devotes half of its cover to an extremely muscular, shirtless teenager who is not playing a sport (he appears to be hoisting a mast on a pleasure cruise). *Teen-Age Stories of*

Action devotes its entire cover to an extremely muscular, shirtless teenager standing on a log with a grappling hook.[28]

Occasionally the stories involve girls, but when the stories are about Boys Next Door or Adventure Boys, they omit girls altogether from references, backgrounds, and relationships. Instead, there are pairs of classmates, sports stars and rivals, greenhorns and cowboys, mistrusting and then trusting, disrespecting and then respecting, acting rashly and being rescued, taking the blame for the other's misdeeds, learning to care for each other, learning to love each other, reveling in the twilight of the homoromantic Arcadia.

Some even tread an oddly queer homoeroticism. In "Boy Meets Buoy," jock Johnny asks the class aesthete, Spud, to be his partner in an upcoming boat race. Spud, a sissy boy who hates boats, is not the most logical choice, but Johnny persists: "Will you be my ballast?"

"*Will you be my Valentine* is a much prettier sentiment," Spud responds.

When Spud finally acquiesces, Johnny calls him "dream boy," perhaps referring to his laziness, and "beautiful," but maybe he means the boat. Spud thinks that his discussion of boating techniques is "all about luff [love] and very beautiful." And so on, with so much flirtation veiled, misdirected, and masked as a joke that the reader must check to make sure that this is a sports story rather than a sex comedy. At the end Spud declares that he has changed his mind: He now loves boating, and who knows what else?[29]

Teen-adult partnerships with elements of homoromance appeared among Adventure Boys for about a decade after the war. The serials *Superman* (1948), *Batman and Robin* (1949), and *Cody of the Pony Express* (1950) featured adult-teen duos as effusive in their physical interaction as Terry Lee and Pat Ryan in *Terry and the Pirates* nearly a decade before. Indeed, they seem an almost deliberate throwback to the days of homoromantic adventure: Nearly every chapter ends with the teenager tied to something, thrown off something, being beaten up, or otherwise threatened, waiting for the superhero to swoop down to the rescue. Then they walk side by side toward the next adventure, oblivious to the charms of whatever young ladies they have befriended. In feature films, gangly cowboy kid Buzz Henry gazes at adult heroes Eddie Dean,

Charles Starrett, Robert Kellard, and Roy Rogers, but never at a girl.[30] Dickie Jones buddy-bonds with Gene Autry, Errol Flynn, and Jock Mahoney, never romancing a girl on-screen until he is nearly thirty, playing *Buffalo Bill Jr.* on television (1955).[31]

Science fiction television also managed a significant number of quasi-homoromantic relationships. Frankie Thomas of *Tim Tyler's Luck* was twenty-nine years old but still "adolescent" when he bonded with his space academy classmate Jan Merlin in *Tom Corbett, Space Cadet* (1950). Commander Buzz Corey (Ed Kemmer) of the *Space Patrol* (1951) patrolled the galaxy with a teenager named Cadet Happy (Lyn Osborn). Richard Crane as *Rocky Jones, Space Ranger* (1954) patrolled the galaxy with a teenager named Winky (Scotty Beckett). These partners did not demonstrate much intensity or intimacy, but were exclusive, permanent, and domestic, reflecting the superheroes and sidekicks of wartime, and they almost entirely eliminated heterosexual interest.

The homoromantic Arcadia may have endured in these media objects because they were aimed at preteens. In spite of its name, the "Teen-Age Library" was marketed to children, or rather to their parents; the back cover flap includes testimonials like "Highly recommended for all children's rooms and young people's collections" and "Teachers and parents will be pleased." Adults and teenagers were increasingly gravitating to their own niche markets, leaving adventure movies to Saturday morning matinees and adventure television to after-school time blocks favored by preteens.[32] Perhaps teenagers had to be taught to embrace their "natural" heterosexual desire—thus the comic books and science fiction stories still aimed at them carefully promoted girl-craziness—but preteen boys were presumed "presexual," that is, not yet potent and not yet "aware" of girls. Indeed, they were supposed to despise girls. The Penrods and Alfalfas of the earlier generations gave way to Beaver Cleaver on the TV sitcom *Leave It to Beaver.* "Go see a girl? I'd rather smell a skunk! If I had a choice between a three pound bass and a girl, I'd take a three pound bass!"[33] An interest in girls prior to puberty would destabilize that myth that heterosexual desire was a natural, normal, inevitable consequence of biological maturation. Thus, heterosexual practice in media objects aimed at preteens was dangerous, even when the characters were teenagers, so teenage sports heroes and their buddies, spacemen and their teenage sidekicks, could still fly off into the sunset together. At least for a few years.

BOMBA

Johnny Sheffield thought that his loincloth days were over in 1947, when he retired from the RKO Tarzan franchise and enrolled at Hollywood High School. He graduated in 1949 and planned to major in premed at UCLA, but then Walter Mirisch of Monogram Studios approached him to star in an adaptation of *Bomba the Jungle Boy*, the book series from the 1920s. Assured that filming could fit around his classes (it didn't), Johnny strapped on his loincloth again to play Bomba in twelve features (1949–1955), all written and directed by movie-serial maven Ford Beebe.

The features drew little inspiration from the books, which had been out of print for a decade. Instead they presented a teenage Tarzan. Bomba lives in Africa instead of South America, has a pet chimpanzee, swings on vines, and at first talks in Weissmuller's trademark "Me Tarzan" style. But Johnny Sheffield, now aged eighteen to twenty-six, wears a skimpier loincloth than Weissmuller, and his close-ups are more frequent, so the viewer is privy to many more details of his body, not only the curve of his chest and the bulge of his biceps but his thighs and buttocks, often filmed from beneath as he climbs trees. When Bomba is tied up by an ivory poacher or jungle warlord, his muscles taut and straining against the ropes, the camera waits for thirty seconds or more for the viewer to get a good look. While he sleeps cradled by a tree branch, prone and immobile, the camera again waits, for nearly a minute, inviting the viewers to commit his body to memory inch by inch, muscle by muscle. No doubt they did, for little else appeared to occupy their attention. The plots are minimal, the action scenes dull, the characters stock, the footage of African wildlife constantly recycled; most of each seventy- or eighty-minute movie is spent on pinup poses of Bomba's body.

Though director Ford Beebe explicitly displays Bomba as an object of desire, there are no men or boys in Bomba's world to actualize that desire by falling in love with him. The men in the jungle are either colonial administrators (this is still the era of empires, after all), cordial and benevolent but too old for a teen-adult homoromance, or else unscrupulous hunters, escaped criminals, desert-kingdom tyrants, and Russian agitators, who usually have Bomba strung up and tortured by the second reel. Bomba takes a big-brotherly interest in a barely pubescent scientist's son in *The Lost Volcano* (1950), and he befriends the teenage son of an assassinated chief in *Bomba and the Jungle Girl* (1952), but with none of the intensity or intimacy of a peer homoromance. And there are no other boys near his own age anywhere in the series.

However, there are lots of girls his own age. Bomba is partnered with at least one, sometimes two, in every installment—the daughter of a wildlife photographer, the niece of the colonial administrator, the sister of an agricultural expert, a scientist's maid, a Hollywood starlet, on and on, present in Africa on the flimsiest of excuses or no excuse at all, except to give the Jungle Boy an opportunity to demonstrate that he is a "typical teenager" and therefore girl-crazy. At first Bomba seems delighted just to meet someone his own age, regardless of gender; he calls the girl a "friend," leading the viewer to expect a nonromantic buddy. But they do not buddy-bond so much as go out on jungle-teen dates: They peek at cute baby animals; they dive into lagoons and synchronized-swim like Tarzan and Jane; they lie on the ground side by side to talk about their dreams, and perhaps Bomba offers the girl a flower, all accompanied by syrupy-sweet, violin-heavy scores. When the bad guys have Bomba strung up, the girl runs for help, and at the denouement, Bomba rescues her from a crocodile, panther, elephant, volcano, or forest fire, just as Tarzan once rescued his Boy.

Bomba's friendships with girls deviate from the conventions of heteroromance in two key points, intimacy and permanence. Bomba never touches his girl friend, except when she hysterically throws herself into his arms after being rescued from something. There is no hugging or hand-holding during the jungle dates, and there is only one kiss, but it doesn't really count, since Bomba has just convinced the girl to reconcile with her fiancé.

Also, since the girl is usually in Africa on a brief visit, their relationship will necessarily end soon.[34] Only once does Bomba ask a visiting girl to stay (she refuses), and on those rare occasions when the girl happens to be a permanent resident of Africa, he ignores any attempt to define their relationship as heteroromantic love. In *Elephant Stampede* (1951), native girl Lola (Donna Martel) tries to seduce Bomba while teaching him to read, but he cunningly pretends to be oblivious. She tries to trick him into confessing his "true" hetero-desire by assigning him the sentence, "I love Lola." He reads, "I love . . . I love . . . ," and pretends to be stuck on the last word, while Lola waits, breathless with anticipation. Then, brightening, he says, "I love . . . to go swimming!" and dives into the lagoon.

When the Bomba series ended, Johnny Sheffield had spent nearly three-quarters of his life in a loincloth. He knew that he would never be seriously considered for a fully-clothed role, and though he was pleasantly muscular, he was not sufficiently mountainous to compete with the technologically enhanced bodybuilders of the Cold War marketplace: Contemporary Tarzan Gordon Scott had a bigger bust than Jayne Mansfield, and only titled Mr. Universes need apply to star in the Italian sword-and-sandal epics. Johnny tried to continue his career on television with pet zebra and magic ring in *Bantu the Zebra Boy*, but the pilot was not picked up. A few years later, he and his father produced a syndicated television series, *Zim Bomba*, by chopping up the old movies, but in effect his show biz career was over. When MGM was looking for a new Tarzan in 1959, Johnny didn't even bother to audition (beach boy Denny Miller was cast). He enrolled at UCLA after all, studied business instead of medicine, and enjoyed considerable success in a second career in real estate.[35]

THE VANISHING SIDEKICK

In the years after the war, when many teenagers and young adults were still reading comic books, most of the superheroes retired or lost their Adventure Boy sidekicks. In 1946, Captain America replaced Bucky with the Golden Girl. The Black Terror's "young partner" Tim grew into a man before they both retired in 1947. In March 1948, the Shield and Dusty officially relinquished *Pep* comics to Archie, closed down their fan club, and vanished into civilian life. Toro was still being tied half-naked to things and rescued as late as July 1948, but soon he, too, faded away, leaving the Human Torch a bachelor.

The surviving superhero-teen sidekick teams, Batman–Robin and the Green Arrow–Speedy, became thoroughly heterosexualized.[36] No longer was there any question about the relationship: They were legally appointed guardian and ward. The superhero still spent his alter-ego time at restaurants, the theater, and fancy socialite parties, but now he was explicitly and continuously shown *saying good-bye* to the sidekick and rushing off to meet *a date*. Batman not only dated but embraced heteroromance, falling for reporter Vicki Vale, reformed villain Cat-woman, and superhero competitor Batwoman.[37] The sidekick also inhabited a heteronormative frame: Before and after the call to adventure, Robin and Speedy were shown doing homework, playing on their high school basketball team, grinning at girls at the malt shop, dating and dancing and experiencing the pangs of puppy love. They became so deliberately hetero-horny that by 1954 Frederic Wertham's psychosexual ranting about an inscribed "perversion" in the superhero-sidekick bond seemed like nonsense.[38]

A NEW FOUNDATION

Science fiction magazines and novels were still evoking lyrical homo-romance in 1946, when C. L. Moore published "Daemon," about a Bra-zilian youth named Luiz who might be an extraterrestrial. Shanghaied and forced to become a sailor, he is beaten and burned by his abusive captain. A passenger named Shaughnessy takes an interest in him and intervenes during a particularly brutal beating. Both are exiled on a desert island:

> I put up a hand to touch a star cluster that hung above my head, and the cluster was bright and tingling to feel. Then I saw that it was the Shaughnessy's face.
>
> I said, "Oh, s'nhor," in a whisper. . . . The Shaughnessy smiled at me in the starlight. "Don't whisper, Luiz. We're alone now."[39]

But two years later, in 1948, when Isaac Asimov returned to the far-future Galactic Empire of Foundation, he made heterosexual desire an ordinary part of the world for youngsters and adults alike.[40] More significantly, he denigrated same-sex relationships as uniformly cold and oppressive. The tyrannical ruler of the galaxy, a dwarfish mutant named the Mule (because he is sterile), worries that a mysterious organization called the Second Foundation is threatening his power, so he sends two men out on a search-and-destroy mission. Middle-aged Han Pritcher has been "converted" (brainwashed into loyalty), but youngster Bail Channing is working only for the glory. In earlier stories, the men would form a strong bond of mutual respect and love, but here, in spite of some sentences that can inadvertently be read as pornographic ("The stiff officer felt himself harden against the other"), they despise each other from beginning to end. Every word they say to each other is qualified with "coldly," "coolly," or "derisively." Channing deprograms Pritcher from his brainwashing not to save him but to use him in a power struggle against the Mule. Their story ends during a monumental battle, with one of the men unconscious or dead and the other not grieving.

In the sequel, middle-aged scientist Toran Darrell II and his youngster assistant, Pelleas Anthor, are still trying to find the Second Foundation so it can be destroyed. They not only work together but also share domestic space and never seek out other companions: "[T]he evenings passed in friendly intercourse," Asimov tells us with his usual unintended double entendre, "the days in pleasant unimportance."[41] But when Darrell suspects that Anthor is a spy, he tortures him, graphically and without hesitation. Meanwhile, the head of the Second Foundation turns out to be the benevolent Pappa, explicitly heterosexual, with a wife, Mamma. The Mule could never become anyone's Pappa. Any whisper of homoromance is drowned out by the roars of acclamation as home, hearth, and fatherhood save the galaxy.

In the September 1951 issue of *Astounding Science Fiction*, Alan E. Nourse published "The Universe Between," about a parallel dimension so unimaginable that anyone "crossing over" goes crazy, except for seventeen-year-old Robert Benedict. He began crossing over shortly after his birth, and he always emerges unscathed, though he can't explain anything he experiences on the other side. When the inhabitants of the parallel dimension suddenly begin slicing off large pieces of the Earth, like the lower third of Manhattan, only Robert can try to communicate with them and figure out what's going on. But crossing over is becoming increasingly unpredictable, disturbing, and dangerous; he returns screaming.

The gruff elder scientist in charge of the project treats Robert as a laboratory animal, ignoring his needs and safety, but assistant Dr. Merry takes a personal interest in him. Not much older than Robert himself— usually called "Hank" and first introduced oversleeping and missing his college math class—the young engineer seems quite taken with the handsome teenager. They smile at each other, joke, and enjoy a physical intimacy, with many touches of arm or shoulder. When a crossover goes wrong, Hank rushes to Robert's side much faster than do Robert's parents:

> [Robert] stood shivering, literally blue with cold, gasping for air
> and looking so ill and exhausted that [his mother] stifled a cry and
> Hank leaped across to catch his arm before he fell. "Robert! What
> happened? What did they do to you?" The boy shook his head
> numbly as Hank eased him to the floor and loosened his jacket. "Easy,
> fella," Hank said softly. "Just get your breath and rest a minute."[42]

So far this is a classic Adventure Boy homoromance, requiring only a coda that shows the permanence of Robert and Hank's relationship. But when Nourse revised several of the parallel dimension stories into a novel, *The Universe Between* (1965), he added another sort of coda: years later, Robert and Hank are business partners, transporting people across the galaxy via interdimensional shortcuts (it is perfectly safe as long as they wear blindfolds to avoid going crazy). And the reader finally discovers, in a last-paragraph "tomato surprise," that the parallel dimension is really our own world: Robert is the one who lives in a parallel world, where America never broke away from Britain, there were no Presidents Lincoln or Kennedy, and democracy was never invented, nor capitalism, nor freedom. On one of his crossing-over expeditions, Robert falls in love with someone from our democratic, capitalist, free United States, a girl named Sharnan, "beautiful, with violet eyes." He decides to cross over permanently to be with her. He tells Hank, "I'll be in touch," but no doubt he means that he will send an occasional postcard. Hank has no place on the other side; only Robert has the capacity to look at the intertwining of democracy and heterosexual destiny without a blindfold. So he must reject his buddy for the girl: "Sharnan was waiting for him there. As he had known she would be."[43]

Girl-craziness had triumphed. In "The Big Time" (1958), Fritz Leiber imagines a war between Spiders and Snakes, representing Democracy and Communism, respectively, over control of Time itself. Soldiers of many time periods and species recuperate at a sort of intergalactic USO. When a youngster named Bruce materializes, wounded after a battle, the hostess immediately sends him off with a girl. She explains: "What does a badly hurt and mixed up creature need who's been fighting hard? One individual to look out for him and feel for him . . . and it helps if that individual is of the opposite sex. That's something that goes beyond species."[44]

Later one of the soldiers pretends to be a *maricón*, but only in jest: Everyone "knows" that heterosexual desire is a constant, experienced and expressed by everyone, without exception, human or alien, man or woman, adult or youngster, across the galaxy, across the universe.

12

THE CLASS OF 1957

At Elkhorn High School in Frankfort, Kentucky, the class of 1957 started a new tradition, Mr. and Miss Elkhorn. The honor went to a Big Man on Campus named Doug (class president, captain of the football team) and a booster named Janice (Future Homemakers of America, Pep Club). They receive a full-page photo treatment, descending a staircase somewhere inside the school. Doug is tall and broad-shouldered, with a letterman's jacket and severe crew cut, and he dangles his books at his side in gender-polarized he-man fashion. Janice wears a dark sweater with lace at the neck, a dark skirt, and bobby sox. She carries her books demurely across her chest.[1]

Twelve years have passed since V-J Day; the Baby Boom is in full swing, and teenagers, especially teenage boys, believe that the world was created especially for them. They are everywhere in the spring of 1957. On television, every nuclear family sitcom includes a wisecracking teenage boy: David Nelson, Ricky Nelson, Billy Gray, Dwayne Hickman. At the movies, James MacArthur and Sal Mineo play juvenile delinquents, Michael Landon a teenage werewolf, and Pat Boone a wholesome, girl-crazy Boy Next Door. On the top of the pop charts, teen idols sing about "Teenage Romance," "April Love," and "Young Love." On the top of the bestseller list are two humorous takes on the teen-adult generation gap. A dozen teen magazines tell boys how to get girls and girls how to get boys, in a more lighthearted, self-assured tone than the advice manuals and educational films ever dared.[2] Doug and Janice descend the staircase, smiling. All questions have been answered, all puzzles solved. They know that the meaning of life lies in boys and girls walking side by side into the future.

SPIN AND MARTY

In November 1955, *The Adventures of Spin and Marty* premiered as a serial segment of the late-afternoon kiddie show *The Mickey Mouse Club.* Based on the novel *Marty Markham*, it was originally about a wealthy mollycoddle who arrives at summer camp with chauffeur and butler in tow, and learns to be a regular fella.[3] But when buzz-cut jock Tim Considine auditioned, he was deemed too regular already, yet too charismatic to be relegated to a back-of-the-cabin role, so a new role was invented for him, camp big shot Spin Evans, and Marty was cast with redheaded scrappy-sissy type David Stollery. One expects a tough-sissy homoromance, as in *Tom Brown's School Days* or *Cadets on Parade* a few years before, and the series does waste no time in displaying the boys' barely pubescent muscles, as well as the respectable physique of an older boy; however, there is no instant camaraderie, no moment of falling in love. Throughout most of the series, the two fourteen-year-olds despise each other. They may stare at each other from across the yard, but they come face-to-face only for pranks, taunts, insults, and fistfights, like the men and women on adult TV series who bicker for endless seasons while audiences anxiously await the kiss. Here the "kiss" comes late, in the twentieth episode: As the counselors break up their latest fight by holding them upside down, Spin and Marty seem to really see each other for the first time without posturing, bragging, or hiding behind a shield of rage. They grin, and then laugh, and suddenly, inevitably, they are a pair. In the remaining episodes, they treat each other with amazing tenderness; each tries to sacrifice himself for the other; and in the last scene, as the other campers prepare to go home, they are invited to stay on as ranch hands.

Viewers—grade schoolers and no doubt not a few high schoolers—were mesmerized by this hostility melting into homoromance, and they responded with an urgency unknown in the days of *Tom Brown's School Days* and *Cadets on Parade.* Books, comics, sheet music, and 45-rpm records flew off the shelves, evoking the homoromantic Arcadia for years after the series ended. Today, when the other serials on *The Mickey Mouse Club* have faded into obscurity, many Baby Boomers recall Spin and Marty fondly, as their long-lost friends. Many recall them, clearly and unequivocally, as a gay couple.[4]

Boy Next Door homoromance was vanishingly rare in 1955. No doubt this one was possible only because *The Mickey Mouse Club* aired on weekday afternoons, for grade schoolers who wore Mousketeer ears and shouted "Hi, Mickey!" at the screen. Presexual, predesiring preteens could still watch teenage boys desiring each other, while their older brothers must subsist on a diet of never-ending girl-craziness.

In November 1956, Tim Considine and David Stollery returned for a second season, *The Further Adventures of Spin and Marty*. Now the Boys Next Door are nearing their sixteenth birthdays; Spin has an impressively tight, hard-lined chest and stomach, while Marty is lean, lanky, and decidedly feminine. Both are on display as often and earnestly as Mickey Rooney nearly twenty years earlier. However, the homoromantic Arcadia is threatened by a girls' camp that just opened up across the lake. The tough guy is not interested, but the sissy falls for Mousketeer Annette (Annette Funicello). When Annette prefers Spin anyway, Marty seethes with jealousy and breaks up with him. Then, when Marty is drowning, Spin rushes to the rescue. They realize how much they care for each other and renew their commitment, swearing off trivial distractions like girls. Homoromance has triumphed over girl-craziness.

But not for long. When Annette starred in her own serial on the *Mickey Mouse Club* that spring, Tim Considine played the cute jock she had a crush on and David Stollery the gawky string bean who had a crush on her, with no hint of a romantic bond between them. The last of the Boys Next Door had been ejected from Arcadia. In *The New Adventures of Spin and Marty* (November 1958), seventeen-year-old Spin is dating Annette, and Marty is dating her fellow Mousketeer Darlene (Darlene Gillespie). Whatever passion they once felt for each other has been forgotten; they are not, and never have been, more than buddies. A fourth season was scripted but never filmed; instead Tim Considine went on to star as the eldest of the sons on *My Three Sons* on television (1960), and marry twice. David Stollery left Disneyland to become an automobile designer and marry once. They still run into each other from time to time, at fan conventions, but they have not stayed in touch.[5]

SUPERMAN'S BOY PAL

The 1954 Comics Code Authority forbade mature, controversial, or unpleasant situations in comic books, virtually assuring that only very young children would be interested in reading them. That same year, Superman's erstwhile "boy pal" Jimmy Olsen received his own title. Although he is working full time as a cub reporter for the *Daily Planet*, Jimmy is still a teenager, still living in an orphanage under adult supervision. He is as girl-crazy as Boys Next Door Archie, Oogie, and Buzzy, but his hetero-desire is more often framed as a threat: Archie may be terrified at the prospect of marrying a girl, but Jimmy is forced to marry apes, insect-girls, and sundry monsters; or else his girlfriends have murderous intentions; or else they disapprove of Superman and insist that the duo break up.

Like *Spin and Marty*, the series recalls, to a great extent, the conventions of the homoromantic Arcadia. Nearly every story finds some reason to strip the extremely buffed Adventure Boy out of his clothes, displaying him as an object of desire as overtly as Robin, Bucky, and Toro in the 1940s. And just as those superheroes were constantly threatened with torture or execution, Jimmy is constantly undergoing weird transformations: He becomes a genie, a ghost, a giant, a merman, a gorilla, a werewolf, an alien, an octopus-boy, a porcupine-boy, an elastic boy, and a fat boy. However, Superman does not swoop down to save the day, like Captain America and the Human Torch once did; X-ray vision and super strength cannot cure bodily transformations, so he must stand by helplessly. The humorous stories only serve to accentuate the reader's discomfort with the more serious stories. Sometimes Jimmy is dying.

Superhero and "boy pal" display the intensity, intimacy, and exclusivity of homoromance, but their relationship seems only to create problems. Jimmy is wooed by another superhero. Superman courts another boy. Jimmy develops amnesia and cannot understand why this famous superhero is taking such an interest in him. They switch roles, the boy becoming the superhero and the man his pal. Jimmy reveals Superman's true identity, paralyzes him with kryptonite, tries to kill him, sides with a villain against him. Though equilibrium is always restored by the last panel, when the amnesia is cured or the betrayal turns out to be a ruse necessary to catch a crook, these stories suggest an anxiety over same-sex desire only slightly less blatant than the shift away from homoromance in *The Foundation Trilogy*. Though heterosexual romance is problematic, homoromance brings darkness and despair. Men can be chummy "pals," but they can never fully trust each other. Every masculine smile hides the potential for backstabbing and malice.

JUVENILE SCIENCE FICTION

Between 1945 and 1965, Isaac Asimov, Lester Del Rey, Robert Heinlein, and other science fiction professionals catered to the Baby Boomer generation with dozens of "juvenile" novels. They were marketed mostly to preteens and young teenagers, distributed through book clubs, middle school libraries, and *Boys Life* more often than bookstores, and they starred not structural "youngsters" but real sixteen- or seventeen-year-old Adventure Boys, with parents and curfews and homework.[6] Their rip-roaring adventures often read like throwbacks to the serial novels of the authors' youth. However, their heterosexualization is not a throwback at all.

The heroes of the stories lack the magnificent physiques of prewar Adventure Boys. Indeed, their bodies are nearly absent; they are characterized almost entirely by personality and hair color. Jim, the title character in *Rocket Jockey* (1952), is described more vividly than usual, but still his body (short and slim) vanishes in favor of "carrot-red hair," "a freckled face," and "eyes that stood out from behind glasses." When a superior physique is required for the plot, it appears through a colorless "wiry build," or even through implication, as when Jerry in *Undersea Quest* (1954) is told, "[M]aybe I haven't got as many muscles as you do—who does?"[7]

Girls are nearly absent from juvenile science fiction plots, as they were in the boys' books. But they are not out of mind. The high schooler chosen for an interplanetary voyage in *Secret of the Ninth Planet* (1959) may be the sole exception: He visits his home town to say good-bye, sees only boys, and kisses no one except his mother. More commonly, the frame stories contain dates, girlfriends, flirtations, and rejections, and during the adventure, there are allusions to girls back home and wolf whistles at the female denizens of outer space. While on leave at a space station, the teenagers of *Space Cadet* (1948) try to pick up a "tall, willowy blonde, dressed in some blue wisps of nothing much." *The Colors of Space* (1963) opens with teenage Bart Steele saying good-bye to his space-academy chum ("[I]n some indefinable way, the parting marked the end of their boyhood.") and closes with heterosexual fulfillment: "[H]e looked down at the pretty Mentorian girl . . . and suddenly he knew he would never be lonely again." Isaac Asimov's *Lucky Starr* series (1952–1958) is set five thousand years in the future, but the culture of the late 1940s has never gone out of style: There are big bands playing on the radio, dinners of veal chops and mashed potatoes, packs of cigarettes in everyone's front pocket, and endless set-piece descriptions of pretty secretaries and businessmen's wives.[8]

Some Adventure Boys ruggedly opine that girls and space do not mix, but they are careful to establish that their disdain in no way signifies lack of heterosexual interest. In *Tunnel in the Sky* (1955), about high school students space-wrecked on a savage planet, chief Adventure Boy Rod doesn't date, but only because he is too busy acting as "mayor" of their new society. He clarifies: "There's nothing better at a picnic or a hayride. I'm the biggest supporter of the female gender." In *The Rolling Stones* (1952), teenage twins Castor and Pollux discuss whether they should let their sister tag along on their amateur space flight. Pollux disapproves:

> "We can't drag her all around the system; girls are a nuisance."
> "You've got that wrong, Junior. You mean 'sisters.' Girls are okay."
> Pollux considered this. "Yeah, I guess you're right."
> "I'm always right."[9]

Though friendships between the space teens are common, they rarely approach the intensity, intimacy, exclusivity, or permanence of

homoromance. Robert Silverberg's *Revolt on Alpha C* (1955) gives protagonist Larry Stark three companions rather than just one, and he
forms no passionate bond with any of them. In *Undersea Quest*, Jerry
seems to care deeply for his aquatic academy roommate. However, when
the boy returns after being lost undersea and presumed dead, all Jerry
can muster is a handshake ("I pumped his hand in a storm of warm
feeling"), and when they are expelled from the academy together, they
go their separate ways. In *The Mysterious Planet* (1953), space cadet Bob
befriends a teenage civilian, with some clutching of arms and grabbing
of shoulders. But in the end they part. A promise of future visits ("I'll
be seeing you every summer. Maybe we can all take another trip next
year. . . .") is a pale reflection of the prewar Adventure Boys, who always
returned to the mundane world together and continued to share houses
and lives through middle age.[10]

Lester Del Rey's *Tunnel Though Time* (1956) sends the narrator, a
high school jock named Bob, twenty thousand years into the past to
help a classmate named Pete rescue his stranded scientist-father. At first
Bob isn't too keen on the chess-playing class brain: "[W]hile I didn't
especially like him, that wasn't to say I disliked him. We were just separate types." They grow to respect and even care for each other, but they
assiduously, almost deliberately, avoid falling in love. Dad does all of the
rescuing, there are no war-whooping embraces, and the book does not
end with a fade-out "where shall we go next?" The boys go their separate ways without comment, and Bob waxes misty-eyed over a girl they
met in the past: "I hoped she would remember me."[11]

In the *Lucky Starr* series, youngster Lucky has an exclusive, permanent, domestic relationship with a diminutive Martian named Bigman.
They frequently rescue each other; villains force Lucky to do things by
threatening to harm Bigman, or vice versa; their friends invite them to
parties and dinners as a couple. Yet Asimov seems determined to demonstrate their utter lack of homoromantic intensity or intimacy. They
have little physical contact other than the punches of feigned attacks.
They frequently comment on each other's ugliness, as a means of displaying affection by displacing it. The aftermath of a rescue or an escape
is a joke rather than an embrace:

Lucky let Bigman remove his sea suit and managed a smile as the little Martian looked up worriedly at him.

"I never thought I'd see you again, Lucky," said Bigman, gulping noisily.

"If you're going to cry," said Lucky, "Turn your head away. I didn't get in out of the ocean just to get all wet in here. How are the main generators coming along?"[12]

Heinlein's *Time for the Stars* (1956) may represent the nadir of the juvenile science fiction flight from homoromance. Teenage twins Tom and Pat Bartlett sign on as a telepathic communications link for an interstellar exploration mission: Tom, aboard the ship, will zap instant messages to Pat, back home. Since the ship travels at near light speed, Tom ages only a few years, while seventy years pass on Earth. Within months (from Tom's point of view), Pat is a middle-aged businessman. Telepathy only works for children and teenagers, so Pat's daughter must take over the communication, and then his granddaughter, and finally his spunky teenage great-granddaughter. (The reason Pat has no male descendents is obvious: The telepathic link is described as intimate and sensual, so a strange boy linking with Tom would become perilously erotic.) When the brothers are finally reunited, Tom is still young and strong, of college age, but Pat is an emaciated, bitter, wheelchair-bound old man.

One might look for a metaphoric comparison of deadening, soul-destroying heteronormativity and the wild homoerotic freedom of space, except that Tom doesn't experience a moment of homoerotic freedom. Other than his uncle, who dies halfway through the book, the men and boys Tom encounters are all bullies or insufferable snobs. However, he seems obsessed with investing every relationship with heterosexual innuendo: He jokingly calls the female psychiatrist who evaluates him his "girlfriend," gets a real hand-holding, kissing-at-the-movies girlfriend aboard the ship, and advises his pet pig to "find a lady pig" during a stay on an amenable planet. When he returns to Earth, he barely has a moment to reunite with his brother before great-grand-niece Vicky pulls him aside and tells him (via telepathy):

"After we are married, there will be none of this light-years-apart stuff . . . understand me? I go where you go!"

"Huh? When did you decide to marry me?"

"You seem to forget that I have been reading your mind since I was a baby . . ."

Our "courtship" had lasted all of twenty seconds. Without letting go my hands Vicky spoke aloud. "Tom and I are going downtown and get married. We'd like you to come along."[13]

SWISS FAMILY ROBINSON

Between 1955 and 1965, Walt Disney personally auditioned a veritable army of young men to model girl-craziness for preteens and their families, and he seemed to concentrate on the previously underhetero-sexualized Adventure Boy. Nearly half of the twenty-nine Disney live-action films released to children and families during the decade feature Adventure Boys, and they all, without exception, fall in love with girls. Strangely, Disney often selected boys who had played gay or gay-stereo-typed roles on-screen. Michael Anderson Jr. played Robert Mitchum's shy, sensitive (i.e., gay) son in *The Sundowners* (1960) before Disney cast him in *In Search of the Castaways* (1962). Peter McEnery played a young gay man who committed suicide in *Victim* (1962) before Disney cast him in *The Moon-Spinners* (1964). Surely it is no coincidence that, al-though many young actors who portrayed aggressively heterosexual characters were available, so many of the Disney Adventure Boys were hired directly from roles with implicit or explicit sexual ambiguity. It seems that Disney was attempting to instill adolescent heterosexual de-sire as a form of personal and national salvation, to demonstrate that even "sissies" could become "red-blooded, all-American men," that America retained, or (at the very least) could invent, a masculine, com-petitive, successful presence in the world.

Swiss Family Robinson (1960, dir. Ken Annakin), about a family ship-wrecked on a tropical island, seems designed specifically to demonstrate to children that Adventure Boys could (and should) be girl-crazy. The only nod to homoromance comes in the form of beefcake: The two

Robinson teenagers, James MacArthur (playing Fritz) and Tommy Kirk (playing Ernst) are bare-chested and bronzed in nearly every scene. However, there are no boys (or girls) their own age on the island. The lack of boys bothers no one, but early on, Father and Mother Robinson (John Mills, Dorothy McGuire) worry about the lack of girls:

> Father: Don't you sometimes feel this is the life we were meant to live?
>
> Mother: It's wonderful now, but what about tomorrow? What about our sons? What future is there for them? What if we were never to get away? They'd never know what it is like to be married . . . what it's like to have a family.

Hetero-horniness precipitates Fritz and Ernst's plan to sail to the other side of the island, where there might be some girls. Instead, they encounter a puzzlingly sissified boy, Bertie, but fortunately for their hetero-hormones, "he" turns out to be a "she," Roberta (Janet Munro), traveling in drag to avoid assault. There is a girl in the original novel, an "English cousin" whom Fritz marries in the last lines, almost as an afterthought, but in the Disney version Fritz and Ernst spend the rest of the movie posturing, flirting, and fistfighting over her.[14] Roberta is always talking about how she misses London, with its color and excitement, but in the end, when the rescue boat arrives, she refuses to go home. Instead she and Fritz (the older brother) will stay and found a new colony.

> Roberta: Two people, if they have each other, what more could they want?
>
> Fritz: I guess . . . to be alone. [They kiss. Ernst, coming to fetch them, grimaces.]

Ernst goes off to Europe to be educated. Fritz and Roberta and their heterosexual desire are all that is necessary to bring American-style civilization to the tropics, and brothers and boy-pals are merely a hindrance.

JUNGLE COMICS

Dell and Gold Key comics were aimed at grade-school boys: Their clean, uncluttered art and stories that concluded within one issue made them an ideal alternative to the complex DC and Marvel comic universes favored by their older brothers. Yet by the 1960s, even Dell and Gold Key comics were insuring that their Adventure Boys expressed hetero-passion. Not that same-sex pairings were unknown, especially in the jungle: *Turok Son of Stone* (1956), a Native American teenager trapped in a lost world with dinosaurs and savages, traveled with an older buddy; *The Jungle Twins* (1972), heirs to a Central European throne, preferred to jaunt loincloth-clad around the veldt; and *Brothers of the Spear* (1972), the white Dan-El and the black Natongo, became corulers of the jungle kingdom of Aba-Zulu. All had superb physiques and the intense, intimate, exclusive bonds that suggest homoromance rather than friendship. But there were also GGA girls to rescue, shy boy-girl flirtations, invitations for the girl to stay in the jungle or the boy to return to civilization with her. Dan-El and Natongo even had wives.

Korak, Son of Tarzan (1964) traveled alone, without a same-sex partner, but he, too, encountered endless GGA girls, jungle princesses and scrappy scientists' daughters. Evidently that was not sufficient: When DC Comics took over the series in 1972, he received an ongoing heteronormative motive. He searches for his lost girlfriend Meriam, who, according to the opening narration, "gives his life meaning." He elaborates: "I seek a girl . . . without whom my life is nothing. And nothing else in life holds value for me!"[15] Dethroning tyrants, rescuing lost expeditions, killing monsters, ending plagues, and otherwise improving the quality of life for vast numbers of jungle residents means nothing. The only thing that holds value is heterosexual practice.

SABUS

South Asian Adventure Boys were especially popular in Europe, where white Western teenagers commonly traveled with turban and dhoti-clad sidekicks, reenacting the old Sabu–Jon Hall bond but without a heteronormative triangulation. The blond Breton Corentin and his

Hindu sidekick Kim premiered in the comic magazine *Tintin* in 1946 and adventured in various danger-filled colonial locales for nearly thirty years.[16] In 1948, *Tintin* paired the "beau, jeune, et intrépide" Roman citizen Alix with the muscular, brown-skinned Egyptian Enak (perhaps Rome and Egypt had a relationship equivalent to modern-day France and its colonies). Thirty years of adventures, translated into a dozen languages (not English), displayed the teenage bodies much more blatantly than any American comic would dare, with endless panoramas of chests, biceps, shoulders, and thighs, even occasional frontal and rear nudity. There were constant buddy-bonding rescues, separations, reunions, and vows of permanent commitment, but no heteroromance until Alix fell for a Pacific Island lass in *Les Proies du volcan* (1976). Though their creator, Jacques Martin, vociferously opposed any homoromantic reading of the pair, an article in *Le Palace* called them "herós homosexuel de notre enfance."[17] They continue to globe-trot to this day, with just an occasional wink at a girl to spare them from the "stigma" of gay rumor.

In the spring of 1954, USC college student Nino Marcel played a South Asian named Gunga Ram in the feature film *Sabaka*, displaying a lean, muscular physique in dhoti and turban as he traversed India to avenge his murdered family. He never expressed any interest in girls or boys. But that fall, when he was hired to star in live-action segments of the children's television program *Andy's Gang*, a minor character in the original movie, Rama, was promoted to sidekick (dialect comedian Vito Scotti was thirty-six years old but still able to play adolescent).[18] Rama spent most scenes permanently attached to Gunga's wrist or shoulder, or hugging him from behind so tightly that one wonders how they could walk that way. Along with the amazingly revealing beefcake and the amazingly expressive intimacy came hints of hetero-desire, but only hints: Rama protests that he isn't going to a village festival "just to see the girls," and when the pair rescues two backward-talking white girls from forced goddess-hood, they ride off on elephants, each girl hugging her boy from behind as he tries to teach her English (or perhaps Hindustani).

Homoromance between white Western and South Asian Adventure Boys appeared in media aimed at children as late as the 1960s. In MGM's *Maya* (1966, dir. John Berry), fifteen-year-old ex–Dennis the

Menace Jay North, grown into a leggy redhead, plays Terry, who travels the Indian bush in search of lost treasure while accompanied by the titular elephant and a brown, wiry mahout named Raji (fourteen-year-old Sajid Khan). Neither expresses the slightest heterosexual interest, years after gasping after girls had become de rigueur, but they do form an unusually overt homoromantic bond. Their picaresque run-ins with scoundrels, scalawags, and assorted wild animals are notable for their intimacy: They hug, clasp each other from behind, and hold hands—with fingers interlocking. And there is a homoromantic conclusion. Terry takes Raji in his arms as if he intends to kiss him:

> Raji: [Gazing into his eyes.] I never knew what the treasure was.
>
> Terry: [Huskily.] Now we know.

The chemistry between Jay North and Sajid Khan spun them into a 1967–1968 television series in which the increasingly buffed Raji and the increasingly gaunt Terry roam around India, now in search of Terry's kidnapped dad instead of treasure, but still never glancing at a girl. Just as the thundering gods and demons of ancient myth decayed into nursery-tale bogies, the thundering passion of the homoromantic Arcadia had become a kiddie-show amusement. But *Maya* was the last holdout: The hints of homoromance were becoming too dangerous even to displace onto children.

THE SUMMER OF LOVE

In 1966 and 1967, as the first of the Baby Boomers were driving off to college or flying off to Vietnam, jungle-bred Adventure Boys were as common as tie-dye T-shirts and patchouli incense. With few exceptions they were looking for the women who would give their life meaning. Jai (Manuel Padilla Jr.), who traveled with Ron Ely's lanky television *Tarzan*, was excused, perhaps because he was only ten years old; yet Disney's ten-year-old Mowgli in *The Jungle Book* was drawn from the wild into civilization through the smile of a sari-clad girl. When DC comics gave *Bomba the Jungle Boy* his own title in 1967, he had a girlfriend in every story.[19]

In *Island of the Lost* (1967), the teenage native Tupana (Jose De Vega) befriends a shipwrecked anthropologist and his clan. He grins at hula-dancing castaway Judy (Irene Tsu), and kisses her, and holds her hand. When the rescue boat arrives, he says good-bye, but at the last minute he decides to forsake his homeland and swims out to join her. At least that is how the scene *can* be read. But Tupana also grins at another castaway, Stu (*Flipper* star Luke Halpin in tight jeans), and touches his shoulder, and takes him fishing. It is Stu who actually pulls him aboard the rescue boat. We are not *absolutely* certain, amid the fade-out hugs, which one Tupana has decided to follow.

A similar pattern appears everywhere in 1966 and 1967, among Boys Next Door, Lost Boys, and Adventure Boys:

College freshman Bobby Vee woos the dean's daughter, but he also gleams at his grinning, redheaded boy friend.

Tommy Kirk plays a teenage Casanova who trolls the beach in search of babes, but he also has a remarkably expressive bond with his best buddy.

Gang leader Peter Fonda is so distraught over the death of his pal that his girlfriend leaves him.

In Renaissance Ireland, Peter McEnery rescues a princess, but he also spends an inordinate amount of time being rescued by an older man.

Robin and Jimmy Olsen date girls, but they are heartbroken when they believe that their superhero pals have found someone else.

Korak Son of Tarzan rescues a young African diplomat and introduces him to a girl, but not before the duo spends many panels gazing at each other with unparalleled delight.[20]

During the Summer of Love, and after, nearly every teenage boy in mass culture, whether he was drawn for children, teenagers, or adults, whether he was star, sidekick, or villain, would be portrayed as aggressively and unequivocally girl-crazy. The homoromantic Arcadia had vanished. But homoerotic desire could not vanish; teenage boys in mass culture still often, perhaps usually, desired each other or fell in love with each other. Their bonds were emotionally passionate, physically intimate, yet always tentative, fragile, easily disrupted, and always submerged beneath a girl-crazy façade. They would gaze at each other while discussing how much they liked girls, or while competing over the same girl, or while consoling each other when their attempts at getting girls faltered. They would express their desire through hints and innuendos, through subtexts and double entendres, through ambiguities in spectacle or plot, through moments stolen from the "main" story, lest anyone notice. Lest anyone realize that they once walked into fade-out sunsets together, proudly and openly, and that they could again.

Notes

Chapter 1

1. Hurlock, E. B., and E. R. Klein, "Crushes." *Child Development* 5.1 (March 1934): 63–80.
2. Herman-Giddens, M. E., E. J. Slora, R. C. Wasserman et al. "Secondary Sexual Characteristics and Menses in Young Girls Seen in Office Practice." *Pediatrics* 99 (1997): 505–12.
3. Ariès, Philippe. *Centuries of Childhood: A Social History of Family Life.* Tr. Robert Baldick. New York: Knopf, 1962; Hanawalt, Barbara A. "Historical Descriptions and Prescriptions for Adolescence." *Journal of Family History* 17.4 (1992): 341–51; Fox, Vivian C. "Is Adolescence a Phenomenon of Modern Times?" *Journal of Psychohistory* 5.2 (1977): 271–90.
4. Demos, John, and Virginia Demos. "Adolescence in Historical Perspective." *Journal of Marriage and the Family* 31 (1969): 632–38; Bakan, David. "Adolescence in America: From Idea to Social Fact." *Daedalus* 100.4 (1971): 979–96.
5. Haines, W. Scott. "The Development of Leisure and the Transformation of Working-Class Adolescence, Paris 1830–1840." *Journal of Family History* 17.4 (1992): 451–56; Hiner, N. Ray. "Adolescence in Eighteenth-Century America." *History of Childhood Quarterly* 3.2 (1975): 253–80; Kett, Joseph F. "Adolescence and Youth in Nineteenth-Century America." *Journal of Interdisciplinary History* 2.2 (1971): 283–98; Stokvis, Pieter R. "From Child to Adult: Transition Rites in the Netherlands ca. 1800–1914." *Paedagogica Historica* 29.1 (1993): 77–92.
6. Bullough, Vern L. "Age of Consent: A Historical Overview." Pp. 23–42 in Vern L. Bullough and Helmut Graupner, eds., *Adolescence, Sexuality, and the Criminal Law.* Binghamton, NY: Haworth Press, 2005; Heywood, Colin. *A History of Childhood: Children and Childhood in the West from Medieval to Modern Times.* Cambridge: Polity Press, 2001: 30–31; Goodsell, W. *A History of Marriage and the Family.* New York: MacMillan, 1934: 475–76.
7. Handlin, Oscar. *Facing Life: Youth and the Family in American History.* Boston: Little, Brown, 1971; Kett, Joseph F. *Rites of Passage: Adolescence in America, 1790 to the Present.* New York: Basic Books, 1977; Palladino, Grace. *Teenagers: An American History.* New York: Basic Books, 1996.
8. Stoler, Ann Laura. *Race and the Education of Desire.* Durham: Duke University

Press, 1995; Banton, Michael. *Racial Theories.* Cambridge: Cambridge University Press, 1998.

9.   In 1918, the last state in the United States passed a mandatory education law, requiring children to attend school until they reached the age of sixteen.

10.   Fornas, Johan, and Goran Bolin. *Youth Culture in Late Modernity.* New York: Sage, 1995; McRobbie, Angela. *Feminism and Youth Culture.* New York: Routledge, 2000; Moran, Jeffrey P. *Teaching Sex: The Shaping of Adolescence in the Twentieth Century.* Cambridge: Harvard University Press, 2000; Pilkington, H. "Youth Cultural Studies." *Sociology Review* 7.1 (1997).

11.   Puberty is quantified through the Tanner Stages, from 1 (prepubescent) through 5 (adult). The mean age for boys' attainment of Tanner Stage 4 in pubic hair is 13.9, axillary hair 14.0, penis 13.2, testes 14.0, height 13.8, and voice 14.1. Cameron, Noël. *Human Growth and Development.* San Diego, CA: Academic Press, 2002: 367–76.

12.   Rollin, Lucy. *Twentieth Century Teen Culture by Decade: A Reference Guide.* Westport, CT: Greenwood Press, 1999; Schrum, Kelly. *Some Wore Bobby Sox: The Emergence of Teenage Girls' Culture, 1920–1945.* New York: Palgrave Macmillan, 2004; Palladino, *Teenagers*; Fass, Paula S. "Creating New Identities: Youth and Ethnicity in New York City High Schools in the 1930s and the 1940s." Pp. 95–117 in Austin, Joe, and Michael Willard, eds. *Generations of Youth: Youth Cultures and History in 20th Century America.* New York: New York University Press, 1998.

13.   Dalzell, Tom. *Flappers 2 Rappers: American Youth Slang.* New York: Merriam-Webster, 1996.

14.   Stowe, David L. *Swing Changes: Big Band Jazz in New Deal America.* Cambridge: Harvard University Press, 1996: 116.

15.   Maynes, Mary Jo. "Adolescent Sexuality and Social Identity in French and German Lower-Class Autobiography." *Journal of Family History* 17.4 (1992): 397–418; Stokvis, "From Child to Adult"; Cohen, Eleanor. "From Solitary Vice to Split Mind: Psychiatric Discourses of Male Sexuality and Coming of Age, 1918–1938." *Australian Historical Studies* 30.112 (1999): 79–95; Moran, *Teaching Sex.*

16.   Cather, Willa. "Paul's Case." In *Youth and the Bright Medusa* (1905). www.gutenberg.org/files/13555/13555-8.txt.

17.   There were a few exceptions, such as Carl Ed's *Harold Teen* comic strip, which ran from 1919 through 1959: Harold lives with his parents and participates in teen culture (he actually invented much of teen culture of the 1920s, from the derogatory term "pantywaist" to yellow raincoats). Yet he has a girlfriend, Lillums.

18.   Lancaster, E. G. *The Psychology and Pedagogy of Adolescence.* Worcester, MA: O. B. Wood, 1897; Hall, G. Stanley. *Adolescence.* New York: Appleton, 1904; Swift, James. *Youth and Race: A Study in the Psychology of Adolescence.* New York: Scribners, 1912; King, Irving. *The High School Age.* Indianapolis: Bobbs-Merrill, 1914; Starr, Louis. *The Adolescent Period.* Philadelphia: Blakiston's, 1915; Steadman, Henry. *Mental Pitfalls of Adolescence.* Boston: Hygiene Society, 1916; Paget, Stephen. *Adolescence.*

New York: Business Press, 1917; Tracy, Frederick. *The Psychology of Adolescence.* New York: Macmillan, 1920.

19. At the time masturbation was considered extremely dangerous, leading to physical emaciation and insanity.

20. Hall, G. Stanley. "How and When to Be Frank with Boys." *Ladies Home Journal,* September 1907; Ferenczi, Sandor. *Sex in Psychoanalysis.* Tr. with intro. by Ernest Jones. Boston: Badger, 1922; Ellis, Havelock. *Havelock Ellis on Life and Sex: Essays of Love and Virtue.* Garden City, NY: Doubleday, 1921: 50; Lindsey, Ben B., and Wainwright Evans. *The Revolt of Modern Youth.* New York: Boni & Liveright, 1925.

21. During this period the term "petting" meant kissing between partners who were not engaged or pinned. It does not seem to be a euphemism for more intimate activities—kissing was scandalous enough in itself. In *This Side of Paradise* (1920), F. Scott Fitzgerald tells us: "Amory had come into constant contact with that great current American phenomenon, the 'petting party.' None of the Victorian mothers—and most of the mothers were Victorian—had any idea how casually their daughters were accustomed to be kissed. . . . Amory found it rather fascinating to feel that any popular girl he met before eight he might quite possibly kiss before twelve." New York: Signet Classics, 1996: 71–72. The popular song "Pettin' in the Park" from *Gold Diggers of 1933* was made into a Warner Brothers cartoon in 1934.

22. Lynd, Robert Staughton. *Middletown: A Study in Modern American Culture.* 1929. New York: Harvest/HBJ Books, 1959: 137.

23. Lewis, Frederick Allen. *Only Yesterday: An Informal History of the 1920's.* 1931. New York: Wiley, 1997: 68.

24. Stratton-Porter, Gene. *Freckles.* 1904. Bloomington: Indiana University Press, 1986; Stratton-Porter, Gene. *Girl of the Limberlost.* 1911. Bloomington: Indiana University Press, 1984.

25. Anonymous ("By a Mother"). "When a Girl Became a Girl to My Boy." *Ladies Home Journal,* February 1907.

26. "Bernice Bobs Her Hair." *Saturday Evening Post,* May 22, 1920. Bryer, Jackson F., ed. *F. Scott Fitzgerald: Novels and Short Stories, 1920–1922.* New York: Penguin, 2000: 356–81; "The Four Fists." *Scribner's Magazine,* June 1920. Bryer, *F. Scott Fitzgerald,* 417–34.

27. Everett High School *Neskia,* 1925. http://thirdstbooks.com/everetths/ evhs25index.html; Otter Creek High School *Otterian,* 1928. http://165.138.44.11/ onlinearchives/schoolpubs/otterian.

28. Lewis, Sinclair. *Babbit.* 1922. New York: Bantam, 1998.

29. O'Neill, Eugene. *Ah, Wilderness!* 1933. New York: Samuel French, 1979.

30. Deitcher, Dave. *Dear Friends: American Photographs of Men Together, 1840–1918.* New York: Harry N. Abrams, 2001; Katz, Jonathan Ned. *Love Stories: Sex between Men before Homosexuality.* Chicago: University of Chicago Press, 2003.

31. Columbus, Indiana, High School *Log,* 1929. www.historiccolumbusindiana.org/

yearbooks/yearbooks.htm; Clarksville, Tennessee, High School *Purple & Gold,*
    1933. www.tngennet.org/montgomery/index.html.

32.   Maugham, W. Somerset. *Of Human Bondage.* 1915. New York: Bantam, 1991: 68.

33.   Taylor, Barnard. *Joseph and His Friend* (1869); Forster, E. M., *Maurice* (1911–1914),
    quoted in Fone, Byrne. "The Other Eden: Arcadia and the Homosexual
    Imagination." Pp. 13–34 in Stuart Kellog, ed., *Literary Visions of Homosexuality.*
    New York: Haworth, 1983: 16–17; Gide, André. *Saül.* 1906. Paris: Gallimard, 1942;
    Grahame, Kenneth. *The Wind in the Willows.* 1908. New York: Simon & Schuster,
    1983. Cf. Rosenmeyer, Thomas G. *The Green Cabinet: Theocritus and the European
    Pastoral Lyric.* Berkeley: University of California Press, 1969. Ettin, Andrew V.
    Literature and the Pastoral. New Haven: Yale University Press, 1984; Cook, Matt.
    London and the Culture of Homosexuality, 1885–1914. Cambridge: Cambridge
    University Press, 2003.

34.   Kincaid, James R. *Erotic Innocence: The Culture of Child Molesting.* Durham: Duke
    University Press, 1998; Higgonet, Anne. *Pictures of Innocence: The History and Crisis
    of Ideal Childhood.* London: Thames and Hudson, 1998; Vicinus, Martha. "The
    Adolescent Boy: Fin de Siécle Femme Fatale?" *Journal of the History of Sexuality*
    5.1 (1994): 90–114.

35.   See, for instance, Martin, Robert K., and George Piggford, eds., *Queer Forster.*
    Chicago: University of Chicago Press, 1997; Sedgwick, Eve Kosofsky. *Novel
    Gazing: Queer Reading in Fiction.* Durham: Duke University Press, 1997; Barrios,
    Richard. *Screened Out: Playing Gay in Hollywood from Edison to Stonewall.* New
    York: Routledge, 2002.

36.   Buhle, Paul, and David Wagner. *Radical Hollywood: The Untold Story behind America's
    Favorite Movies.* New York: New Press, 2003: 15.

37.   Sedgwick, Eve Kosofsky. *Between Men: English Literature and Male Homosocial
    Desire.* New York: Columbia University Press, 1986.

38.   Burstein, Stanley M. *A Brief History of Ancient Greece: Politics, Society, Culture.*
    Oxford: Oxford University Press, 2004: 190–91.

39.   Douglas, Ann. *The Feminization of Culture.* New York: Farrer, Strauss, & Giroux,
    1998; Leske, Nancy. *Act Your Age! A Cultural Construction of Adolescence.* New York:
    Routledge-Falmer, 2002: 35; Bederman, Gail. *Manliness and Civilization: A Cultural
    History of Gender and Race in the United States, 1880–1917.* Chicago: University of
    Chicago Press, 1995: 79.

40.   Calinescu, Matei. *Faces of Modernity: Avant-garde, Decadence, Kitsch.* Bloomington:
    Indiana University Press, 1977; Constable, Liz, Dennis Denisoff, and Matt Potolsky,
    eds. *Perennial Decay: On the Aesthetics and Politics of Decadence.* Philadelphia:
    University of Pennsylvania Press, 1999; Showalter, Elaine. *Gender and Culture at the
    Fin-de-Siècle.* New York: Viking, 1990.

41.   Morgan, David. *Protestants and Pictures: Religion, Visual Culture, and the Age of
    American Mass Production.* Oxford: Oxford University Press, 1999; Mitchell,
    Lee Clark. *Westerns: Making the Man in Fiction and Film.* Chicago: University of

NOTES TO PAGES 19–22   247

Chicago Press, 1996; Winter, Thomas. *Making Men, Making Class: The YMCA and Workingmen, 1877–1920*. Chicago: Univerisity of Chicago Press, 2002; MacDonald, Robert H. H. *Sons of the Empire: The Frontier and the Boy Scout Movement, 1890–1918*. Toronto: University of Toronto Press, 1993; Putney, Clifford. *Muscular Christianity: Manhood and Sports in Protestant America, 1880 to 1920*. Cambridge: Harvard University Press, 2003.

42. In other books I have used the term "homoerotic Eden" to refer to a somewhat different convention common among teenagers in mass culture after World War II: same-sex eroticism evoked simultaneously with girl-craziness. In Arcadia, heterosexual interest is absent, at least in the teenage partner, and the relationship therefore is more likely to be exclusive and permanent.

CHAPTER 2

1. Lewis, Sinclair. *Main Street*. 1920. New York: Penguin, 1998: 3.
2. Origin: 21% Northwest Europe, 4% Ireland, 25% Central Europe, 18% Russia and Eastern Europe, 32% Italy and Southern Europe, 1% elsewhere. Occupation: 3% managers, technicians, and professionals; 13% skilled craftsmen,;47% laborers; 14% other occupation; 23% no occupation. Only adult men were counted. Bureau of the Census, *Historical Statistics of the United States: From Colonial Times to 1970*. Washington, DC: Bureau of the Census, 1989.
3. Roediger, David R. *The Wages of Whiteness: Race and the Making of the American Working Class*. London: Verso, 1999; Frye, Matthew. *Whiteness of a Different Color: European Immigrants and the Alchemy of Race*. Cambridge: Harvard University Press, 1999; Perry, Curtis L., Jr. *Apes and Angels: The Irish in Victorian Caricature*. Washington, DC: Smithsonian Books, 1996; Lagumina, Salvatore; *Wop: A Documentary History of Italian Discrimination*. Toronto: Guernica Editions, 1999; Daniels, Roger. *Guarding the Golden Door: American Immigration Policy and Immigrants since 1882*. New York: Hill & Wang, 2004: 49–51.
4. Race and ethnicity data from Department of the Census; religious affiliation from Ahlstrom, Sydney E. *A Religious History of the American People*. New Haven: Yale University Press, 1973: 1002.
5. Date is given for the first book in the series only. See Johnson, Deidre. *Edward Stratemeyer and the Stratemeyer Syndicate*. New York: Twayne, 1993; Billman, Carol. *The Secret of the Stratemeyer Syndicate: Nancy Drew, the Hardy Boys, and the Million Dollar Fiction Factory*. New York: Ungar, 1986; Dizer, John T. *Tom Swift & Company*. Jefferson, NC: McFarland, 1982.
6. Overton, Mark. *Jack Winters' Gridiron Chums*. 1919. www.blackmask.com; Breckenridge, Gerald. *The Radio Boys on the Mexican Border*. 1922. www. gutenberg.org; Cox, Stephen Angus. *The Dare Boys of 1776*. 1910. www.gutenberg. org.

7. Chapman, Allan. *The Darewell Chums in the Woods, or, Frank Roscoe's Secret.* 1908. www.gutenberg.org.

8. Fitzhugh, Percy Keese. *Roy Blakely.* 1920. www.gutenberg.org.

9. Hancock, H. Irving. *Dave Darren at Veracruz.* 1914. www.gutenberg.org.

10. Hancock, H. Irving. *The Young Engineers in Arizona.* 1912. www.blackmask.com. All six were reunited for the *Uncle Sam's Boys* series (1916), but the contours of the "particular friendships" remain clear.

11. Eunice Fuller Barnard, "Children of Hollywood's Gold Rush." *New York Times,* October 4, 1936: 10

12. Kincaid, James R. *Child-Loving: The Erotic Child and Victorian Culture.* New York: Routledge, 2002; Robson, Catherine. *Men in Wonderland: The Lost Girlhood of the Victorian Gentleman.* Princeton: Princeton University Press, 2001; Birkin, Andrew. *James Barrie and the Lost Boys: The Real Story behind Peter Pan.* New Haven: Yale University Press, 2003.

13. Cooper, Jackie, with Dick Kleiner. *Please Don't Shoot My Dog: The Autobiography of Jackie Cooper.* New York: Morrow, 1981: 49.

14. From the author's collection.

15. The titular Tough Guy is not Jackie Cooper, but Joseph Calleia, redeemed by the innocent love of Jackie and his dog Rin Tin Tin.

16. For instance, when he writes of Tyrone Power, he might have said, "I never saw any sign that he was gay," but instead he says the excoriating, "I never saw even a hint of the supposed homosexuality he has been accused of practicing." Cooper, *Please Don't Shoot,* 188.

17. Cooper, *Please Don't Shoot,* 85. They shared her with two of Mickey's usual brothel-buddies, William Tracy and Sidney Miller.

18. Illustrations are available at http://histclo.hispeed.com/style/suit/faunt/faunt.html.

19. I have not seen the 1976 Glenn Anderson version, but the 1980 Ricky Schroeder and the 1994 George Baker versions both minimize the relationship between the two boys, making Mr. Hobbs, the adult grocer, Cedric's main friend.

20. Again, recent versions omit any suggestion that Dick stays in England with Cedric.

21. Churchill, Douglas W. "Life of the Child Star." *New York Times,* May 22, 1938: 118.

22. Clark, Gerald. *Get Happy: The Life of Judy Garland.* New York: Random House, 2000: 117–20.

23. Strindberg, August. *Zones of the Spirit: A Book of Thoughts.* Tr. Claud Fielde. 1917. New York: Haskell House, 1974: 171.

24. Drake, Robert. *The Gay Canon.* New York: Anchor Books, 1998: 167; Hughes, Thomas. *Tom Brown's Schooldays.* 1857. Oxford: Oxford University Press, 1999: 306–7, 376.

25. Played by Billy Halop from the Dead End Kids. George MacDonald Fraser has

written a series of best-selling novels (1969–) that carry Flashman into adulthood, where he becomes a swashbuckling Indiana Jones–style adventurer.

26. The term was slang for the passive partner in a same-sex encounter, or for gay men in general. See entry "Film Noir" in the Gay Online Encyclopedia, www.glbtq.com/arts/film_noir.html.

27. Mann, William J. *Wisecracker: The Life and Times of William Haines, Hollywood's First Openly Gay Star.* New York: Penguin, 1999: 320; Wallace, David. *Hollywoodland.* New York: St. Martin's, 2003: 56; McNulty, Thomas. *Errol Flynn: The Life and Career.* Jefferson, NC: McFarland, 2004.

28. Hoerle, Helen Christine. *The Story of Freddie Bartholomew.* Akron, OH: Saalfield, 1935; Best, Marc. *Those Endearing Young Charms: Child Performers of the Screen.* New York: A. S. Barnes, 1971: 15–19; Parish, James Robert. *The Great Child Stars.* New York: Ace Books, 1976: 1–8; "Ronald Sinclair, Child Actor, Film Editor." *Los Angeles Times,* December 3, 1992: B-8; Bond, Tommy, with Ron Genini. *Darn Right It's Butch: Memories of Our Gang.* Wayne, PA: Morgin Press, 1994: 99–100.

29. The most famous girls' book series, Nancy Drew, stars a teenage girl, but not unexpectedly her boyfriend is a college "man," Ned Nickerson.

30. Their ages are inconsistent. Frank ranges between sixteen and eighteen, and Joe is a year younger. When the original series was revised during the 1960s, they became eighteen and seventeen throughout.

31. And evidently untranslatable to other media. There have been two Hardy Boys television series, but never a radio series or feature-length motion picture.

32. Dixon, Franklin W. (pseud.). *The House on the Cliff.* New York: Grossett & Dunlap, 1927: 50; Dixon, Frank W. (pseud.). *The Shore Road Mystery.* New York: Grossett & Dunlap, 1928: 4.

33. Kismaric, Carole, and Marvin Heiferman. *The Mysterious Case of Nancy Drew and the Hardy Boys.* New York: Simon & Schuster, 1998: 36, 90.

CHAPTER 3

1. Whitman lived in Manhattan or Brooklyn until 1860. Schmidgall, Gary. *Walt Whitman: A Gay Life.* New York: Dutton, 1997: 110–18.

2. Sante, Luc. *Low Live: Lures and Snares of Old New York.* New York: Farrer, Strauss, & Giroux, 2003: 306; Riis, Joseph A. *How the Other Half Lives.* 1890. New York: Penguin, 1997: 193.

3. Platt, Anthony. *Child Savers: The Invention of Delinquency.* Chicago: University of Chicago Press, 1980: 15–18.

4. Alger, Horatio. *Ragged Dick.* 1868. New York: Signet, 1990: 4.

5. Furia, Philip. *The Poets of Tin Pan Alley.* Oxford: Oxford University Press, 1992; Buhle, Paul. *From the Lower East Side to Hollywood: Jews in American Popular Culture.*

New York: Verso, 2004; Negra, Diane. *The Irish in Us: Irish, Performativity, and Popular Culture*. Durham: Duke University Press, 2006.

6. Scharnhorst, Gary, and Jack Bales. *The Lost Life of Horatio Alger, Jr.* Bloomington: Indiana University Press, 1985.

7. Schwartzman, Roy. "Recasting the American Dream through Horatio Alger's Success Stories." *Studies in American Culture* 23:2 (2000): 75–91; Hendler, Glenn. "Pandering in the Public Sphere: Masculinity and the Market in Horatio Alger." *American Quarterly* 48.3 (September 1996): 415–38; Moon, Michael. "'The Gentle Boy from the Dangerous Classes': Pederasty, Domesticity, and Capitalism in Horatio Alger." *Representations* 19 (Summer 1987): 87–110.

8. Jameson, Frederic. *Postmodernism, Or, the Cultural Logic of Late Capitalism* Durham: Duke University Press, 1992: 25.

9. Alger, Horatio. *Facing the World*. 1893, 1917. www.gutenberg.org.

10. One story has several MGM teen stars visiting a prostitute together. The others stay in the room for only a few seconds, but Mickey Rooney takes half an hour. Later they ask the prostitute if he was really so sexually proficient. She tells them that he spent thirty seconds on the sexual act itself and the rest of the time trying out comedy material.

11. Coghlan, Frank. *They Still Call Me Junior: Autobiography of a Child Star.* Jefferson, NC: McFarland, 1993: 89.

12. "News of the Screen." *New York Times,* October 25, 1937: 23.

13. *Headline Crasher* (1937) is an exception: Kane Richmond plays a sleazy reporter tailing rich-kid Frankie in the hopes of catching him doing something scandalous and thereby discrediting his senator father. They team up briefly to capture some bank robbers, but they never become intimate. In the last scene, Frankie asks his father to reward "that reporter" who helped him.

14. Frankie Darro biography, http://members.aol.com/darrofan/frankie.

15. Phillips, Gene D. "A Profile of Adolescent Delinquents: Dead End as Play and Film." Pp. 19–35 in Michael A. Oliker and Walter P. Krolikowski, eds., *Images of Youth: Popular Culture as Educational Ideology*. New York: Peter Lang, 2001.

16. Leo Gorcey was twenty years old, Huntz Hall nineteen, Gabriel Dell eighteen, Billy Halop seventeen, Bernard Punsly fourteen, and Bobby Jordan fourteen.

17. Vallet, François. *L'image de l'enfant au cinéma*. Paris: Les Éditions du Cerf, 1991: 141.

18. Reuter, Donald F. *Shirtless: The Hollywood Male Physique*. New York: Universe Publishing, 2000: 48.

19. Berger, Martin A. *Man-Made: Thomas Eakins and the Construction of Gilded Age Masculinity*. Berkeley: University of California Press, 2000: 97; Dutton, Kenneth R. *The Perfectible Body: The Western Ideal of Male Physical Development*. New York: Continuum, 1995: 158; Kasson, John F. *Houdini, Tarzan, and the Perfect Man: The White Male Body and the Challenge of Modernity in America*. New York: Hill & Wang, 2001: 211.

20. Wlodarz, Joe. "Rape Fantasies: Hollywood and Homophobia." Pp. 62–80 in Peter Lehman, ed., *Masculinity: Bodies, Movies, Culture*. New York: Routledge, 2001: 69.

21. Russo, Vito. *The Celluloid Closet: Homosexuality in the Movies*. Rev. ed. New York: Harper & Row, 1987: 32–40; Doherty, Thomas. *Pre-Code Hollywood: Sex, Immorality, and Insurrection in American Cinema, 1930–1934*. New York: Columbia University Press, 1999: 123–24.

22. Springhall, John. *Youth, Popular Culture, and Moral Panics: Penny Gaffs to Gangsta-Rap, 1830–1996*. New York: St. Martins Press, 1998: 106–7.

23. Kingsley, Sidney. "Dead End." 1937. Pp. 75–166 in *Five Prizewinning Plays*. Columbus: Ohio State University Press, 1995: 96, 103.

24. Farrell, James T. *Studs Lonigan*. New York: Random House, 1938: 6, 55, 68. The first part, "Young Lonigan," was published in 1932.

25. Borde, Raymond, and Etienne Chaumeton. *A Panorama of American Film Noir, 1941–53*. Tr. Paul Hammond. 1955. San Francisco: City Lights Books, 2002: 144; cf. Doherty, *Pre-Code Hollywood*, 146–47.

26. Dyer, Richard. "Homosexuality and Film Noir." Pp. 52–72 in *The Matter of Images*. New York: Routledge, 1993; Oliver, Kelly, and Benigno Trigo. *Noir Anxiety*. Minneapolis: University of Minnesota Press, 2003: 37–39; Shadoian, Jack. *Dreams and Dead Ends: The American Gangster Film*. 1977. New York: Oxford University Press, 2003: 38.

27. Nasaw, David. *Children of the City at Work and Play*. New York: Oxford University Press, 1986: 142.

28. Leske, Nancy. *Act Your Age! A Cultural Construction of Adolescence*. New York: Routledge-Falmer, 2002: 39.

29. Lee, Raymond, and B. C. Van Hecke. *Gangsters and Hoodlums: The Underworld in the Cinema*. New York: Castle Books, 1971: 15.

30. *Newsboy's Home* (1939), *Little Tough Guy* (1940).

31. *Boy of the Streets* (1938), *Reformatory* (1938), *The Little Tough Guys in Society* (1939).

32. *Juvenile Court* (1938), *Wanted by the Police* (1938), *Boys' Reformatory* (1939), *Off the Record* (1939), *You Can't Get Away with Murder* (1939)

33. Leske, *Act Your Age!*, 66.

34. DePastino, Todd. *Citizen Hobo: How a Century of Homelessness Shaped America*. Chicago: University of Chicago Press, 2003: 86–89; Boag, Peter. *Same-Sex Affairs: Constructing and Controlling Homosexuality in the Pacific Northwest*. Berkeley: University of California Press, 2003: 40–42.

CHAPTER 4

1. Weaver, John C. *The Great Land-Rush and the Making of the Modern World, 1650–1900*. Toronto: McGill-Queens University Press, 2003; Stoler, Anne L., ed. *Tensions*

of Empire: Colonial Cultures in a Bourgeois World. Berkeley: University of California Press, 1997

2.   Kipling, Rudyard. "The White Man's Burden." 1899. In *Rudyard Kipling: Complete Verse.* New York: Anchor, 1989: 321.

3.   Said, Edward W. *Orientalism.* 1979. New York: Knopf, 2000. Cannadine, David. *Ornamentalism: How the British Saw Their Empire.* Oxford: Oxford University Press, 2001.

4.   DeForest, Tim. *Storytelling in the Pulps, Comics, and Radio: How Technology Changed Popular Fiction in America.* Jefferson, NC: McFarland, 2004; Johnson, Deidre. *Edward Stratemeyer and the Stratemeyer Syndicate.* New York: Twayne Publishers, 1993: 23; Macaigne, Bernard, "From Tom Sawyer to Penrod: The Child in American Popular Literature, 1870–1910." *Revue Francaise d'etudes Americaines* 8.17 (1983): 319–31.

5.   Duffield, J. W. *The Radio Boys in the Thousand Islands.* 1922. www.blackmask.com. This is a different series from *The Radio Boys at the Mexican Border.*

6.   Johnson, *Edward Stratemeyer,* 103.

7.   The narrator is careful to establish that the act is to be taken as rude, not as criminal. The girl is indignant but not frightened: There is no threat to her honor or safety.

8.   Appleton, Victor (pseud.). *Don Sturdy in the Land of Volcanoes:* New York: Grosset & Dunlap, 1925: 135.

9.   Sherman, Harold. *Tahara, Boy Mystic of India.* Chicago: Goldsmith, 1933: 112.

10. Though the whiz-kid Tom Swift in the popular adventure series (1910) is sometimes referred to as a boy, he does not meet the criteria for adolescence. He does not require adult supervision during the adventures, and he is not in school during the frame stories. Sidekick Ned is an adult who works in a bank.

11. Salmonson, Jessica Amanda. "The Great Marvel Series: A Discursive Bibliography." www.violetbooks.com/greatmarvels-bib.html.

12. Rockwood, Roy (pseud.) *Five Thousand Miles Underground.* 1908. www.gutenberg. org.

13. Robert Aldrich suggests that this arrangement may mirror real life: Many of the nineteenth-century colonizers were gay or at least established their most significant emotional bonds with men. *Colonialism and Homosexuality.* New York: Routledge, 2002: 23.

14. See also Nelson, Claudia. "David and Jonathan—and Saul—Revisited: Homodomestic Patterns in British Boy's Magazine Fiction, 1880–1915." *Children's Literature Association Quarterly* 23.3 (1998): 120–27.

15. All-Story had published his "Under the Moons of Mars" in six parts earlier that year.

16. Burroughs, Edgar Rice. *Tarzan of the Apes.* 1912. New York: Signet, 1990.

17. For instance, Balasopoulos, Antonis. "Progress, Regression, Repetition: Edgar Rice Burroughs' Tarzan of the Apes and the Ambivalences of Imperial Modernity."

Imaginaires: Revue du Centre de Recherche sur l'Imaginaire dans les Littératures de Langue Anglaise 9 (2003): 199–213; Berglund, Jeff. "Write, Right, White, Rite: Literacy, Imperialism, Race, and Cannibalism in Edgar Rice Burroughs' Tarzan of the Apes." *Studies in American Fiction* 27.1 (1999): 53–76; Gleason, William. "Of Sequels and Sons: Tarzan and the Problem of Paternity." *Journal of American & Comparative Cultures* 23.1 (2000): 41–51; Jurca, Catherine. "Tarzan, Lord of the Suburbs." *Modern Language Quarterly* 57.3 (1996): 479–504; Mayer, Ruth. "The White Hunter: Edgar Rice Burroughs, Ernest Hemingway, Clint Eastwood, and the Art of Acting Male in Africa." Pp. 247–65 in West, Russell, ed. and Frank Lay, ed., *Subverting Masculinity: Hegemonic and Alternative Versions of Masculinity in Contemporary Culture.* Amsterdam, Netherlands: Rodopi, 2000.

18. Kline, Otis Adelbert. *Jan of the Jungle.* 1931. New York: Ace Books, 1963: 6–7; Richards, Harvey D. *Sorak and the Clouded Tiger, or, How the Terrible Ruler of the North is Hunted and Destroyed.* New York: Cupples & Leon, 1934: 3; Rockwood, Roy (pseud). *Bomba the Jungle Boy among the Slaves.* New York: McLoughlin Brothers, 1929:2–3.

19. No episodes of the radio series have survived, but some of them were used for the plot of the Big-Little book, in which Nada is considerably younger than Og and not an object of romantic interest.

20. Kline, *Jan of the Jungle,* 53.

21. Rockwood, Roy. *Bomba the Jungle Boy on the Underground River.* New York: Cupples & Leon, 1930: 179.

22. Carter, Lin. *Imaginary Worlds.* New York: Ballantine Books, 1973: 2. He is quoting from two Lovecraft stories, "Celephaïs" (1920) and "The Silver Key" (1926).

23. Lovecraft, H. P. "The Quest of Iranon." 1921. www.dagonbytes.com/thelibrary/lovecraft/thequestofiranon.htm.

24. Weinberg, Robert. *The Weird Tales Story.* New York: Wildside Books, 1999.

25. Howard, Robert E. "The Tower of the Elephant." *Weird Tales* (March 1933). Pp. 59–82 in *The Coming of Conan the Cimmerian.* New York: Ballantine Books, 2003. Several later writers have filled in Conan's childhood and adolescence. See "The Hyperborean Age of Conan." www.dodgenet.com/~moonblossom/hyborian.htm.

26. Later writers give Conan an insatiable appetite for brutal, barbarian-style rapine, but Howard's Conan is far more likely to reject women's advances, and when he does succumb, any activity beyond kissing is left to the imagination.

27. Robert E. Howard committed suicide in 1936 at the age of thirty. His close relationship with his mother and his having minimal girlfriends led to psychosexual speculation that he was "abnormal," that is, gay. See Lord, Glenn. *The Last Celt: A Bio-Bibliography of Robert E. Howard.* West Kingston, RI: Donald M. Grant, 1976; de Camp, L. Sprague, and Catherine Crook de Camp. *Dark Valley Destiny: The Life of Robert E. Howard.* New York: Bluejay Books, 1983. However, more suggestive to contemporary readers is his obsession with describing the

broad chests and iron thews of his heroes, while glossing over the descriptions of the women.

28. DeForest, Tim. *Storytelling in the Pulps, Comics, and Radio: How Technology Changed Popular Fiction in America.* Jefferson, NC: McFarland, 2004.

29. Carter, Lin. *Beyond the Gates of Dream.* New York: Belmont Press, 1969: 11, 13. He identifies the time period as the 1930's, but the mass media objects listed in the three-page-long pastiche all appeared between 1940 and 1943, except for the Leigh Brackett novel, which appeared in *Thrilling Wonder Stories,* not *Startling Stories,* in 1949.

30. Some Old-Time Radio websites suggest that Jimmie is interested in a character named Barbara, but in the original series she is an acquaintance, the older sister of a class chum, who appears in a few continuities to give the duo someone to chastely rescue. When a new version of the series was broadcast in 1946, she did become Jimmie's girlfriend.

31. Bederman, Gail. *Manliness and Civilization: A Cultural History of Gender and Race in the United States, 1880–1917.* Chicago: University of Chicago Press, 1995: 101.

32. Harmon, Jim. *The Great Radio Heroes.* Garden City, NY: Doubleday, 1967: 247; cf "The Pulp Heroes," www.geocities.com/jjnevins/pulpsa.html.

33. Frankie Thomas went on to play Nancy Drew's sidekick for Warner Brothers and, in the 1950s, *Tom Corbett, Space Cadet* on TV. Later he became a renowned bridge expert and mystery novelist. See his interview on the Tom Corbett website, www.slick-net.com/space/interviews/thomas.phtml.

34. The 1979 *Buck Rogers in the 25th Century* heterosexualizes Buck entirely by eliminating Buddy altogether.

CHAPTER 5

1. Auden, W. H. "September 1, 1939." In Mendelson, Edward, ed., *Selected Poems of W. H. Auden.* Knopf, 1989: 86.

2. Of 10,000,000 draftees, 70,000, or less than 0.01 percent, applied for conscientious objector status. During the Vietnam War, the figure was closer to 20 percent.

3. Works consulted: Adams, Michael C. C. *Best War Ever: America and World War II.* Baltimore, MD: Johns Hopkins University Press, 1993. Keegan, John. *The Second World War.* New York: Penguin, 1990; Mercer, Derrek, ed. *World War II Day by Day.* New York: DK Publishing, 2004; Murray, Williamson. *A War to Be Won: Fighting the Second World War.* Cambridge, MA: Belknap Press, 2001; Stokesbury, James L. *A Short History of World War II.* New York: Harper, 1980; Terkel, Studs. *The Good War: An Oral History of World War II.* New York: New Press, 1997.

4. Schultz, Gladys. "So Long, Folks, I Have a Date: Shall Parents Have a Say in the Social Life of Their Teen-Agers?" *Better Homes and Gardens* 17 (February 1939): 34–35; Ellenwood, James Lee. "When Boy Meets Girl." *Parents Magazine* 15

(March 1940): 18–20; Popenoe, Paul Bowman. "Your Son at Seventeen." *Hygeia* 18 (September 1940): 766–69.

5.   Warfield, Frances. "Crushes, and What to Do About Them." *Good Housekeeping* 114 (February 1942): 29–31; Ellenwood, James Lee. "Boys and Girls Need to Like Each Other." *Parents Magazine* 17 (March 1942): 22–24; Whitman, Howard. "Puppy Love Is the Real Thing." *Good Housekeeping* 115 (August 1942): 27; Richmond, Winifred Vanderbilt. "The Boy-Girl Question." *Parents Magazine* 18 (November 1943): 18–19.

6.   Mackenzie, C. "The Awkward Age." *New York Times Magazine,* November 5, 1944: 33; Hankins, Dorothy. "Adolescence: What Is It?" *Parents Magazine* 20 (April 1945): 30–31.

7.   Zachery, Caroline B. "Customary Stresses and Strains of Adolescence." *Annals of the American Academy of Political and Social Science* 236 (November 1944): 136–44.

8.   Ramsey, G.V. "The Sexual Development of Boys." *American Journal of Psychology* 56 (1943): 217–33; Gardner, G. E., and H. Spencer, "Reactions of Children with Fathers and Brothers in the Armed Forces." *American Journal of Orthopsychiatry* 14 (1944): 36–44.

9.   Clarksville, Tennessee, High School *Purple & Gold*, 1939. www.tngennet.org/montgomery.

10.   Richard Halliburton swam the Hellespont, climbed Popocatepetl, traced the footsteps of Ulysses, photographed Mount Everest, and had many other adventures, recounting them in lectures, books, and magazine articles evidently as an afterthought. I have been unable to establish a direct kinship, but they both came from northern Tennessee, so it is very likely. At least Johnnie must have felt an affinity for the famous adventurer who shared his last name. Halliburton, Richard. *Richard Halliburton: The Story of His Life's Adventures.* Garden City, NY: Doubleday, 1942; Townsend, Guy. "Richard Halliburton: The Forgotten Myth." *Memphis Magazine,* August 1977. www.memphismagazine.com.

11.   Selah, Washington, High School *Fruitspur* (1940). www.thirdstbooks.com.

12.   Accardi, Marian. "Love at First Flight: For Local Man, Aviation Not Just a Career, It's His Life." *Huntsville Times,* January 27, 2000.

13.   Columbus, Indiana, High School *Log* (1945). www.historiccolumbusindiana.org.

14.   "Graduation Day" (1956), words and music by Ross Barbour.

15.   Barbour, Ross. *Now You Know: The Story of the Four Freshmen.* Lake Geneva, WI: Tiare Publications, 2000.

16.   Husain, Syed, et al. "Stress Reactions of Children and Adolescents in War and Siege Conditions." *American Journal of Psychiatry* 155 (December 1998):1718–19; Kushnir, T., and S. Melamed. "The Gulf War and Its Impact on Burnout and Well-being of Working Civilians." *Psychological Medicine* 22.4 (November 1992): 987–95.

17.   Blum, John Morton. *V Was for Victory: Politics and American Culture during World War II.* New York: Harvest/HBJ Books, 1977; Lingeman, Richard R. *Don't You Know There's a War On? The American Home Front, 1941–1945.* New York: Nation

Books, 2003; Perret, Geoffrey. *Days of Sadness Years of Triumph: The American People, 1939–1945*. Madison: University of Wisconsin Press, 1985; Winkler, Alan. *Homefront U.S.A.: America during World War II*. Wheeling, IL: Harlan Davidson, 2000; Yellin, Emily. *Our Mothers' War: American Women at Home and at the Front during World War II*. New York: Free Press, 2004.

18. Shapiro, Peter, ed. *A History of National Service in America*. Center for Political Leadership and Participation, 1994. Some 238,000 women also served.

19. "Right Handling Can Reduce Youth Crime" and "Toledo Court's Methods Combat US Youth Crime Wave." *Life*, October 26, 1942.

20. Northwestern University Collection of World War II Posters, www.library. northwestern.edu/govpub/collections/wwii-posters/.

21. Chauncey, George. *Gay New York: The Making of the Gay Male World, 1890–1940*. London: Harper Collins, 1994; Lewis, David Levering. *When Harlem Was in Vogue*. New York: Penguin, 1997; Mann, William J. *Behind the Scenes: How Gays and Lesbians Shaped Hollywood, 1910 to 1969*. New York: Penguin, 2001.

22. Hamilton, D. M. "Some Aspects of Homo-Sexuality in Relation to Total Personality Development." *Psychiatric Quarterly* 13 (1939): 229–44; Wuff, M. "A Case of Male Homosexuality." *International Journal of Psycho-Analysis* 23 (1942): 112–20; Bergler, E. "Eight Prerequisites for the Psychoanalytic Treatment of Homosexuality." *Psychoanalytic Review* (31): 1944: 253–86; Liebman, S. "Homosexuality, Transvestism, and Psychosis." *Journal of Nervous & Mental Disease* 99 (1944): 945–58.

23. Kimmel, Michael. *Manhood in America*. New York: Free Press, 1996: 221–60; Corber, Robert J. *Homosexuality in Cold War America: Resistance and the Crisis of Masculinity*. Durham: Duke University Press, 1997: 23–30; Terry, Jennifer. *An American Obsession: Science, Medicine, and Homosexuality in Modern Society*. Chicago: University of Chicago Press, 1999: 329–42.

24. "Columbia Launches War Health Program: Students to Be Made Fit for Army, Navy." *New York Times*, January 30, 1942: 24; "27th Division Brigade Wins Civilian Praise: West Coast Legion is Manly, Well Behaved." *New York Times*, February 20, 1942: 12; "Milquetoast Men Spurned by Ickles." *New York Times*, May 13, 1942: 10.

25. Terry, Jennifer, *American Obsession*, 304–12; Wylie, Philip. *Generation of Vipers*. New York: Rinehart & Co., 1942.

26. Maskin, M. H., and L. L. Altman. "Military Psychodynamics." *Psychiatry: Journal for the Study of Interpersonal Processes* 6 (1943): 263–69; Anderson, C. "On Certain Conscious and Unconscious Homosexual Responses to Warfare." *British Journal of Medical Psychology* 20 (1944): 161–74; Beck. B. M. "Personnel Selection." *Mental Hygiene* 28 (1944): 568–70; Loeser, L. H. "The Sexual Psychopath in the Military Service." *American Journal of Psychiatry* 102 (1945): 92–101; Berube, Allan. *Coming Out under Fire: The History of Gay Men and Women in World War II*. New York: Plume, 1991: 149.

27. Barahal, H. S. "Constitutional Factors in Male Homosexuals." *Psychiatric Quarterly*

13 (1939): 391–400; Ellis, A. "The Sexual Psychology of Human Hermaphrodites." *Psychosomatic Medicine* 7 (1945): 108–25.

28. Cuber, John F. "The College Youth Goes to War." *Marriage and Family Living* 5.1 (February 1943): 5–7, 10.

29. Neustadt, R., and A. Myerson. "Quantitative Sex Hormone Studies in Homosexuality, Childhood, and Various Neuropsychiatric Disturbances." *American Journal of Psychiatry* 97 (1940): 524–51; Greco, M. C., and J. C. Wright. "The Correctional Institution in the Etiology of Chronic Homosexuality." *American Journal of Orthopsychiatry* 14 (1944): 295–308; Williams, E. G. "Homosexuality: A Biological Anomaly." *Journal of Nervous & Mental Disease* 99 (1944): 65–70; Moore, T. V. "The Pathogenesis and Treatment of Homosexual Disorders." *Journal of Personality* 14 (1945): 47–83.

30. Green, E. W., and L. G. Johnson. "Homosexuality." *Journal of Criminal Psychopathology* 5 (1944): 467–80.

31. Kirkendall, L. A. *Sex Adjustments of Young Men*. Oxford: Harper, 1940.

32. Bender, L., and S. Paster. "Homosexual Trends in Children." *American Journal of Orthopsychiatry* 11 (1941): 730–44; Waggoner, R. W., and D. A. Boyd Jr. "Juvenile Aberrant Sexual Behavior." *American Journal of Orthopsychiatry* 11 (1941): 275–92; Hennessey, M. A. R. "Homosexual Charges against Children." *Journal of Criminal Psychopathology* 2 (1941): 524–32; Cline, Edward Curtis. "Social Implications of Modern Adolescent Problems." *School Review* 49.7 (September 1941): 511–14; Henry, G. W., and A. A. Gross. "The Homosexual Delinquent." *Mental Hygiene* 25 (1941): 420–42.

33. Bellarmann, Harry. *King's Row*. 1940. New York: Kingdom House, 2002: 23.

34. Wolfe, Thomas. *The Web and the Rock*. New York: Sun Dial Press, 1940: 35, 38, 173–74.

35. Jackson, Charles. *The Lost Weekend*. 1944. New York: Manor Books, 1973: 150, 40.

36. Jackson, *Lost Weekend*, 191.

CHAPTER 6

1. FDR expressed disapproval of monopolies in many of his fireside chats.

2. Rouverol, Aurania. *Skidding*. New York: Samuel French, 1925: 6.

3. Charles Eaton was the youngest of the famous "Seven Little Eatons," sibling performers in vaudeville and on Broadway. Sister Doris published her memoirs at the age of ninety-three: Travis, Doris Eaton. *The Days We Danced: The Story of My Theatrical Family from Florenz Ziegfeld to Arthur Murray and Beyond*. Norman: University of Oklahoma Press, 2003.

4. Zierold, Norman J. *The Child Stars*. New York: Coward-McCann, 1965: 216. The hulking Wallace Beery was well-known for his lack of handsomeness.

5. Kay Van Riper worked mainly in radio before MGM hired her for the Andy

Hardy series. She also scripted *Babes in Arms, Strike up the Band,* and *Lady Be Good.* A brief biography is available at www.oscars.org/mhl/sc/vanriper_182.html.

6.   In *Hoosier Schoolboy* (August 1937), *Thoroughbreds Don't Cry* (November 1937), *Hold That Kiss* (May 1938), *Lord Jeff* (June 1938), and *Boys Town* (September 1938).

7.   Nugent, Frank S. "Trust in the Movies: Reviews in Brief." *New York Times,* July 24, 1938: 10.

8.   The custom of "dating," unchaperoned outings between unmarried men and women with the eventual goal of selecting a marital partner, started among immigrant youth and only filtered into the middle classes during the 1930s. It was still considered somewhat unseemly in 1938, especially for high schoolers; Andy Hardy had very progressive parents. Bailey, Beth L. *From Front Porch to Back Seat: Courtship in Twentieth-Century America.* Baltimore: Johns Hopkins University Press, 1989: 17–19.

9.   Zinman, David H. *Saturday Afternoon at the Bijou.* New York: Arlington House, 1973: 369; Steinberg, Cobbett. *Reel Facts: The Movie Book of Records.* New York: Vintage, 1978: 23.

10. The series is critiqued in: Kahn, E. J. "Andy Hardy Comes to Camp." *New Yorker* 18 (June 13, 1942): 55–56; Zinman, *Saturday Afternoon at the Bijou,* 383–97; and Jordan, D., and E. Connor. "Judge Hardy and Family: An American Story." *Films in Review* 25.1 (January 1974): 1–10. More recent references tend to confuse the Andy Hardy series with the MGM Barn Musicals. Robert Ray entitled his 1996 study of film theory *The Avant Garde Finds Andy Hardy,* and Martin Arnold has produced a fifteen-minute experimental film, "Life Wastes Andy Hardy," which manipulates images of the Andy Hardy opus in order to provide a sense of "melancholy." See Lippit, Akira M. "Martin Arnold's Memory Machine." *Journal of Media Arts and Cultural Criticism* 24.6 (1997): 8–10.

11. Cross, Robin. *The Big Book of B Movies.* New York: St. Martin's Press, 1981:60.

12. Levy, Emanuel. *Small-Town America in Film: The Decline and Fall of Community.* New York: Continuum, 1991: 71.

13. Crowther, Bosley. *Hollywood Raja: The Life and Times of Louis B. Mayer.* New York: Henry Holt, 1960: 239.

14. *Love Finds Andy Hardy* (1938); *You're Only Young Once* (1937).

15. Sklar, Robert. *Movie Made America: A Cultural History of American Movies.* New York: Vintage, 1994: 99.

16. Joe Yule Jr. was actually half Scottish, half Anglo-American. His mother and the MGM publicity department came up with "Mickey Rooney," probably from his character in the "Mickey McGuire" comedy shorts and the famous waif "Little Annie Rooney." He originally hated the stage name, but he never changed it, and he has frequently claimed an Irish ethnicity (or failed to correct the mistake).

17. Rooney, Mickey. *Life Is Too Short.* New York: Villard Books, 1991:199.

18. Cohan, Steven. *Masked Men: Masculinity and Movies in the Fifties.* Bloomington: Indiana University Press, 1997: 165; Davis, Melody D. *The Male Nude in*

Contemporary Photography. Philadelphia: Temple University Press, 1991; Dyer, Richard. "Don't Look Now: The Male Pin-Up." Pp. 267–76 in *The Sexual Subject: A Screen Reader in Sexuality*. New York: Routledge, 1992.

19. Hoffman, Bob. *The Big Chest Book*. New York: Strength and Health, 1941. New editions appeared in 1944, 1950, and 1967.

20. He does have a brief swimsuit scene as a young adult in *16 Fathoms Deep* (1946).

21. Cf. the Historical Swimsuit Website, "History of Men's Swimwear," www.ocf. berkeley.edu/~roseying/ids110/MENHIS.HTM.

22. In *Love Finds Andy Hardy*, audiences are favored with a close-up of the front of Andy's swimsuit. Teenage movies in the 1940s zoomed in on the fronts of male stars' swimsuits or undershorts quite often, perhaps for the same reason that teen idols in the 1970s were often photographed with real or artificial bulges in their pants.

23. *The Hardys Ride High* was the original title of *Out West with the Hardys* (1938) and still appears on some lobby cards.

24. John King was the star of the 1936 Bulldog Drummond serial, Aramis in *The Three Musketeers* (1939), and "Dusty" King in a series of B-Westerns. He retired from acting in 1946 and opened a waffle house in La Jolla, California.

25. Dempsey, Michael. "Sex and Drugs and. . . ." Pp. 167–69 in Ann Lloyd, ed., *Movies of the Fifties*. London: Orbis, 1982.

26. A debutante was an upper-class girl introduced into adult society on her eighteenth birthday. Younger teenage girls were called sub-debs.

27. The character appears in *The Courtship of Andy Hardy* (1942), but as an anonymous classmate at the alumni dance, not one of Andy's friends.

28. Crowther, Bosley. "Andy Hardy Becomes a Man at the Capitol." *New York Times*, August 22, 1941: 19.

29. Coincidentally, when Ray McDonald died unexpectedly in February 1959, the media quickly asserted that he had committed suicide, despondent over his career failure. According to his daughter, however, his career was fine and he accidentally choked to death.

30. His character's name, Dr. Standish, probably derives from the high school favorite of the time, Longfellow's "The Courtship of Miles Standish" (1858), about a man who sends a friend to deliver his plaints of love to Priscilla Mullins, only to have her choose the friend. Film versions appeared in 1910 and 1923, and a Looney Tunes parody in 1940.

31. In 1940, 11.6 percent of girls but only 1.7 percent of boys aged fifteen to nineteen. Sources: Department of the Census.

32. Crowther, Bosley. "Same Old Andy." *New York Times*, January 8, 1947: 28.

33. Another version was piloted in 1961, with perennial sitcom kid Jimmy Hawkins playing Andy, but no network picked it up, perhaps worrying that the old-fashioned Andy Hardy could not compete with the hipster generation of Dobie Gillis and "Kookie" Byrnes.

34. In adulthood, Mickey Rooney won two Emmies, two Golden Globes, and a special Oscar for lifetime achievement. In 1995 he parodied Andy Hardy's longevity on *The Simpsons*, auditioning at the age of eighty for the role of superhero Radioactive Man's teenage sidekick: "I can do this! I can do this!" he exclaims, certain that he can still play a believable adolescent.

CHAPTER 7

1. Flanner, Janet. "The Real Parents of Henry Aldrich." *Ladies' Home Journal* 59 (September 1942): 132–33; "The Case of Henry Aldrich." *Time* 53 (April 25, 1949): 67–68; Redman, Ben Ray. "The Education of Henry Aldrich." *American Mercury* 69 (August 1949): 236–44; Harmon, Jim. *The Great Radio Comedians.* Garden City, NY: Doubleday, 1970: 87–90; Zinman, David H. *Saturday Afternoon at the Bijou.* Arlington House, 1973: 367–70; Ward, L. E. "The Boys Next Door." *Classic Images* 195 (September 1991): 54.

2. Nachman, Gerald. *Raised on Radio.* Berkeley: University of California Press, 1998: 215 et seq.

3. The Crossley rating system, introduced by Archibald Crossley in 1929, was based on a telephone survey in which respondents identified what programs (if any) they listened to the prior evening, and later, what they were listening to at that moment. A rating of 10 to 20 percent was considered excellent. The Eddie Cantor show got the highest Crossley rating of all time, 58 percent, in its 1932–1933 season. Newman, Kathy M. *Radio Active: Advertising and Consumer Activism, 1935–1947.* Berkeley: University of California Press, 2004.

4. Other Henrys included future director Norman Tokar, *Pinocchio* Dickie Jones, and Bobby Ellis from the *Meet Corliss Archer* series.

5. Goldsmith, Clifford, "What a Life." Pp. 332–360 in Mantle, Burt, ed., *The Best Plays of 1937–39.* New York: Dodd, Mead, 1938: 333.

6. Billy Halop in *They Made Me a Criminal* (January); Roger Daniel in *Boy Slaves* (February), Jackie Moran in *Buck Rogers*, Mickey Rooney in *The Adventures of Huckleberry Finn*, and Frankie Thomas in *Nancy Drew—Reporter* (February); Jackie Cooper in *Spirit of Culver* (March); Jackie Cooper in *Streets of New York*, Frankie Thomas in *Code of the Streets*, and Mickey Rooney in *The Hardys Ride High* (April); Frankie Darro in *Boys Reformatory* (May).

7. He played Ronald Coleman's brother in *Lost Horizon* (1937) and starred in *Bulldog Drummond* serials. Later he became the real-life headmaster of a private school, Highland Hall.

8. In spite of the title, it is a Lost Boy melodrama, starring practically every teenage actor in Hollywood: Bonita Granville, Gene Reynolds, June Preisser, William Tracy, Tommy Kelly, and Leo Gorcey.

9.   Later Rod Cameron moved into movie serials and Westerns, where he was ranked in the top five Western stars in 1953–1955, according to *Box Office* magazine. He even got his own comic book title.

10. Crowther, Bosley. "Target for Tonight; A Fine Film about the RAF at the Globe; Comedy at the Central." *New York Times,* October 18, 1941: 22

11. Henry's mother would become his mother-in-law in real life: In 1952 Jimmy Lydon married Olive Blakeny's daughter, Betty Lou Nedell.

12. In *Love Laughs at Andy Hardy* (1947), Andy is just returning from military service, but no one states that he has been fighting in a *war.* One gets the impression that he enlisted in a peacetime army.

13. Girls do kiss him on the cheek, and on a few occasions he skittishly backs away as they attempt to kiss him on the mouth, resulting in a sort of half-kiss.

14. In *Henry Aldrich Gets Glamour,* a girl coos, "You're very strong!" and in *Henry Aldrich Boy Scout,* a boy exclaims, "I wish I had your muscles!" Of course, both are trying to butter up the hapless hero, but in every episode Jimmy Lydon lifts heavy objects and does some amazing stunt work.

15. More subtly, Dizzy, who also refused to fight the bully and consistently protests his fear of the old house, rushes into danger twice, to save Elise from a walking suit of armor and to save Henry from the "Neanderthal."

16. Darryl even considered becoming a monk, and spent some time in a monastery.

17. Darryl Hickman's age might have been an inhibiting factor. Preteens in mass culture rarely established homoromantic bonds. Their exclusive friendships with peers usually lacked passion and intimacy, and their romantic "crushes" on teenagers or men were usually unrequited.

18. "Freddie Bartholomew: Child Film Star," *Los Angeles Times,* January 25, 1992: A-22.

19. The adult James Lydon was never a has-been. He played Skeezix in two adaptations of the *Gasoline Alley* comic strip; he starred in *Rocky Jones, Space Ranger, The Real McCoys,* and other television series. He wrote for *Hawaii Five-O* and directed *The Six Million Dollar Man.* His production company, Spectrum, helped create a number of surprisingly liberal television series, including *M*A*S*H.* He has been married to Betty Lou Nedell for fifty years. Lamparski, Richard. *Whatever Became Of? Eighth Series.* New York: Crown, 1982; Collura, Joe. "Interview with Jimmy Lydon." *Films of the Golden Age* 8 (1997): 26–32.

CHAPTER 8

1.   Clum, John. *Something for the Boys: Musical Theater and Gay Culture.* New York: St. Martin's Press, 1999; Mates, Julian. *America's Musical Stage: Two Hundred Years of Musical Theatre.* Westport, CT: Greenwood, 1985.

2.   Feuer, Jane. *The Hollywood Musical.* Bloomington: Indiana University Press, 1993;

Altman, Rick. *The American Film Musical.* Bloomington: Indiana University Press, 1989.

3.   Nolan, Frederick *Lorenz Hart: A Poet on Broadway.* New York: Oxford University Press, 1995; Clum, John M. *Something for the Boys: Musical Theatre and Gay Identity.* New York: St. Martin's Press, 2001: 49–68.

4.   Though minstrel shows with black performers were a relic of the nineteenth century, white performers in blackface remained a staple of working-class entertainment through the vaudeville era, and were revisited as racist nostalgia through the 1940s. Rogin, Michael. *Blackface, White Noise: Jewish Immigrants in the Hollywood Melting Pot.* Berkeley: University of California Press, 1998: 125–27.

5.   Adams, Rachel. "Great Female Singers of Our Time . . . and Place: Woman and Nation in Latin America." Master's thesis, University of Manchester, 2002. www. llc.manchester.ac.uk/Research/Centres/CentreforLatinAmericanCulturalStudies/ Research/Dissertations/RachelAdams/. In Brazilian Portuguese, "Eu quero" has a sexual connotation. When no sexual desire is intended, the proper phrase is "Te amo."

6.   Evidently no one realized that Argentinians play *fútbol* (soccer), not American-style football.

7.   Neither actor in the homoromantic plotline was well-known for off-camera gay interests. In 1939, during a national tour of *What a Life*, Eddie Bracken met and married Constance Nickerson, and they stayed together until her death sixty-two years later. Yet he played many characters "hilariously" lacking in heterosexual interest. Desi Arnaz was infamous for his heterosexual affairs, yet his most famous character, Ricky Ricardo, appeared in *I Love Lucy,* a series with a strong gay subtext.

8.   *Meet Me in St. Louis* cannot be strictly classified as a Boy Next Door musical, since the main characters are all girls or women, or a barn musical, since teenagers do not save or win anything. However, it does feature a Boy Next Door heteroromance.

9.   The 1959 TV version also cast a gay man, Tab Hunter, as the boy next door. The 1966 version cast beefcake model-turned-actor Michael Blodgett, who often starred in gay-friendly projects.

10.   Their daughter, Liza Minnelli, also has the habit of marrying gay men.

11.   "The Boy Next Door," words and music by Hugh Martin and Ralph Blane.

12.   It seems amazing that Dickie Moore would hold off on kissing girls until he was seventeen. In his memoirs, he claims that a campaign of parental and studio disinformation kept him innocent of heterosexual practice during his adolescence, yet many other Hollywood teenagers, just as closely monitored by the studios, had no trouble acknowledging and acting upon hetero-erotic desire at a much earlier age. We might suggest an intrinsic lack of heterosexual interest, except that Dickie (now Dick) describes many adult heteroromances. He has been married

three times, most recently since 1988. Moore, Dick. *Twinkle, Twinkle, Little Star; But Don't Have Sex or Take the Car.* San Francisco: HarperCollins, 1984: 25–32.

13. Dir. Edward G. Ulmer, December 1943. Dickie also had a small part in the Twentieth Century Fox musical *Sweet and Low Down* (1944).

14. Donald O'Connor Tribute, www.muppetlabs.com/~davidj/tnt/oconnor/donald. htm.

15. Brint, Steven, and Jerome Karabel. *The Diverted Dream: Community Colleges and the Promise of Educational Opportunity.* New York: Oxford University Press, 1989; Frye, John H. *The Vision of the Public Junior College, 1900–1940: Professional Goals and Popular Aspirations.* Westbury, CT: Greenwood Press, 1991.

CHAPTER 9

1. Vallet, François. *L'image de l'enfant au cinéma.* Paris: Les Éditions du Cerf, 1991: 150.

2. Sklar, Robert. *City Boys: Cagney, Bogart, Garfield.* Princeton: Princeton University Press, 1992: 15.

3. A square-jawed action stalwart, Dick Purcell worked with Frankie Thomas, Jimmy Lydon, Tommy Bupp, and a number of other teen actors before his tragic death in 1944 at the age of thirty-six. In his memoirs, Mickey Rooney relates that one night he and Purcell went out together and awoke the next morning naked in bed together. He insists that nothing sexual happened; they were just drunk.

4. Bogle, Donald. *Toms, Coons, Mulattoes, Mammies, and Bucks: An Interpretive History of Blacks in American Films.* 3rd ed. New York: Continuum, 1995: 72–74.

5. Directed by Howard Bretherton: *Chasing Trouble* (January 1940), *On the Spot* (June 1940), *Laughing at Danger* (August 1940), *Up in the Air* (September 1940), *You're Out of Luck* (January 1941). Directed by Jean Yarbrough: *The Gang's All Here* (June 1941), *Let's Go Collegiate* (September 1941).

6. *Tomboy* (1940), *Haunted House* (1940), and *The Old Swimming Hole* (1940) had Marcia Mae Jones as a fast-talking urban sophisticate who courts rural Boy Next Door Jackie Moran. In *The Gang's All Here* (1941), Marcia is the daughter of the owner of a trucking company, and Jackie the hunky mechanic she has a crush on. In *Let's Go Collegiate* (1941), they are ordinary college sweethearts.

7. Major, Clarence. *Juba to Jive: A Dictionary of African-American Slang.* New York: Penguin, 1994.

8. In *Bringing Up Baby*, an exasperated Cary Grant answers the door in a lady's dressing gown (because his clothes have been stolen) and explains to the caller, "I've just gone gay all of a sudden! I am standing in the middle of Time Square, waiting for a bus!"

9. Keye Luke played Number One Son to Warner Olandt's Charlie Chan (1935–1938), Kato in two *Green Hornet* serials (1940–1941), Detective Wong in *The Phantom of Chinatown* (1940), and, at the end of his career, a number of aphorism-

spouting "Orientals." Through the war he was sought after for small parts that involved walking onto the set, waiting for the gasps of horror to subside, and explaining that he was Chinese, not Japanese.

10. With Billy Halop: *Little Tough Guy* (dir. Harold Young, July 1938), *Call a Messenger* (dir. Arthur Lublin, November 1939), *You're Not So Tough* (dir. Joe May, July 1940), *Give Us Wings* (dir. Charles Lamont, November 1940), *Hit the Road* (dir. Joe May, June 1941), *Mob Town* (dir. William Nigh, October 1941), *Tough as They Come* (dir. William Nigh, June 1942), *Mug Town* (dir. Ray Taylor, January 1943). With Frankie Thomas: *The Little Tough Guys in Society* (dir. Erle C. Kenton, November 1938), *Code of the Streets* (dir. Harold Young, April 1939). With Bobby Jordan: *Keep 'Em Slugging* (dir. Christy Cabanne, March 1943).

11. Directed by Ford Beebe and John Rawlins: *Junior G-Men* (August 1940), *Sea Raiders* (October 1941). Directed by Lewis D. Collins and Ray Taylor: *Junior G-Men of the Air* (May 1942). Billy Halop also had a minor role as a young adult in *Sky Raiders* (April 1941).

12. In 1940, the FBI employed 654 special agents, nicknamed "G-Men," in forty-two American cities, but none were "Junior G-Men" (boys and teenagers). It was a media convention, probably invented in 1934 for a radio series. FBI website, www.fbi.gov.

13. After he returned from military service in World War II, he came out as gay, divorced his wife, and retired from acting. See the biography written by his daughter Stephanie, "Biography for Kenneth Howell," Internet Movie Database, http://us.imdb.com/name/nm0398006/bio.

14. After the war, Hally Chester produced the Joe Palooka series, about the hunky but naive comic strip boxer, and a few other movies, notably *School for Scoundrels* (1957). Aside from a professional interest in beefcake, there is no indication that the actor was gay in real life.

15. Although whales have been spotted as far south as Hawaii, there is no commercial whaling in the tropics. Somebody goofed.

16. As director of *Arabian Nights* (1942), John Rawlins found countless close-ups of Sabu's bare chest necessary for the plot, and Ford Beebe's film credits read like an encyclopedia of teenage and adult beefcake: *The Vanishing Legion, Jungle Jim, Tim Tyler's Luck, Buck Rogers, The Green Hornet,* and so on.

17. Directed by Joseph H. Lewis: *Boys of the City* (July 1940), *That Gang of Mine* (September 1940), *Pride of the Bowery* (December 1940). Directed by William West: *Flying Wild* (March 1941). Directed by Wallace Fox: *Bowery Blitzkrieg* (August 1941), *Let's Get Tough* (May 1942), *Smart Alecks* (August 1942), *'Neath Brooklyn Bridge* (November 1942), *Kid Dynamite* (February 1943). Directed by Phil Rosen: *Spooks Run Wild* (October 1941). Directed by William Nigh: *Mr. Wise Guy* (February 1942). Directed by William Beaudine: *Clancy Street Boys* (April 1943), *Ghosts on the Loose* (July 1943).

18. Oates, Joyce Carol. *On Boxing.* Expanded edition. New York: Ecco, 1994.

19. Dyer, Richard. *Now You See It: Studies on Gay and Lesbian Film*. New York: Routledge, 2002: 112.

20. Hayes, David. *The Films of the Bowery Boys*. Secaucus, NJ: Lyle Stuart, 1987: 57.

21. Ziesemer, Brandy Gorcey. "Split Image: The Dual Life of Leo Gorcey, Dead End Kid." Master's thesis, University of California, Chico, 1983: 8. Gorcey, Leo, Jr. *Me and the Dead End Kid*. Ashland, OR: Leo Gorcey Foundation, 2003.

22. Gorcey, Leo. *An Original Dead End Kid Presents: Dead End Yells, Wedding Bells, Cockle Shells and Dizzy Spells*. New York: Vantage Press, 1967: 32.

23. *Boys of the City, That Gang of Mine, Pride of the Bowery, Flying Wild*. In the original *East Side Kids* (1940), which predates Leo Gorcey, Algy is an outrageously lisping, mincing "pansy" who responds to the gang's taunts by beating them up, whereupon gang leader Harris Berger ironically asks, "Do you want to join our gang? It will make a man out of you."

24. "The Films of William Keighley," Michael E. Grost, http://members.aol.com/MG4273/keighley.htm.

25. Sunshine Sammy Morrison was drafted at the same time as Bobby Jordan and left the series, appearing only for a dream sequence in *Follow the Leader* (1944). After the war, he declined an offer to play Scruno with the Bowery Boys and retired from acting.

CHAPTER 10

1. To illustrate Seabury Quinn's "Suicide Chapel," John Russell Fearn's "The Master of the Golden City," and part 2 of Jack Williamson's *The Legion of Time*, respectively. The cover dates for these issues are June, but they appeared on newsstands in March or April.

2. Daniels, Les. *Superman: The Complete History*. San Francisco: Chronicle Books, 1998. Dooley, Dennis, and Gary Engle. *Superman at Fifty: The Persistance of a Legend*. Cleveland, OH: Octavia Press, 1987; Siegel, Jerry. *Superman Archives, Volume 1*. New York: DC Comics, 1997.

3. Wright, Bradford W. *Comic Book Nation: The Transformation of Youth Culture in America*. Baltimore: Johns Hopkins University Press, 2001: 14.

4. Jones, Gerald. *Men of Tomorrow: Geeks, Gangsters, and the Birth of the Comic Book*. New York: Basic Books, 2005.

5. A 1945 survey found that 95 percent of young boys, 87 percent of teenage boys, and 41 percent of young men bought comic books regularly. For women, the percentages were 91 percent, 81 percent, and 28 percent, respectively. Wright, *Comic Book Nation*, 31, 47.

6. There were also a few little-boy superheroes and adult sidekicks. Female superheroes usually went solo, and the only male-female pairing seems to be Catman and Kitten.

7. "Superman on Radio," *Superman Through the Ages!*, http://superman.ws/fos/thescreen/radio/.

8. Comics purists may note that an unnamed office boy character appeared earlier, and that Jimmy Olsen was originally blond.

9. "Robin the Boy Wonder," *Don Markstein's Toonopedia,* www.toonopedia.com/robin.htm.

10. First appearance of the Eagle's Buddy, *Science Comics* 1 (February 1940); Uncle Sam's Buddy, *National Comics* 1 (July 1940); Toro, *Human Torch* 2 (Fall 1940); Wasplet, *Shadow Comics* 7 (November 1940); Dusty, *Pep* 33 (February 1941); Bucky, *Captain America* 1 (March 1941); Rusty, *USA Comics* 1 (August 1941); Speedy, *More Fun* 73 (November 1941); Eaglet, *America's Best Comics* 2 (September 1942).

11. Robin originally used a slingshot, a childlike sort of weapon, but he quickly switched to kicking and scissor holds. After the war, he abandoned the practices, perhaps because they were deemed too effeminate; later they became the trademark of Batgirl on television.

12. With the exception of Yank and Doodle, sons of the Black Owl.

13. First appearance of Kid Cobra, *Dynamic Comics* 1 (October 1941); Sandy the Golden Boy, *Adventure Comics* 69 (December 1941); Sleepy, *Clue Comics* 1 (Fall 1943); Davey, *Super-Mystery Comics* 1 (July 1940); Tim Roland, *Exciting Comics* 9 (May 1941).

14. *Captain America* 6 (September 1941).

15. *Captain America* 4 (June 1941), 8 (November 1941), 10 (January 1942), 17 (August 1942), 26 (May 1943), 28 (July 1943).

16. Toro: *Marvel Mystery Comics* 27 (January 1942), *Marvel Mystery Comics* 31 (May 1942), *Marvel Mystery Comics* 34 (August 1942); Roy the Super Boy: *Shield-Wizard Comics* 3 (Spring 1941); *Shield-Wizard Comics* 5 (Winter 1941–1942); Dusty the Boy Detective: *Shield-Wizard Comics* 8 (Fall 1942), *Shield-Wizard Comics* 11 (Summer 1943); Tim: *Exciting Comics* 26 (April 1943), *Black Terror* 3 (August 1943), *Exciting Comics* 33 (June 1944), *Exciting Comics* 42 (December 1945); Pinky: *Wow Comics* 5 (April 1942), internal illustration, not the cover.

17. Asimov, Isaac, ed. *Before the Golden Age: 8 Science Fiction Classics of the Thirties.* New York: Fawcett/Doubleday, 1974; Aldiss, Brian. *Billion Year Spree.* Garden City, NY: Doubleday, 1973: 227–29; Carter, Paul A. *The Creation of Tomorrow: Fifty Years of Magazine Science Fiction.* New York: Columbia University Press, 1977: 16–19.

18. Molson, Francis J. "Children's and Young Adult Science Fiction." Pp. 329–374 in Neil Barron and Brian W. Aldiss, *Anatomy of Wonder: A Critical Guide to Science Fiction.* New York: Bowker, 1987; Sullivan, C. W., III. "Heinlein's Juveniles: Still Contemporary after All These Years." *Children's Literature Association Quarterly* 10.2 (1985): 64–66; Svilpis, Janis. "Authority, Autonomy, and Adventure in Juvenile Science Fiction." *Children's Literature Association Quarterly* 8.3 (1983): 22–26; Erisman, Fred. "Stratemeyer Boys' Books and the Gernsback Milieu." *Extrapolation: A Journal of Science Fiction and Fantasy* 41.3 (2000): 272–82.

19. Williamson, Jack. "The Legion of Time." *Astounding Science Fiction* (May-July 1938). Expanded version: New York: St. Martin's Press, 1985; Williamson, Jack. "Darker Than You Think." *Unknown Fantasy Fiction*, December 1940. Expanded version: New York: St. Martin's Press, 1984; Sturgeon, Theodore. "It." First published in *Unknown Fantasy Fiction*, August 1940. Pp 125–48 in Isaac Asimov, ed., *Isaac Asimov Presents the Great SF Stories 2 (1940)*. New York: Daw Books, 1979.

20. Asimov, Isaac. "Marooned Off Vesta." *Amazing Stories* (March 1939).

21. He does say that he wants to install a Multivac, Jr. (a home computer), "for the kids. Homework and things." But mentioning kids while carefully avoiding any mention of a wife becomes all the more suspicious. Asimov, Isaac. "Anniversary." First published in *Amazing Stories* (March 1959). *The Best of Amazing*. New York: Doubleday, 1967.

22. Van Vogt, A. E. "The Weapon Shop" (1942). *Astounding Science Fiction* (September 1942). Pp. 403–41 in Isaac Asimov, ed., *Isaac Asimov Presents the Great SF Stories 4 (1942)*. New York: Daw Books, 1980. Heinlein, Robert. "The Unpleasant Profession of Jonathan Hoag." First published in *Unknown Worlds* (October 1942). Expanded version: New York: Ace Books, 1989.

23. Rocklynne, Ross. "Backfire." *Astounding Science Fiction* (January 1943). Pp. 100–116 in Groff Conklin, *Omnibus of Science Fiction*. New York: Crown, 1952: 100–116; Geier, Charles S. "Environment." *Astounding Science Fiction* (May 1944). Pp. 327–40 in Ibid.

24. Kuttner, Henry, and C. L. Moore (writing as Lawrence O'Donnell). "Clash By Night." First published in *Astounding Science Fiction* (March 1943). Pp. 113–71 in Isaac Asimov, ed. *Isaac Asimov Presents the Great SF Stories 5 (1943)*. New York: Daw, 1981; Boucher, Anthony. "Q.U.R." *Astounding Science Fiction* (March 1943). Pp. 476–97 in Raymond Healy and J. Francis McComas, eds., *Adventures in Time and Space*. New York: Random House, 1950.

25. All in *Amazing Science Fiction*: "Foundation" (May 1942), "Boots and Saddle" (June 1942), "The Big and The Little" (August 1944), "The Wedge" (October 1944), "Dead Hand" (April 1945). Asimov, Isaac. *The Foundation Trilogy*. New York: Avon, 1981. Raja Thiagarajan has documented the differences between the novels and the original stories in "The Stories that Make up *The Foundation Trilogy*," *Bloomington, Indiana, Science Fiction Discussion Group*, www.pannis.com/SFDG/TheFoundationTrilogy/theFoundationStories.html.

26. Asimov, Isaac. "The Story behind the Foundation." *Isaac Asimov's Science Fiction Magazine* (December 1982).

27. The strip was famous for cheesecake shots of Burma, Normandie Drake, April Kane, and the Dragon Lady, and for a while Caniff drew a special R-rated version for distribution on military bases.

28. First appearance: *Captain America* 1 (March 1941).

29. First appearance: Wambi, *Jungle Comics* 1 (January 1940); Beebo, *Shadow Comics* 9 (December 1942); Zudo, *Marvel Mystery Comics* 51 (January 1944).

30. Bill and Steve Dale, the Jungle Twins (*Nickel Comics* 1, May 1940), had each other, but they were actually Adventure Boys exploring the jungle; it was not their home. Congo Bill had a teenage sidekick, Janu the Jungle Boy, but they didn't meet until 1954. See Cazedessus, Camille E., "Lords of the Jungle." Pp. 256–88 in Richard A. Lupoff and Don Thompson, eds., *The Comic-Book Book*. Carlstadt, NJ: Rainbow Books, 1998; and Black, Bill. *The Comic Book Jungle: An Illustrated History of Jungle Comics*. Longwood, FL: Paragon Publications, 1999.

31. Lewis Sargent may have been scripted as adolescent in *The New Adventures of Tarzan* (1935): He twirled a yoyo, complained about his bottomless-pit stomach, required constant rescue, and ignored girls, but he was three years older than Tarzan Herman Brix.

32. One wonders why Tarzan and Jane didn't just get married. The answer may be that every movie climaxes with a rescue. Audiences were happy to watch a single girl captured and threatened with various tortures, but not a married lady, certainly not a mother.

33. Weissmuller, Johnny, Jr., William Reed, and R. Craig Reed. *Tarzan, My Father*. Toronto: ECW Press, 2002: 47.

34. MGM, directed by Richard Thorpe: *Tarzan Finds a Son!* (1939), *Tarzan's Secret Treasure* (1941), *Tarzan's New York Adventure* (1942). RKO, directed by William Thiele: *Tarzan's Desert Mystery* (1943), *Tarzan Triumphs* (1943); directed by Kurt Neumann: *Tarzan and the Amazons* (1945), *Tarzan and the Leopard Woman* (1946), *Tarzan and the Huntress* (1947).

35. One such full-body shot lasts for a full five minutes, as Boy lounges on a raft that Tarzan is poling downriver.

36. Since he was adopted as an infant and never knew his birth parents, Boy might be expected to call his adopted parents "Father" and "Mother," but he always refers to them as Tarzan and Jane, as if to emphasize that he is not their natural son.

37. Boy and Jane together: *Tarzan's Secret Treasure, Tarzan and the Leopard Woman*. Boy alone: *Tarzan's New York Adventure, Tarzan Triumphs, Tarzan and the Amazons, Tarzan and the Huntress*, The other post-Boy movie, *Tarzan's Desert Mystery*, has Cheetah making the climactic rescue of Tarzan, Boy, and a GGA jungle princess.

38. "A Hero of Modern Arabian Nights." *Screen Thrills Illustrated* 2.4 (May 1964): 28–33.

39. Crowther, Bosley. "The Elephant Boy in Modern Dress." *New York Times*, September 8, 1938: 159.

40. Strauss, Theodore. "New Arabian Nights: Sabu the Elephant Boy Today Travels Via a Twin-Motored Flying Carpet." *New York Times*, September 15, 1940: 135

41. "Screen News Here and in Hollywood." *New York Times*, May 28, 1938: 9.

42. London Films, December 1940, dir. Ludwig Berger and Michael Powell. See Rovin, Jeff. *The Fabulous Fantasy Films*. South Brunswick and New York: A. S. Barnes, 1977: 140.

43. For instance, Keye Luke (1904–1991) often played secret agents, detectives, and

spies, but as the sidekick of the white secret agent, as often subject to capture and daring rescues as the leading lady. He played a doctor alongside Van Johnson in the Dr. Gillespie series, but as a sort of comic relief sidekick.

44. Nga, Thi Thanh. "Long March from Wong to Woo: Asians in Hollywood." *Cineaste* 21.4 (1995): 38–40; Fung, Richard. "Looking for My Penis: The Eroticized Asian in Gay Video Porn." Pp. 115–34 in David L. Eng and Alice Y. Hom, eds., *Q&A: Queer in Asian America*. Philadelphia: Temple University Press, 1998.

45. "Remembering Sabu the Elephant Boy." *Thai Guys Magazine* (Pattaya). www.thaiguys.org

46. Dutton, Kenneth R. *The Perfectible Body: The Western Ideal of Male Physical Development*. New York: Continuum, 1995: 156.

47. *Arabian Nights* (1942, dir. John Rawlins), *White Savage* (1943, dir. Arthur Lubin), and *Cobra Woman* (1944, dir. Robert Siodmak).

48. In *Ali Baba and the Forty Thieves* (1944), *Gypsy Wildcat* (1944), and *Sudan* (1945). After the war, Sabu returned to the formula in *Tangier* (1946), with Paul Kenyon taking the place of Jon Hall.

49. Lewis, Reina. *Gendering Orientalism: Race, Femininity, and Representation*. New York: Routledge, 1995; Yegenoglu, Meyda. *Colonial Fantasies: Toward a Feminist Reading of Orientalism*. Cambridge: Cambridge University Press, 1998; Aldrich, Robert. *Colonialism and Homosexuality*. New York: Routledge, 2003.

50. After the war, Sabu played heavily muscled, usually half-naked Jungle Men who get girlfriends in *End of the River* (1947), *Man-Eater of Kumaon* (1948), and *Savage Drums* (1951). He appeared briefly in his own comic book title, as a sort of South Asian Tarzan who rescues GGA blondes from savage tribesmen. Later in the 1950s he invested in a real estate business and took whatever minor roles he could find that did not require wearing a loincloth. Days after filming Disney's *A Tiger Walks* (1964), he died of a heart attack, only thirty-nine years old.

CHAPTER 11

1. The sailor has never been identified, though over twenty men claim the honor (there was a lot of kissing going on that day). Ms. Shain was embarrassed by her "indiscretion" and did not come forward until 1980. "V-J Kiss." www.life. com/Life/special/kiss01.html; Taibbi, Mike. "The Famous Kiss." *MSNBC*, http:// msnbc.msn.com/id/8930699/.

2. Brokaw, Tom. *The Greatest Generation*. New York: Random House, 1998; Hamill, Peter. *Downtown: My Manhattan*. New York: Little, Brown, 2004: 172; Kozloff, Max. *New York: Capital of Photography*. New Haven: Yale University Press, 2002: 35.

3. "Boys and Girls Like You and Me," words and music by Rodgers and Hammerstein. Transcribed from *Meet Me in St. Louis,* DVD special edition. It was also cut from *Oklahoma*.

4. Modell, John, and Duane Steffey. "Waging War and Marriage: Military Service and Family Formation, 1940–1950." *Journal of Family History* 13.2 (1988): 195–218.

5. Vidal, Gore. *The City and the Pillar*. 1948. New York: Random House, 1998; Barr, James. *Quatrefoil*. New York: Greenburg, 1950; Hughes, Langston. "Café: 3 am." 1951. P. 406 in *Collected Poems of Langston Hughes*. New York: Vintage, 1995; Ginsberg, Alan. *Howl and Other Poems*. San Francisco: City Lights, 1956. Sangarin, Edward (writing as Donald Cory). *The Homosexual in America: A Subjective Approach*. New York: Greenburg, 1951; Westwood, Gordon. *Society and the Homosexual*. New York: Dutton, 1953.

6. Terry, Jennifer. *An American Obsession: Science, Medicine, and Homosexuality in Modern Society*. Chicago: University of Chicago Press, 1999: 329–42; Corber, Robert J. *Homosexuality in Cold War America: Resistance and the Crisis of Masculinity*. Durham: Duke University Press, 1997; Grant, Julie. "A Thought a Mother Can Hardly Face: Sissy Boys, Parents, and Professionals in Mid-Twentieth Century America." Pp. 117–30 in Alid M. Black, ed., *Modern American Queer History*. Philadelphia: Temple University Press, 2001.

7. Jerseyville, Illinois, Community High School *Album* (1949). www.geocities.com/jerseyvillealbum1949/.

8. The hit song "Tutti Frutti," which both Little Richard and Pat Boone recorded in 1956, is rumored to be about a man who enjoys anal sex. It certainly has nothing to do with ice cream. White, Charles. *The Life and Times of Little Richard*. New York: Omnibus Press, 2003: 39.

9. It doesn't last. During the rest of the series, Lee displays no interest in girls, but he never falls in love with a boy, either.

10. Munter, Pam. *When Teens Were Keen: Freddie Stewart and the Teen Agers of Monogram*. Los Angeles: Nicholas Lawrence Books, 2005.

11. Aylesworth, Thomas. *Hollywood Kids*. New York: Dutton, 1987: 46–47; "Frankie Darro." *Variety*, January 19, 1977: 94.

12. Betz, Betty. *Your Manners Are Showing: The Handbook of Teen-Age Knowhow*. New York: Grossett & Dunlap, 1946; Sadler, William. *A Doctor Talks to Teen-Agers*. St. Louis: C.V. Mosby, 1948; Shryock, Harold. *On Becoming a Man*. Hagerstown, MD: Review and Herald Press, 1951; Duvall, Evelyn Mills. *Facts of Love and Life for Teen-Agers*. New York: Popular Library, 1957; Graham, Billy. *Billy Graham Talks to Teen-Agers*. Grand Rapids, MI: Zondervan, 1958; Van Buren, Abigail. *Dear Teenager*. New York: Cardinal, 1959; Boone, Pat. *'Twixt Twelve and Twenty*. Upper Saddle River, NJ: Prentice-Hall, 1958.

13. Justin and Mary Landis, *Teenager's Guide for Living*. Englewood Cliffs, NJ: Prentice-Hall: 1957: 113.

14. Head, Gay. *Boy Dates Girl*. New York: TAB Books, 1952; White, Betty. *Betty White's Teen-Age Dance Book*. New York: Perma Books, 1959.

15. Many educational films do not list directors or the names of the actors.

16. *Pep* 24 (February 1942); *Pep* 27 (May 1942); *Pep* 30 (August 1942).

17. *Pep* 36 (February 1943); *Pep* 40 (August 1943).

18. Later, teenage comics would be aimed at an audience of preteens, but during this period, the intended reader seems to be a teenager. Ads sell engagement rings, trade schools, and muscle-building equipment rather than toys. There are no positive child characters: Younger siblings are bratty, manipulative monsters with names like Allergy and Asphalt.

19. *Archie* 19 (March-April 1946); *Leave It to Binky* 4 (August 1948); *A Date with Judy* 21 (February-March 1951); *A Date with Judy* 25 (October-November 1951); *Buzzy* 43 (May 1952).

20. *Leave It to Binky* 31 (March-April 1953); *Gabby* 2 (September 1953); *A Date with Judy* 39 (February-March 1954).

21. *A Date with Judy* 37 (October 1953).

22. *A Date with Judy* 13 (October-November 1949); *A Date with Judy* 24 (August-September 1951); *Leave It to Binky* 25 (March 1952); *Here's Howie* 4 (July-August 1952).

23. *Archie* 39 (July-August 1949); *Ginger* 2 (August 1951); *Wilbur* 58 (January 1958).

24. *Oscar* (1947) occasionally displays a muscular physique, but his comic lasted for only thirteen issues. More surprisingly, Mazie's boyfriend Stevie appeared in a six-issue series (*Stevie,* 1952) with a naturalistic butt and crotch.

25. Why, then, do teenage boys get any attention at all from the girls? Often the girls are triangulating their own homoromantic desire. When Betty asks Veronica, "What do you like most about Archie?" Veronica responds, "You!"

26. Lamparski, Richard. *Whatever Became Of? Third Series.* New York: Crown, 1971: 187–89; Aylesworth, Thomas. *Hollywood Kids.* New York: Dutton, 1987: 149–53.

27. In *Blues Busters* (Monogram, 1950, dir. William Beaudine).

28. Owen, Frank, ed. *Teen-Age Sports Stories.* New York: Grossett & Dunlap, 1947; Owen, Frank, ed. *Teen-Age Stories of Action.* New York: Grossett & Dunlap, 1948. Both cover illustrations by Frank Vaughn.

29. Chute, B. J. "Boy Meets Buoy." Owen, *Teen-Age Sports Stories,* 20–35. Originally published in *Boys' Life.* Barbara Joy Chute was a prolific writer of children's fiction who also taught creative writing at Barnard College.

30. In *Wild West* (1946), *Law of the Canyon* (1947), *Tex Granger* (1948), and *Heart of the Rockies* (1951).

31. In *The Strawberry Roan* (1948), *Rocky Mountain* (1950), and *The Range Rider* (1951).

32. There were many "adult" Westerns on prime time, of course, but their heroes frequently romanced women and never had teen sidekicks.

33. Mathers, Jerry, with Herb Fagen. *And Jerry Mathers as the Beaver.* New York: Berkeley Press, 1998: 90.

34. The fact that a new girl will be needed for the next feature is irrelevant. Many series had women agreeing to stay with men at the end of one installment, only to be absent without comment at the beginning of the next. Continuity was not a major goal.

35. "Tarzan Co-Stars," www.mergetel.com/~geostan/costars.html; "Bomba Speaks: An Interview with Johnny Sheffield." *Matt's Bomba the Jungle Boy Movie Guide*, www.tarzanmovieguide.com/sheffint.htm.

36. Three new sidekicks appeared in DC comics about a decade later. One of the Flash's teenage fans was accidentally zapped into Kid Flash (*The Flash* 110, December 1959–January 1960); Aquaman took in Aqualad, a teenage refugee from Atlantis (*Adventure Comics* 269, February 1960); and Wonder Woman was partnered with Wonder Girl, "The Amazon Teenager" (*Wonder Woman* 112, February 1960).

37. *Batman* 49 (October–November 1948), *Batman* 62 (December 1950–January 1951), *Detective Comics* 233 (July 1956).

38. Wertham, Frederic. *Seduction of the Innocent.* New York: Rinehart, 1954; Brooker, Will. *Batman Unmasked: Analysing a Cultural Icon.* New York: Continuum, 2000: 101–71. Wertham contends that comic book images caused children to become violent, sadistic, and sexually abnormal, and that the domestic relationship of Batman and Robin in particular led to "homosexuality."

39. Moore, C. L. "Daemon." *Famous Fantastic Mysteries* (October 1946). Pp. 286–308 in Isaac Asimov, Martin H. Greenberg, and Charles Waugh, eds., *Isaac Asimov's Magical Worlds of Fantasy #10: Ghosts.* New York: NAL/Signet, 1988.

40. Asimov, Isaac. "Now You See It." *Astounding Science Fiction* (January 1948); "Now You Don't." *Astounding Science Fiction* (December 1949–January 1950). Reprinted in Asimov, Isaac. *Second Foundation.* New York: Bantam, 1981.

41. Asimov, "Now You Don't," in *Second Foundation*, 130.

42. Nourse, Alan E. "The Universe Between." *Astounding Science Fiction* (September 1951). Expanded edition: *The Universe Between.* New York: David McKay Company, 1965: 145.

43. Ibid., 208. Tomato Surprise is a fan term for a trick ending. The reader is supposed to react with an astonished "You mean *they* were the aliens all along?"

44. Leiber, Fritz. "The Big Time." *Galaxy* (March–April 1958). *The Big Time.* New York: Orb Books, 2001:42.

CHAPTER 12

1. Elkhorn High School *Elk*, 1957. http://get.to/kyyb/elkhorn1957/index.htm#

2. All in the spring of 1957. Television: Ricky and David Nelson, *The Adventures of Ozzie and Harriet*; Billy Gray, *Father Knows Best*; Dwayne Hickman, *The Bob Cummings Show*. Movies: James MacArthur, *The Young Stranger*; Michael Landon, *I Was a Teenage Werewolf*; Sal Mineo, *Dino*; Pat Boone, *Bernardine*. Music: Tommy Sands, "Teenage Romance"; Pat Boone, "April Love"; Tab Hunter, "Young Love." Books: Robert Paul Smith, *Where Did You Go? Out. What Did You Do? Nothing*; Max Shulman, *Rally 'Round the Flag, Boys.*

3. Watkin, Lawrence E. *Marty Markham*. London: Frederick Muller Ltd., 1947.

4. Wyatt, David A. *List of Gay/Lesbian/Bisexual Televison Characters*, http://home. cc.umanitoba.ca/~wyatt/tv-characters.html.

5. Smith, David R. "Spin and Marty." *Persistence of Vision*. www.disneypov.com/ issue10/spin.html.

6. Reid, Suzanne Elizabeth. *Presenting Young Adult Science Fiction*. Boston: Twayne, 1998; Sands, Karen, and Marietta Frank. *Back in the Spaceship Again: Juvenile Science Fiction Series since 1945*. Westport, CT: Greenwood, 1999; Westfahl, Gary. *Science Fiction, Children's Literature, and Popular Culture: Coming of Age in Fantasyland*. Westport, CT: Greenwood, 2000.

7. Del Rey, Lester. *Rocket Jockey*. 1952. New York: Del Rey Books, 1978: 2; Pohl, Frederick, and Jack Williamson. *Undersea Quest*. 1954. New York: Del Rey Books, 1982: 34.

8. Wollheim, Donald A. *Secret of the Ninth Planet*. 1959. New York: Paperback Library, 1973. Heinlein, Robert. *Space Cadet*. 1948. New York: Del Rey Books, 1981: 93; Bradley, Marian Zimmer. *The Colors of Space*. Derby, CT: Monarch Books, 1963: 12, 124.

9. Heinlein, Robert. *Tunnel in the Sky*. 1955. New York: Del Rey Books, 1977: 185; Heinlein, Robert. *The Rolling Stones*. 1952. New York: Del Rey Books, 1977: 25.

10. Del Rey, Lester. *The Mysterious Planet*. 1953. New York: Del Rey Books, 1978: 33; Pohl and Williamson, *Undersea Quest,* 183.

11. Del Rey, Lester. *Tunnel through Time*. Philadelphia: Westminster Press, 1956. The girl was only eight years old, so Bob is not expressing heterosexual yearning; still, he neatly deflects attention away from his relationship with Pete.

12. Asimov, Isaac (writing as Paul French). *Lucky Starr and the Oceans of Venus*. New York: Doubleday, 1954: 94.

13. Heinlein, Robert. *Time for the Stars*. 1956. London: Pan Books, 1968: 189–90.

14. Wyss, Jonathan. *The Swiss Family Robinson*. 1812. New York: Everyman's Library, 1994.

15. *Korak, Son of Tarzan* 50 (January–February 1973).

16. "Paul Cuvelier," http://membres.lycos.fr/pcuvelier/.

17. Groensteen, Thierry. *Avec Alix: L'Univers de Jacques Martin*. Paris: Castermann, 2002: 14.

18. Originally *Smilin' Ed's Gang,* but renamed *Andy's Gang* when Smilin' Ed died in 1955 and cowboy sidekick Andy Devine took over.

19. He was advertised as "TV's new teen sensation" even though there was no regular Bomba program on TV at that time.

20. *C'mon, Let's Live a Little* (1966); *It's a Bikini World* (1966); *The Wild Angels* (1966); *The Fighting Prince of Donegal* (1966); *Batman* 185 (October–November 1966); *Jimmy Olsen* 94 (July 1966); *Korak Son of Tarzan* 20 (December 1967).

INDEX